'This competent and fascinating documentary of Thomas Hodgskin by a prominent European scholar of free peoples and institutions is a substantive contribution to the history and understanding of the development of classical liberal thought.'
  –**Vernon L. Smith**, *Professor, George L. Argyros Endowed Chair in Finance and Economics, Chapman University, 2002 Nobel laureate in Economics, Author of* Rationality in Economics

'Mingardi's book is a brilliant portrait of a man and a time in the history of economics, deepening, our understanding of the era of classical economics and showing us cross-currents neglected in the standard accounts. Elegantly and engagingly written, it is a classic.'
  –**Deirdre N. McCloskey**, *UIC Distinguished Professor of Economics and of History Emerita, University of Illinois at Chicago, Author of* The Bourgeois Era *trilogy*

'In this fascinating and beautifully written book, Mingardi has shed new light on Thomas Hodgskin, a fascinating and highly original nineteenth century economist and social thinker, whose writings managed to influence both Marxists and Libertarians. A proponent of both free trade and workers' rights, Hodgskin wrote intelligently about economic progress, human capital, and population. Mingardi does justice to this unduly neglected writer. A must read for anyone interested in the evolution of modern economic thought.'
  –**Joel Mokyr**, *Professor of Economics and History, Northwestern University, Author of* The Enlightened Economy

'Thomas Hodgskin was a workingman's libertarian, but a libertarian nonetheless. In this engaging and scholarly book, Alberto Mingardi rescues him from those socialists who claim him as one of their own, and restores him to his rightful place in the pantheon of great classical liberal thinkers.'
  –**George Selgin**, *Director, Center for Monetary and Financial Alternatives, The Cato Institute. Author of* Good Money

'In this splendid book Alberto Mingardi explains the economic and political views of Thomas Hodgskin, one of the most important classical liberals of the nineteenth century. Mingardi disposes the old myth that Hodgskin was a Ricardian socialist, when in fact his major intellectual debts were to John Locke and Adam Smith. Mingardi also explores, in considerable detail, Hodgskin's theories of free trade, money, banking, capital, and spontaneous order. Especially interesting are Mingardi's discussions of the relationship between Hodgskin and Herbert Spencer, and the similarities between Hodgskin's theories and the later theories of F.A. Hayek. This book is essential reading for anyone interested in the radical wing of classical liberalism.'
  –**David Boaz**, *Executive Vice President, The Cato Institute. Author of* The Libertarian Mind: A Manifesto for Freedom

'Today classical liberalism couldn't be more relevant, whether to a U.S. election or to ruction in international markets. Mingardi reveals that black swans are not black: market events such as a virus in China are not entirely unpredictable, and are therefore largely avoidable. Useful and incisive, this book not only traces the origins of classical liberalism, but also connects the past with thinkers relevant today, such as Friedrich Hayek. The result is to give the reader not only the "what" of classical liberalism but the "why" – why classical liberal thought is the most relevant for parsing reality today. The pleasure here is not only Hodgskin, but also Mingardi. Alberto Mingardi is one of those rare men, an international mind who sees through nations to truths that hold across borders and over the course of history. Read anything Mingardi writes.'

–**Amity Shlaes**, *author of* Great Society: A New History

Classical Liberalism and the Industrial Working Class

Thomas Hodgskin (1787–1869) is today a largely unknown figure, sometimes considered to be a forerunner of Karl Marx. Yet a closer look at Hodgskin's works reveals that he was actually a committed advocate of *laissez-faire* economics and enthusiastic about labor-saving machinery and the Industrial Revolution, with a genuine interest in the well-being of the working classes. This book places him in the tradition of classical liberalism, where he belongs—as a disciple of Adam Smith, but even less tolerant of government power than Smith was.

Classical Liberalism and the Industrial Working Class: The Economic Thought of Thomas Hodgskin will be of interest to advanced students and scholars in the history of economic thought, economic history and the history of political thought.

Alberto Mingardi is associate professor of the history of political thought at IULM University in Milan, Italy. He is also a presidential scholar in political theory at Chapman University, director general of the Istituto Bruno Leoni, a think tank in Milan, and an adjunct fellow at the Cato Institute.

Routledge Studies in the History of Economics

The Economic Thought of Michael Polanyi
Gábor Biró

Ideas in the History of Economic Development
The Case of Peripheral Countries
Edited by Estrella Trincado, Andrés Lazzarini and Denis Melnik

Ordoliberalism and European Economic Policy
Between Realpolitik and Economic Utopia
Edited by Malte Dold and Tim Krieger

The Economic Thought of Sir James Steuart
First Economist of the Scottish Enlightenment
Edited by José M. Menudo

A History of Feminist and Gender Economics
Giandomenica Becchio

The Theory of Transaction in Institutional Economics
A History
Massimiliano Vatiero

F.A. Hayek and the Epistemology of Politics
The Curious Task of Economics
Scott Scheall

Classical Liberalism and the Industrial Working Class
The Economic Thought of Thomas Hodgskin
Alberto Mingardi

For more information about this series, please visit www.routledge.com/series/SE0341

Classical Liberalism and the Industrial Working Class
The Economic Thought of Thomas Hodgskin

Alberto Mingardi

LONDON AND NEW YORK

First published 2021
by Routledge
2 Park Square, Milton Park, Abingdon, Oxon OX14 4RN

and by Routledge
52 Vanderbilt Avenue, New York, NY 10017

Routledge is an imprint of the Taylor & Francis Group, an informa business

© 2021 Alberto Mingardi

The right of Alberto Mingardi to be identified as author of this work has been asserted by him in accordance with sections 77 and 78 of the Copyright, Designs and Patents Act 1988.

All rights reserved. No part of this book may be reprinted or reproduced or utilised in any form or by any electronic, mechanical, or other means, now known or hereafter invented, including photocopying and recording, or in any information storage or retrieval system, without permission in writing from the publishers.

Trademark notice: Product or corporate names may be trademarks or registered trademarks, and are used only for identification and explanation without intent to infringe.

British Library Cataloguing-in-Publication Data
A catalogue record for this book is available from the British Library

Library of Congress Cataloging-in-Publication Data
A catalog record has been requested for this book

ISBN: 978-0-367-19362-1 (hbk)
ISBN: 978-0-429-20189-9 (ebk)

Typeset in Bembo
by Taylor & Francis Books

Contents

Acknowledgments ix

1 A life in the storm 1

   The early life of Thomas Hodgskin 1
   Utilitarian (and useful) friendships 4
   A journalistic career 6
   An Essay on Naval Discipline 10

2 Thomas Hodgskin's peculiar blend of "socialism" 32

   Hodgskin: a Ricardian socialist? 32
   Capital and privilege 36
   The issue of machinery 43
   A theorist of human capital? 50

3 Political economy and free trade 66

   A defender of political economy 66
   Labor, knowledge and a principle of population 69
   A long-time opposition to the Corn Laws 76
   Hodgskin, Cobden, and the League 81
   Hodgskin's free trade manifesto 84

4 Free trade in banking 98

   Some thoughts on the business cycle 98
   Free banking 101

5 Between liberalism and anarchism   114

   Private property, good and bad: Hodgskin as a Lockean 114
   Against "scientific" government 120
   Public opinion and the middle classes 123

   Conclusion   136

   Herbert Spencer and Thomas Hodgskin 137
   The anti-utilitarianism of Spencer and Hodgskin 140
   A distinct tradition of classical liberalism? 142

   Index   147

Acknowledgments

My love affair with Thomas Hodgskin began in my university years, when I was working on a dissertation on Herbert Spencer's political thought, but it was only later, while pursuing my research under the guidance of Luigi Marco Bassani at the University of Milan, that I came to like (and, I hope, to understand) Hodgskin better. This is but one of the many things for which I am grateful to Marco, a mentor and a friend like no other.

Steve Davies was kind enough to read the manuscript of this book, and provided the most useful comments. I would like to thank George Selgin and Larry White for doing the same with the free banking chapter. Over the years, I've talked about Hodgskin with Emilio Pacheco, whose wisdom enlightened me in this area, too.

I'm grateful to colleagues at IULM University in Milan, particularly Emilio Mazza and Angelo Miglietta, and at ESI at Chapman University, particularly Dave Potter, Vernon L. Smith, and Daniele Struppa, for their support and patience over the years.

Sincere thanks are due to the librarians of the Sterling Memorial Library at Yale, the Seymour Library at Knox College, and the British Library in London for their many kindnesses.

Filippo Cavazzoni, David Perazzoni, and particularly Jane Shaw Stroup have greatly helped me in streamlining this book. I owe them a great deal. All the shortcomings of this work are, of course, exclusively my fault.

If this book is written in English (sort of), I shall thank the late Lord Harris of High Cross, who taught me the little English I speak, and how to smoke a pipe. Ralph was a great champion of the free market who came from a modest, working-class background. This book is dedicated to his memory.

1 A life in the storm

The early life of Thomas Hodgskin

Running away to sea "is, for the English, the traditional break from parental authority—the road to adventure" (Borges [1935] 1975, 31).

In Thomas Hodgskin's case, a life on the sea meant something entirely different. Rather than getting rid of the parental authority, it was the parental authority that got rid of him—ushering in a painful initiation to his relationship with authority and power.

Hodgskin's political reflections were shaped and molded by this youthful experience. It shaped his lifelong attempt to build a political philosophy in which government plays no positive role whatsoever. Hodgskin was the advocate of an uncompromisingly radical kind of classical liberalism, one that foreshadows modern libertarianism.[1] It stemmed especially from his military experience, which he regarded as his own encounter with tyranny.

Thomas Hodgskin was born on December 12, 1787, in Chatham, Kent, a city dominated by its naval docks since the Elizabethan era. Like many Chatham residents, Hodgskin's father worked at the dockyards, in his case as an administrative clerk. He was an assistant to a storekeeper, and in 1800 he would become a storekeeper himself at the Sheerness shipyards. He also had a small annuity from land he had inherited.

Although John Hodgskin was an example of white-collar respectability, his habits were those of a spendthrift: "My father is not a sneak, but he is an ignorant man," wrote his son in 1817. "He is greedily fond of distinction ... but knows no means to procure it but by being generous to strangers at the expense of justice to his family and by presiding at a circle of smokers more ignorant than himself" (Hodgskin to Place, June 29, 1817). Thomas and his siblings[2] suffered through a joyless childhood ("youth had not been for me the happiest period of existence" [Hodgskin 1820, I, 29–30]), but he kept a grateful memory of their mother who "for thirty years struggled patiently but vainly to conceal the thriftlessness and misconduct of the head of the family" (Driver n.d., 1).

At the age of twelve, the young Hodgskin had to leave school and his childhood surroundings: his father enlisted him as a cadet (a junior trainee) on a warship. The feeling of never having experienced the love of his father, according to Cecil H. Driver (1900–1958), left a "permanent mark" on Hodgskin's character and temperament and may explain his disdain for authority (1). The same can be said of his experience in the Royal Navy.

In his view, as Hodgskin wrote later, the discipline imposed by the navy was nothing less than "one universal system of terror" (Hodgskin 1813, ix). His years in the navy provided him with a perspective on the ways of life and the economic habits of populations with whom he would never have come into contact otherwise.[3]

Whatever excitement young Thomas derived from serving in an almost invincible fleet that defeated every opponent who dared to put to sea, the twelve years he spent in the navy prevented Hodgskin from receiving a formal education. Yet he was eager for education. He tried to get hold of a book whenever he could; there were no such things as "on-board libraries" available then; they were established only after he had retired from active duty.[4] In those years "a book of any kind on a ship's lower deck was a great rarity; and in any of the messes that had one, it was read and re-read, and lent from mess to mess, until it became difficult to tell its original colour" (Bechervaise 1847, 34). One can well understand the frustration of a clever boy, kept apart from those very things that could offer him the opportunity to educate himself as well as provide some leisure time.[5]

Hodgskin passed the lieutenant's exam in 1806,[6] during his sixth year aboard the frigate *Active*, when he was nineteen years old.[7] Since 1801, the *Active* had been stationed in the Mediterranean, and was used "by Lord Nelson for several intelligence operations off the coast of Toulon … in connection with the long-drawn-out strategy that culminated in the Battle of Trafalgar" (Driver, 2). Later, Hodgskin served on the *Combatant*, the *Star*, and the *Nymphe*. His mission aboard the *Nymphe* was the peak of his naval career. That ship was charged with maintaining the blockade on the Tagus River after the second invasion of Portugal by Napoleon's armies. Hodgskin developed an admiration and friendship for his captain, Conway Shipley, whom he later praised for being "as genuinely pious as he was brave; he was as honourable and humane as he was ardently courageous" (Hodgskin 1813, 47^{fn}). Shipley lost his life while attempting to board the brig-covette *Garotta*, a Portuguese vessel that had been requisitioned by the French and was anchored in a bend near the Belem tower. "Captain Shipley, having sprung into the *Garotta*'s fore-rigging, was in the act of cutting away the boarding-netting, when he received a musket-ball in his forehead and fell dead into the water" (James 1837, V, 39).

Less amiable was Hodgskin's relationship with those commanders under whom he later served. His experience on the frigate *Nemesis* was probably crucial to his future thinking. David Stack (1998, 38) pointed out that "Hodgskin was twenty-one years old when he joined the *Nemesis*, old enough to reflect upon the consequences of such a system [of naval discipline] but still young enough to keep his misgivings to himself rather than jeopardize a promising career." As much as he disapproved of the iron fist of his captain, William Ferris, he was implicated in the trial for the death of a fifteen-year-old crew member.[8]

On November 26, 1809, Hodgskin had ordered one of his underlings to clean up a young man named Bentley, who was suffering from a bad case of diarrhea. "Despite the rough seas and snow, Fenton took Bentley to the head, made him strip naked, and lowered him into the sea" (Stack 1998, 38). According to the ship's doctor, the cause of death was a head injury; probably, the sergeant in charge of "cleaning" the boy had failed to persuade him by the sheer force of his arguments to take a plunge into the chilly sea waters (his version of the facts, however, was that the boy had slipped and injured himself once back on board). In any case, Hodgskin's responsibility did not go beyond the initial order given, as he had not specified how the boy had to be "cleaned up." He did not even present a defense at the trial, so confident he felt of his innocence.

In hindsight, as David Stack (1998, 39) suggests, it is likely that those events—and having been, in fact, at least morally responsible for murder—had affected Hodgskin deeply; but at the time, he did not yet possess the necessary intellectual resources to reject the system altogether. A few months later, in July 1810, he received an honorable mention for his bravery in action. The *Nemesis* was decommissioned in April 1811 and, for the first time in his entire adult life, Hodgskin was forced to return ashore. He tried in every way to get another shipboard job, and eventually succeeded that same year in October, as third lieutenant on the *Menelaus*.

Aboard that ship, his career came to a screeching halt as he ended up being dragged before a navy court martial. He was accused of allowing a prisoner to escape and of having mentioned his commander, Peter Parker (1785–1814), in disrespectful terms in one of his letters. At first, relations between Hodgskin and Parker were good, to the point that Hodgskin was quickly promoted to second lieutenant. The moment, however, a certain Pevison was preferred as a first lieutenant, something cracked. A heated argument ensued between Hodgskin and his captain, and when Hodgskin asked Parker whether he was responsible for the denied promotion, he was told no. That was enough to push Hodgskin to write a letter to the commander of the fleet. In the letter he aimed to defend his position. The missing promotion, he maintained, was an insult to his professionalism, but it was unlikely that anyone would pay attention to a "lieutenant, unknown to the world, destitute of fortune, or of rank" who "should dare to lift up the brow of honest indignation against destructive injustice, unmerited insult, and vulgar abuse" (Hodgskin 1813, 113).

This moment of friction was followed by an incident that crippled any hope of future career advancement in the navy. On April 8, 1812, Hodgskin was entrusted with custody of a prisoner by the name of John Frederick, accompanying him ashore at Port Mahon (Minorca) to retrieve his clothes from the consul. Apparently, while his unwitting guardian was engaged in a conversation, Frederick managed to pack up his things and flee. Hodgskin defended himself by explaining that he had no idea Frederick was a prisoner; he was not in shackles and was not presented to him as such. To the court martial he sent only a written statement, possibly because at this point he felt his destiny was already decided and fighting against the hierarchy was useless. The court demoted him, undermining the possibility of any future promotions, and allowed him an annuity of 66 pounds a year. His experience in the Royal Navy was over, and—at age 25—he was "a disgruntled and disappointed man" (Hodgskin 1813, xiv).

Forced to return to civilian life, although with the comfort of a modest lifetime stipend, Hodgskin had to face a world that he did not know. He had no education and no job, yet he did not give in to despair. A curious young man, he was attracted to a life of letters; he became an avid, self-educated reader and made his pen the weapon he would use to change the world. We will never know how he was seduced into the idea of denouncing what he perceived as the injustice of the Royal Navy by his pen, but so he did. He wrote a polemical pamphlet, published in 1813, based on his experience in the navy. The aim of that pamphlet is summed up by the title: *An Essay on Naval Discipline, Shewing Part of its Evil Effects on the Minds of the Officers, on the Minds of the Men, and on the Community; with an Amended System, by Pressing which May Be Immediately Abolished*.

The essay is both a scathing critique of the brutality of naval discipline and a plea to the civil authorities for radical reform. His experience with the court martial had scarred him for life. The courts of the Royal Navy, Hodgskin wrote, were "composed of men comparatively destitute of education; corrupted by power, and often strangers to religion and morality: that, as the naval laws and customs, which form their minds, are founded in injustice, as they can have no strong convictions of injustice hereafter to be punished; and as its commission is never punished in the navy; whenever their interest is concerned, they have no motives to be just" (Hodgskin 1813, 132).

Utilitarian (and useful) friendships

At the age of twenty-six, Hodgskin enrolled at the University of Edinburgh as a student of literature (the only other option available to him was to enroll as a medical student), but he attended only some of the courses. It is unknown whether he ever attended any classes in his second year.[9] It was, nevertheless, a fruitful period: he wrote *On Naval Discipline* and *On Mind*, a short treatise of which there is no record left. He also became friends with the poet and Anglican minister James Gray (1770–1830), who introduced him by letter to Francis Place (1771–1854). Place, known as the "radical tailor of Charing Cross," was one of the central figures of the intellectual and political scene in London, a formidable activist and organizer in the events that led to the abolition of the Combination Laws in 1824 and the first Reform Act in 1832.

It was a life-changing encounter. It is easy to see why Place would sympathize with Hodgskin. Like Hodgskin's, Place's father[10] had been unloving and absent—and also an avid gambler (Wallas [1898] 1925, 3), who repeatedly undermined the family finances. This is the sort of similarity that may easily bond men.

Young Francis had started working as an apprentice to a leather-breeches maker and had known extreme poverty first-hand. Endowed with a great talent for organization, in just a few years he had managed to set up a tailor's workshop, first in partnership with a friend, and later on his own, at 16 Charing Cross. Place was a very skilled artisan when it came to crafting breeches but he was, by his own admission, unable to cut a coat. He could, however, hire qualified people for such a purpose, and he knew that "the most profitable part for me to follow was dancing attendance on silly people" (Thale 1972, 216). Devoted as he was to improving his family's living conditions and his own, still Place was never one to turn down a chance for self-education; he was a voracious reader and ended up amassing a remarkable library which became a reference point for radicals in London.

Thus, Hodgskin and Place shared a complex personal history, the experience of poverty, self-education, and the determination, typical of self-educated people, to put enormous effort into achieving what they wanted. Their personality was a curious mixture of a personal ambition for recognition and the public ambition for bringing about a freer and fairer society.

The correspondence between the two is extremely thick, and the elder tried to help the younger fulfil his ambition to live off his writing talents. Hodgskin had begun to submit to the *Morning Chronicle*—which was directed by John Black (1783–1855)—a series of letters (signed "T. H.") on the issue of the forced enlistment of sailors. Through these letters, published between October 26 and December 23, 1815, two years after *An Essay on Naval Discipline*, he tried to synthesize the arguments of the essay for the benefit of a wider audience. Thanks to Place, he later came into contact with Jeremy Bentham (1748–1832) and James Mill (1773–1836). Such associations were definitely beneficial and, at first, Hodgskin showed "an almost childlike admiration" for Place (Stack 1998, 57). It is somewhat surprising that the young, self-taught former sailor did not end up being intellectually subjugated by such famous and influential friends.

Instead, he took a completely different direction and developed his own way of thinking in open opposition to both his eminent friends. As Élie Halévy (1870–1937) noted in the first systematic study of Hodgskin's personality and body of work:

> Against Benthamite Utilitarianism which reduced every deed of virtue to a plain and calculated act of individual prudence, he took up the defence of those moral promptings, which, although doubtless not free from the influence of prejudice and error, are an expression of the total experience of mankind and a prerequisite of knowledge and foresight.
>
> (Halévy [1903] 1956, 35)

Thanks to Place, Hodgskin was able to take a long trip to Europe, first accompanied by Place's son and then alone. In Paris, he stayed at the home of Jean-Baptiste Say (1767–1832), thanks to a recommendation by Place, who had met the great economist in 1814. He attended Say's political economy lectures, which strongly resonated with the young Thomas and permanently influenced his way of thinking (see chapter 3). Within a few months, he began exploring the continent on a larger scale, visiting France, Italy, Switzerland, Tyrol, and southern Germany. He made his grand tour "on foot and generally alone" (Hodgskin 1820, I, 1), living in the simplest accommodations.

Germany was the country that won him over: in October 1817 he decided to stay in Dresden for the winter, a city abundant "with learned and clever men" (Hodgskin 1820, I, 5). In Dresden he had access to magazines and English newspapers like the *Times*, the *Morning Chronicle*, the *Courier* and the *Edinburgh Review* (6), but he mainly devoted himself to the study of philosophy and the German language.

Throughout his stay in Europe he continued to correspond with Place, who, impressed by his letters, forwarded them occasionally not only to Bentham and James Mill, but also to the newspapers.

The outcome of Hodgskin's extended stay in Germany was the publication of the two-volume *Travels in the North of Germany* in 1820. The modest sales of such work, and other awkward attempts to break into the world of the written word, left Hodgskin in a very precarious financial situation from which he emerged only in 1822, when Place and Mill managed to secure for him a position at the *Morning Chronicle* as a parliamentary reporter.

A journalistic career

From then on, Hodgskin's career was that of a journalist. This was a time that has been called the "great age of newspaper triumphalism" (Pettegree 2014, 363) and a place, London, where more than anywhere else magazine publication went through a tumultuous development. In part, such development consisted in reaching a new population of readers: "in the early nineteenth century periodicals became for the first time financially and intellectually accessible to the working-class reader," writes Kathryn Prince (2009, 129–130). This new audience became, for Hodgskin, the readership he wanted to address, persuade, win over. More than others, he could empathize with the personal stories of craftsmen and laborers who were beginning, gradually, to educate themselves thanks to the widespread availability of newspapers and magazines (Rose 2001, 84).

The phenomenon of self-education of the masses was not just limited to the printed media. An instrument of paramount importance in such process was the spontaneous associations formed for the purpose. The Society for the Diffusion of Useful Knowledge, founded by Lord Brougham (1778–1868) in 1826, with its weekly *Penny Magazine*, is one of the best-known examples. The Mechanics' Institutes, technical schools established in the early 1820s and designed to transfer useful and practical knowledge to adults, by 1850 numbered more than two hundred and were spread all over England (Hilton [2006] 2013, 174).

In 1823, Hodgskin—while remaining a parliamentary reporter for the *Chronicle*—contributed to the foundation of the *Mechanic's Magazine*, collaborating very closely with Joseph Clinton Robertson (1787–1852). The magazine's target audience was made up of "intelligent mechanics, epitomizing the artisan culture of self-improvement in the 1820s. They were the technocratic artisans who had become widely responsible for managing, improving and repairing the increasingly complex machinery on which industrialization depended" (Brake and Demor 2009, 405). The magazine provided both practical information and knowledge that fed their intellectual curiosity.

The inspiration and the "agenda" are clearly stated from the beginning. As described by Christine MacLeod ([2007] 2010, 88–90):

> The frontispiece of the first issue of the *Mechanic's Magazine,* in 1823, paid tribute to Bacon's programme of scientific reform at the same time as it symbolised the new supremacy of steam. Instead of the sailing ship passing through the mythical pillars of Hercules, in the engraving which formed the frontispiece to Bacon's Instauratio magna (1620), a paddle steam battles the waves beneath a cliff, on which stands a bEam engine, pumping water from a mine. Above, the winged figure of Mercury stands over the Baconian motto, 'knowledge is power,' and between two rows of classical columns, inscribed with the surnames of ten men of science from the past two centuries.

Such unequivocal praise of the power of knowledge becomes, in Hodgskin's view, the belief that the redemption of the working classes will be a by-product of the intellectual tools at their disposal. The self-taught former sailor sees in the self-education of the masses the crowbar to break the grip of the dominant class. No regulations and laws will free the people, but the chance to participate in the market process with adequate human capital will.[11]

In 1824, Hodgskin became editor-in-chief of an offshoot of the *Mechanic's Magazine, The Chemist*, likewise published by Knight and Lacey. Once again, articles were anonymous: at a glance, however, the editorial line of this magazine says quite a lot about its editor-in-chief. The core mission of the magazine was the transmission of technical information that was immediately useful for the readers: how to obtain a certain reaction, how to use a certain tool. Such useful knowledge reflected the latest innovations in the industry. Alongside the magazine, a long, serialized "history of chemistry"—presumably written by Hodgskin himself—was published, suggesting that Hodgskin felt a need to reconcile "practical" knowledge with a general, "theoretical" vision.

The magazine did not last long: and neither did, for a number of reasons, the collaboration with Robertson. The latter had pitched the idea of a Mechanics' Institute in London. The first to respond to his appeal was the physician and philanthropist George Birkbeck (1776–1841), whose name is still associated today with what remains of that institution (now Birkbeck College), and who would become its main financier.

Robertson and Hodgskin also involved Francis Place in the project. The group appeared rather well-suited, but soon irreconcilable disagreements began to emerge. The divergence of opinions between Robertson/Hodgskin and Place revealed a different view of how the social emancipation of the workers should be accomplished, and whether the workers themselves ought to be actively involved in the process. Robertson and Hodgskin wanted the Mechanics' Institute to be an institution for the working classes, directly financed by such classes through a modest membership fee; Place, on the other hand, aimed to act on a broader scale, which included accepting donations from the wealthier classes.[12] Place prevailed, eventually. While Robertson would later criticize the institute, and quite harshly, Hodgskin maintained a softer attitude. Something, however, was broken in the relationship with Place, who, increasingly hostile to Hodgskin's ideas (see chapter 2), later tried—and only partially succeeded—in preventing him from teaching at the very institute that he had helped create. (From that series of lectures, which took place in September 1826, in fact, *Popular Political Economy*, his most famous book, would be born.)

In 1827, Hodgskin applied to be a teacher for two new professorships in philosophy at the London University, hopeful and confident of success despite never having earned any "official" qualification. His hopes were soon to be crushed: he was rejected. Similarly, his employment under James Mill as editor for the Library of Useful Knowledge—owned by the Society for the Diffusion of Useful Knowledge founded by Brougham—turned out to be a very unsatisfactory experience for both parties. From then on, Hodgskin's "ideological" detachment from radical philosophers became personal as well.

Following the *Essay on Naval Discipline* and the two volumes of the *Travels*, Hodgskin's three major works—which we will examine more closely in the following chapters—came out in the 1820s and 1830s: *Labour Defended Against the Claims of Capital* (1825), signed as "A Labourer," *Popular Political Economy: Four Lectures Delivered at the London Mechanics' Institution* (1827) and *The Natural and Artificial Rights of Property Contrasted* (1832). Later he published a concise advocacy of the abolition of duties on grain (see chapter 2) and then *Peace, Law and Order: A Lecture Delivered in the Hall of the National Association* (1842). In 1856, his career as an essayist ended officially with the publication of his two lessons on crime and power (see chapter 3); in their own way, they were a seal of a lifetime's reflections.

For the largest part of his career, Hodgskin's primary occupation was anonymous journalism: for the *Morning Chronicle* (where, after 1834, Charles Dickens [1812–1870] was among his colleagues) and the *Courier*, both pillars of the Whig press. For both, he worked essentially as a parliamentary reporter, a disaffected observer of the "ridiculous ceremonies and mummeries practised at Westminster" (Hodgskin 1832, 110).

In 1844, after twenty years at the *Chronicle*, Hodgskin finally landed an arrangement that felt more congruent with his talent and ideas: he was hired as one of the first editors of the *Economist*, which was at the time just being established by James Wilson (1805–1860).[13] Initially Hodgskin reviewed "books and pamphlets on economic and social issues" (Dudley Edwards 1993, 127), but soon became one of its top columnists. Hodgskin shared with Wilson a common militancy in the movement to abolish the corn laws. The most popular business magazine in the world grew out of the need for a magazine that was both independent and yet supportive of the League. Since its foundation, it has followed the method of anonymous journalism. According to Ruth Dudley Edwards, historian of the British magazine,

> there is no evidence about how the relationship between Hodgskin and Wilson was conducted, [but] it is clear [from the pages of *the Economist* that] it worked well. Hodgskin added intellectual tone, and though facts, more facts and yet more facts continued to form the backbone of the paper, it became quirkier, less stolid, more cultivated and less prosaic.
> (Dudley Edwards 1993, 130)

While working at the *Economist*, Hodgskin met Herbert Spencer (1820–1903), a younger colleague.[14] He reviewed the philosopher's first book—*Social Statics* (1851)—with great favor. After leaving the *Economist* in 1857, mainly due to disagreements over Wilson's editorial policy,[15] Hodgskin contributed to several other periodicals and, in particular, to the *Brighton Guardian* for which he wrote from 1856 until his death; from 1861, he wrote for *the Brighton Guardian* a column called "Science."

Earlier, in 1848, he had been hired for a short period as editor-in-chief of a newspaper, the *London Telegraph*. As David Stack convincingly remarked (1998, 166–168), the *London Telegraph* was the closest thing Hodgskin ever had to a political manifesto at his own disposal. The publisher of the *Telegraph* was Herbert Ingram (1811–1860), a liberal politician and "inventor" of the first illustrated weekly magazine, the *Illustrated London News*, progenitor of modern tabloids. According to an eminent columnist, Charles Mackay (1814–1889), who contributed as a foreign policy commentator, the specialty of the *Telegraph* was "the publication of a *feuilleton*, after the fashion of those rendered familiar by the Parisian press, and containing a succession of novels and romances." Hodgskin strictly limited himself "to economical subjects, on which he was a reputed expert, while exercising a general supervision of the editorial columns" (Mackay 1887, 350).

The experience only lasted six months. As Mackay explained (1887, 351–352):

> The new paper was not a success… . The rapid growth of the *Illustrated London News* had accustomed him [Herbert Ingram] to success; and after sacrificing several thousands of pounds in the *Telegraph*, he lost heart and faith in the venture, and resolved to discontinue it. Mr. Hodgskin reported that the disappointed proprietor, in his unreasonable and unreasoning wrath at the failure, accused him of being the cause of it, from his constant use of the word "bureaucracy," which, Mr. Ingram said, had occurred at least ten times in one week in the leading articles!

"Bureaucracy! bureaucracy!" he exclaimed in irate tones. "Such a word is enough to damn any newspaper, and it has damned the Telegraph!"

The Telegraph ceased to appear on the following morning. The name was afterwards adopted ... by Colonel Sleigh, who established the Daily Telegraph, without sufficient means to carry it on, and allowed it perforce to fall into more competent hands, who have made it one of the greatest successes of modern journalism.

Twice a newspaper editor, both times for barely half a year; a frustrated aspiring professor; a discharged navy officer: Hodgskin's career certainly does not look like a constellation of great accomplishments but, rather, of valiant attempts. It is not surprising, therefore, that Hodgskin's name completely slipped into obscurity with the passing of time. When he died, according to Halévy ([1903] 1956, 165), no British newspaper would publish the news of his death,[16] although fortunately that was an exaggeration.

In spite of that obscurity, his life had shown a remarkable commitment to freedom and progress. To discover such commitment, we shall start with his first essay, based on his naval experience.

An Essay on Naval Discipline

By writing *An Essay on Naval Discipline*, and later by sending a few letters based on it to the *Morning Chronicle*, Thomas Hodgskin was taking the measure of his life up to that point. His navy experience would affect his writing for the rest of his life. From the outset of his career as a writer, at the very center of his reflections was violence, which he saw as a typical attribute of an arbitrary and discretionary power. This is not merely a youthful pamphlet. The book allows us to see the backdrop of Hodgskin's later thinking and is in itself an important contribution on an important matter.

Life aboard a ship instilled in Hodgskin an inveterate opposition to arbitrary acts; in fact, from then on, virtually *every* public decision would appear to him as arbitrary. Men-of-war were centers of despotism, where no regulations controlled the man in a position of command:

> The main spring of the coercion in existence is, the power the captains possess of making what they please customs, and punishing them at their pleasure; part of its ill effects are now before the public in a tangible shape, and it is for them to support or abolish it. To have called the attention of the public to the sufferings of an individual would have been trifling with its majesty; but the same principle that has deeply injured me, is now inflicting thousands of cruelties on the seamen; and the mischief it may cause to the community, from the destruction of our national character, is quite incalculable.
>
> (Hodgskin 1813, 112)

In his essay, Hodgskin considered two primary issues. One was the practical management of life on board and, more specifically, the issue of corporal punishment. The navy was, of course, a hierarchical structure and inequalities aboard were sharp: for every lieutenant on the average ship, there were about a hundred other men. Policing them was a necessity, but the method, Hodgskin maintained, questionable. Corporal punishment was ubiquitous and was a hallmark of "despotic power." Cruelty was self-perpetuating, because it was supinely accepted as custom. The other was *impressment*, the practice of forced enlistment.

These represent two different faces of coercion in the navy and they led Hodgskin to approach a subject that always remained at the core of his thought: the relationship between order and coercion. The threat of use of force on the one hand, and the fear of becoming a victim on the other, have no positive role to play in ensuring order or peaceful coexistence between human beings. The echo of the lesson he thought he had learned on British ships would never fade, even through fifty years of intellectual work.

Of the two issues on which Hodgskin focused, impressment is of greater importance—and worthy of some background. In the United Kingdom, the main instrument of expansion and maintenance of British power was not the army but the Royal Navy. The British islands were to be protected by sea, and the monopoly of trade with the colonies established by the Acts of Navigation (the first one promulgated in 1651) had to be guaranteed. In Adam Smith's words (1721–1790), "The maintenance of this monopoly has hitherto been the principal, or more properly perhaps the sole end and purpose of the dominion which Great Britain assumes over her colonies." Such monopoly has caused "the expense of a very considerable naval force which was constantly kept up, in order to guard, from the smuggling vessels of other nations, the immense coast of North America, and that of our West Indian islands" ([1776] 1981, IV.7.150, 614–615).

It is difficult to dispute that "navalism" reflected "Britain's geographical circumstances: as a rich island it needed to defend itself against invasion, and as the seat of a maritime empire it needed to protect its trade and overseas possessions" (Keegan 1993, 225). The Royal Navy occupied a particular place at the heart of the Empire. "The history of England is the history of her Navy. It is to that, under the providence of God, that she stands before the world unrivalled; the asylum of oppressed freedom, the scourge of tyranny, and the emporium of commerce," wrote an "Old Quarter Master" in his naval memoir in 1847 (Bechervaise, 1847, 7). For Lord Halifax (1633–1695), "The first Article of an Englishman's Political Creed must be, That he believeth in the Sea" ([1692] 1700, 2). Of this political creed and such devotion to the sea, the Royal Navy was the cornerstone, the indispensable guardian without which it would have been impossible to guarantee a monopoly of trade with the colonies.

The problem of manning warships was always urgent, but especially during wartime, when impressment occurred. Before the great technological innovations of the industrial revolution and the introduction of steamships, human labor was a dominant factor. "In the labour-intensive era of sail, the Royal Navy simply could not recruit enough volunteers to man its fleets," wrote Nicholas Rogers (2007, 4). Rogers (2007, 5) calculated that, of the 450,000 men who manned the British navy between 1740 and 1815, 40 per cent were coerced.[17]

Such a heavy reliance on conscription had its reasons. While it may have sufficed to give a gun to a man to make a soldier out of him, that was not the case with sailors. On a ship, 40 percent of the crew was necessarily made up of skilled seamen, while the rest were newly enrolled landsmen and servants. Professional sailors were sought after by both the military and the mercantile sectors. Captains needed *competent* men who could operate a vessel. "The Royal Navy drew its manpower from a world-leading mercantile and fishing fleet" (Dancy 2015, 28), and that was no small part of its success.

Indeed, the development of mercantile trade and the Royal Navy were intertwined. Guaranteeing the monopoly in trade subordinated the merchant vessels to the navy, allowing their sailors to be impressed into the navy. The Act of 1660 required that all colonial imports and exports be carried by vessels built in England and operated by a crew that was at least 75 percent English. Likewise, it provided that a number of goods exported from the colonies (including tobacco, rice, sugar, cotton) could only and exclusively be sold on the English market. The Staple Act of 1663 ordered that all goods sent from other European countries to the colonies were first put into port in England, so that it was possible to tax them. Therefore, to some extent, the trade privileges with the colonies had very strict regulations as a trade-off. At a time when the government went so far as to determine the composition of individual crews (at least in terms of nationality) on merchant ships, it was not inconceivable that it would come to regard all sailors as its own proprietary staff.

Forced manning was based on the ancient prerogative of the royal power to freely dispose of the goods and the time of its subjects. Over time, such prerogative was increasingly limited or subjected to parliamentary ratification; "by the early eighteenth century, seamen were the last group of labourers that the monarchy could compel to service without Parliament's approval," writes Denver Brunsman (2013, 21). There was no conscription in the army; in fact, British thinkers opposed it because the idea of a standing army as a tool of arbitrary and absolute power was anathema, but such was not the case with the navy.

The practice was particularly despicable because it was discretionary and therefore unpredictable. It was a process entirely disconnected from any kind of regulatory control or standard procedure and more or less frequent depending on the demand for personnel on British ships. The Admiralty obtained license from the Crown to proceed in procuring sailors whenever there was need. We should not make the mistake of thinking that the seamen to be enrolled received a draft call in the mail or that the navy recruited in good order all male citizens upon their coming of age.

Forced recruitment was messy and improvised; it occurred through the action of small groups (press gangs), composed of fewer than a dozen people, often "organized" for the task by the captain of a ship but not composed of sailors, so as not to detract precious, marine labor. The press gangs were a symbol of naval power on shores. The gangs typically operated from a base, often established in a pub, but scouted the port and patrolled the surroundings, looking for potential sailors. Their work became more frenzied in time of crisis, when "hot presses" ended up with massive recruitment. As an incentive, members of the press gangs received payment for every man they managed to procure, but only after their recruits had passed the scrutiny of the captain. Sometimes the press gangs were corrupt as well as violent—allowing a person freedom in return for a bribe. A person's freedom had a price: whether it was paid by the Royal Navy or by the poor sod himself, it mattered little.

The press gangs were not limited, however, to recruiting in ports and on the docks. They were normally "careless of legal niceties" (Rogers 2007, 27) and had no qualms about violating private property or searching every square inch of a house and village to hunt down deserters and fugitives but also whoever put up any resistance. The easiest way to operate was to recruit directly on board a merchant ship—easier and also more effective, as the need was not just for merely "able bodies" but, rather, able seamen.[18] Herman Melville's Billy Budd is "enlisted by force on Saint George's Channel, taken from a British merchant ship that was on her way home."[19] The ship from which the "Handsome Sailor" is taken away is named, probably not by chance, the "Rights-of-Man."[20]

The Levellers, the radicals who published their pamphlets and petitions during the English civil war, had already brought the issue of impressment into focus, in terms not dissimilar to those used by Hodgskin. As early as 1646, in the *Remonstrance of Many Thousand Citizens*, they exhorted the lawmakers

> to consider what difference there is between binding a man to an oar as a galley-slave in Turkey or Algeria, and pressing of men to serve in your war. To surprise a man on the sudden, force him from his calling where he lived comfortably from a good trade, from his dear parents, wife or children, against inclination and disposition to fight for a cause he understand not and in company of such as he has no comfort to be withal, for pay that will scarce give him sustenance—and if he live, to return to a lost trade, or beggary, or not much better.
> (Overton and Walwyn [1646] 1998, 47–48)

Impressment's overtly arbitrary nature and the fact that it occurred as an unfortunate accident which a citizen could run into without any possibility of appeal made it all the more despicable. It was a practice that—unknown among the Dutch neighbours, frequently brought up as a model—resembles very closely a form of slavery. In the eighteenth century, writes Brunsman (2013, 7), "impressed seamen became second only to African slaves as the largest group of unfree labourers in the ... British Empire."

The comparison with slave labor is not inappropriate. "Impressment … robbed sailors of the one thing, short of property, that made them independent adult men—their freedom of movement" (145). Literally "stuck" on his Majesty's ships, in a period of war they could not leave at the end of a voyage; when their ship came out of service, they were usually transferred to another. Impressed sailors often escaped, trying by any means possible to return to their homes and families. The Royal Navy sought to remedy that by hunting the fugitives down as a slave owner would hunt down his slaves. And yet, it is also true that those very same fugitives often proved to be valiant fighters and sailors, as the success of the British Navy throughout history testifies.

Among the many reasons the British had for disliking impressment, one in particular was related to the mechanics of supply and demand. As Adam Smith ([1776] 1981, I.10.48, 132) explained, "In time of war, when forty or fifty thousand sailors are forced from the merchant service into that of the king, the demand for sailors to merchant ships necessarily rises with their scarcity, and their wages upon such occasions commonly rise from a guinea and seven-and-twenty-shillings, to forty shillings and three pounds a month."[21] Thus, during wartime, impressment decreased the supply of seamen for trading vessels, allowing those who remained to extort higher wages than those forcibly enlisted "at his Majesty's service" had to give up.[22] For Hodgskin, "the high rate of seamen's wages during war *is the effect of impressment*," which always raised the demand for foreign workers (1815c, 4).

The extreme arbitrariness of impressment was profoundly dissonant with that "adjustment" of royal prerogatives that seems to characterize the English idea of freedom. As it "was not subject to any formal civilian supervision," impressment clearly constituted a "vexatious and arbitrary power vested in the hands of the state" (Rogers [1991] 1998, 87). David Hume (1711–1776) considered impressment a "peculiar political habit," eccentric and terrible. It was a case in which the Parliament had obviously failed in curtailing a royal prerogative. Rather than adopt a rule that limited discretion, said Hume ([1752] 1987, 375),

> we continue a practice seemingly the most absurd and unaccountable. Authority, in times of full internal peace and concord, is armed against law. A continued violence is permitted in the crowd, amidst the greatest jealousy and watchfulness in the people; nay proceeding from those very principles: Liberty, in a country of the highest liberty, is left entirely to its own defence, without any countenance or protection.

The Levellers' petition in September 1648 had addressed this point as well, stating as one of its hopes:

> That you would have disclaimed in yourselves and all future Representatives a power of pressing and forcing any sort of men to serve in wars, there being nothing more opposite to freedom.
>
> (Lilburne [1648] 2017, 136)

In his *Thoughts on the Commencement of a New Parliament*, through which he urged Parliament to implement effective reforms, the dissenting clergyman Joseph Towers (1737–1799) included forced recruitment among the "violations of the principles of the Constitution, of justice and humanity." It was "totally repugnant to every idea of liberty and justice" and, through it, "a much greater degree of violence, injustice, and oppression have been exercised upon British subjects, in consequence of the press-warrants lately issued by the Lords of the Admiralty, than have been suffered from the Spaniards by any subjects of the British government" (Towers 1790, 23–24).

The discomfort of impressed sailors was felt throughout the Empire. Only a part of the British fleet was manned by Englishmen: others included Irish, Scots, blacks from the colonies, even Americans.[23] The men boarded on North American ships, by and large, were people who owned some property and looked forward to going back home after their tour of duty (Knollenberg [1960] 2003, 182).[24] Impressment on British soil was legal, but the law was more opaque when it came to impressment in the colonies. In 1708, during the War of the Spanish Succession, the Act for the Encouragement of Trade with America had declared forced enlistment illegal in the American territories, except for those sailors who had deserted from a British ship. The Crown's lawyers believed, however, that this provision would be removed with the end of the war. Impressment in the West Indies was actually forbidden in 1746.

In 1747, a forced enlistment attempt in Boston was followed by a street riot which, in some ways, anticipated the upcoming American uprising. It should not come as a surprise that the matter of impressment was a serious concern of the Founding Fathers.[25] The Declaration of Independence states clearly that, among the faults of the King of England, "He has constrained our fellow Citizens taken Captive on the high Seas to bear Arms against their Country, to become the executioners of their friends and Brethren, or to fall themselves by their Hands."[26]

Not even the successful conclusion of the American revolution solved the Americans' problems with impressment, however. Foreigners were officially exempted from impressment, yet the Royal Navy continued to "recruit" after its own fashion for the duration of the conflict with the French, during which an estimated ten thousand Americans served their former homeland involuntarily. In response to this state of affairs, Thomas Jefferson (1743–1826) promoted the Embargo Act of 1807, which prohibited exports and aimed, in so doing, to hinder Britain.

There is still one more element that can broaden the context for Hodgskin's reflections. He was writing at the conclusion of the Napoleonic wars, most of which he had fought in. The Royal Navy grew enormously during the wars: massive recruitment was possible because of impressment and the Quota Acts of 1795 and 1796, which required parishes to provide certain quotas of men to the necessities of war. War vessels naturally needed bigger crews than merchant ones, if only for the complex operations of managing their guns.

The war between Britain and France was seen by many, republicans excluded, as a conflict between the protection of British liberties and the imperialistic ambitions of Bonapartist France. Thus, as never before, the Royal Navy was considered the true champion of British freedom, a bulwark against despotism. But if the Royal Navy had the task of safeguarding the independence of British citizens, what about the jarring contradiction with the abduction of some citizens in order to force them to defend that very same freedom? Napoleon himself, once at St. Helena, hinted at the contradiction: "You talk of your freedom. Can any thing be more horrible than your pressing of seamen?" (as quoted in O'Meara [1822] 1888, 316).

This contrast between the cause of liberty in Europe, which the Royal Navy fought for, and the practice of impressment was highlighted by Hodgskin (1815e, 4) in one of his letters to the *Morning Chronicle*:

> Since Great Britain possesses in her commerce and her industry a certain and an honourable means of increasing in power and strength, she cannot need aggrandisement by conquest. To her greatness, security but not rapine is necessary. A system of secret and rapid offence may be required by a Bonaparte, but should never be organised by a country whose true greatness consists in the moral quality of her people.

In his *Essay on Naval Discipline*, Hodgskin offers a series of arguments against impressment. First, it leads to the "destruction of our national character" (Hodgskin 1813, 95), which ends up feeding a general resentment within society. Deserters and, more generally, the victims of impressment become a mouthpiece for the injustices they suffered, especially affecting the opinion that the humbler classes had of the Royal Navy and, consequently, influencing their sense of duty to defend the homeland. The loyalty of otherwise good British subjects was put to a test, at the risk of their developing an upfront hostility toward their own country: it is "the man who knows the blessings of liberty, and therefore loves his country, that it teaches to hate it; it is the good citizen whose affections it destroys, and very often converts to a bad man" (7).

Such argument might stir some sympathies but would pale before a clear military threat and the subsequent necessity of sailors.[27] Thus, Hodgskin maintained that it was wrong even when viewed from the perspective of the ruling classes. Those classes had some doubt about the patriotism of the working classes. But Hodgskin argued that the feelings of pride and longing for the British liberties were more prevalent than they seemed, and they might be even greater if only the State strived to elicit such virtues. Resorting to forced enlistment aroused the opposite sentiment in the British people, pushing them away from patriotism and making them feel the victims, rather than the participants, of the defense of British institutions.[28]

As Hodgskin (1813, 13) explains:

> Our rulers, at some period or other, have formed an opinion that we were unwilling to defend our country, but it is they alone who have literally created this unwillingness, and now our people positively think they are incapable of voluntarily defending our country.
>
> When there is so strong a propensity in mankind to fight for their homes, when every man's indignation is even roused by the mention of violence, when this is taught youth as a virtue by their mothers, it begets a wish in many men to go to sea, and contribute to the defence, and share the praise of their countrymen; but when it is known that there is in existence so dreadful a thing as pressing, that this is sanctioned by an authority that men permit to guide all their actions, and when they feel that it is employed to produce a virtue that they already eminently possess, it occurs to them that there is something dreadful at sea which they know nothing about.

The enthusiasm for the defense of freedom is therefore, to some extent, a natural feeling (at least in case of a defensive war). According to Hodgskin (1813, 12),

> Our people have never been passive under injuries; they have never submitted to violence with patience. It is even with difficulty they can be made to bear with pressing and coercion, though patience under them is encouraged, by a general opinion that they are greatly necessary to the welfare of the country; and our people might be safely trusted to this principle of resistance, inherent in our nature, to man our fleets.[29]

Resorting to a contemporary lexicon, we might say that Hodgskin was convinced that the production of the "national defense" public good should come directly from society and therefore the British people as a whole must favor it. It is a *voluntaristic* vision, one that hinges on a widespread sense of responsibility and on a natural propensity to defend one's own life and property and, by extension, the political community in which one lives.[30] A modern, authoritative defender of impressment, J. Ross Dancy (2015, 127), notes that most pamphlets that criticized the practice tended to be written by people with limited knowledge of sea service, who thereby assumed that "the maritime population of Britain was virtually limitless" and that "sailors would volunteer in droves if naval service were made more attractive." Thus, he suggested, only such an assumption would make abolishing impressment feasible. But Lieutenant Hodgskin, with a whole life of experience at sea, can hardly be dismissed as somebody who was unaware of how things *really* worked at sea.

Hodgskin's arguments were founded on his involvement in the navy and in the war. And yet indeed they echo the debate that pitted supporters of a volunteer militia vs. supporters of a standing army, an intense debate within that lively movement of ideas known as the "Scottish Enlightenment."[31]

Adam Ferguson (1723–1816) was perhaps the most eloquent champion of the idea of a popular militia. Hodgskin agrees with Ferguson (1756, 5) that appealing to "so strong a propensity in mankind to fight for their homes" had in the past allowed the people to be "sufficient for their own defence" (and indeed, Ferguson adds, also able to prevail in wars of fortune). But, although Hodgskin believed at the same time that "self-defence is the business of all," he would never condemn, as Ferguson did, the transformation of the nation "into a Company of manufacturers" (12).

The opposite position to that of Ferguson is illustrated by Adam Smith, who advocated a standing army, in homage to the idea of the virtue and effectiveness of the division of labor. Hodgskin stands somewhere in between. Although he believed that there is something noble in the widespread participation in the defense of a fair political system (i.e., the British liberties) when it is under attack, he is also completely immune to that nostalgia for the "liberty of the ancients" that pervades the work of Ferguson. Furthermore, he did not believe that an efficient navy could be exempt from division of labor: on the contrary, it needed a better and fairer division of labor, which could only be guaranteed by workers who *voluntarily* put themselves at the service of a certain goal.

The need for a free and voluntary adhesion to any naval defense scheme anticipates later developments of Hodgskin's thinking. There is a theme that runs through all his work: the role of public opinion, which in his view at times appears almost omnipotent. The whole society, in Hodgskin's scheme, is a complex interlocking of opinions and expectations. Prevailing opinions determine individuals' expectations about the role that other individuals can play in society. He believes that the balance between public and private life can either suppress or open up spaces for individual initiative. The legislator whose goal is "governing too much" would not see "the means of producing the obedience that springs from opinion" (Hodgskin 1813, 158), he wrote in his essay, and yet such means are of paramount importance. How does the drive that connects political *ideas* and *facts* work? How come that opinion may guide the lawmaker?

An Essay on Naval Discipline is not a study of social psychology, nor was it written just to build his skills as a writer. He wanted his ideas to change the political reality. The work that Hodgskin began with this pamphlet—i.e., his work as a polemicist, essayist, political writer—is based on the assumption that "ideas have consequences," to quote the title of an essay written by Richard Weaver (1910–1963) in 1948. It is rather uncanny how the determination of the "unhappy and disappointed" young man that Hodgskin was after his experience in the Navy steered him immediately to this kind of career. It is as if his belief in the power of words in shaping the facts pre-existed his later exploration of how they may actually affect social reality.

His vision is founded on a view of human nature that, although sketchy, we cannot help but find familiar. The assumption of political action that emerges from the pages of the *Essay* is that people respond to incentives; they are interested in obtaining the highest possible satisfaction including positive social recognition. In the second chapter, devoted to the love of Fame, he states that the passion for distinction is "a general passion of our nature" that "will be stronger in our country than in any other; for it is one conspicuous effect of that liberty we enjoy to afford room for the gratification of, and consequently to excite, every human desire" (Hodgskin 1813, 18). In itself, there is nothing wrong with this desire to stand out, this need to soar, but Hodgskin was aware that it could produce very different results depending on situations and contexts.[32] "No laws can restrain action that finds praise in society" (23–24); the opinion of men, the opinion of society as a whole, is the ultimate tribunal.

When he published *An Essay on Naval Discipline*, Hodgskin was, as far as we know, ignorant about economic matters. He had not yet cultivated those connections that would culminate in attending the courses taught by Jean-Baptiste Say in Paris, which matured his thinking. Still, he was well aware that insufficient recruitment by the navy could be explained through economics. He said this most explicitly in his letters to the *Morning Chronicle*, a newspaper traditionally close to the Whig party and therefore particularly attentive to "economistic" arguments.

He argued in the letters that impressment was inefficient as it entailed a number of costs not balanced by the benefits it produced. Drafting people by force implied a burden that outweighed the benefit of an unpaid workforce. Hodgskin's reasoning is perhaps elegant but not fully persuasive.

Forced recruitment, he explains, "employs, as we have seen, press gangs, guards, officers and marines uselessly, and by devoting funds to paying them, takes away from the country the power of procuring and paying useful seamen." At first glance, such math seems odd: there is a blatant numerical disproportion between the press gangs and the personnel required by the fleet. Press gangs would have been ridiculously unproductive if, in their searches in seaside villages and on ships at anchor, they really enrolled so few sailors that their work could not compensate for their living costs. Suffice it to say that, during the Napoleonic wars, the Royal Navy went from 17,000 men in active duty in 1792 to over 130,000 in 1801. "By 1810, British naval manpower had reached over 145,000 men, about 2.7 per cent of Britain's male population" (Dancy 2015, 29).

Hodgskin was well aware that the difficulty of manning the fleet could be the main objection, and had an answer. Much of the activity of the press gangs consisted not only in coercively recruiting sailors, but in retrieving them after they had fled. A rebellious employee, on a ship as in any other situation, is a cause for several possible unpredictable expenses: coercion can lead to varying degrees of active resistance and, consequently, to a series of costs associated with surveillance and "correction of unwanted behavior."

In short, "the employment of impressment makes every man it procures cost as much annually as would hire two" because "many of the men procured by impressment are deserters, or are pressed two or three times" (Hodgskin 1815c, 4). Seizing a man, taking away his freedom of movement, is still not enough to prevent him from trying to return to his homeland or the merchant ship from where he was taken.[33] It is true that ships are enclosed, isolated environments from where it is difficult to escape. But it is also true that they stop at ports, and there are not enough officers to police all the sailors one by one, and civilians can sometimes turn out to be accomplices of the fugitives. A "perfect" police state—one that has total control over the lives of its subjects—is unachievable even on the seas.

That impressed sailors were thus basically slave laborers, victims of a coercive system and not workers, simply recruited by somewhat unorthodox methods is, for Hodgskin, a plain matter of fact. Voluntary participation in any form of division of labor coincides with the effort to gear up for the task at hand with an investment in human capital, as we would say today. But, according to Hodgskin, the use of forced labor implies an attempt to "combine" the factors of production in a very ineffective way, like pieces of a puzzle that a stubborn kid tries to wedge in where they will not fit. Forcing people who have not experienced the apprenticeship of life on board to serve on a warship results in a superficial, untimely training, training that will produce bad sailors, ready to flee at the first opportunity, wasting the time and resources that have been invested in them. When bad sailors are punished with excessive rigor, the navy ends up taking away "from the seamen what is their only reward for all privations, what is the only remuneration for all the injuries they suffer—the respect and praise of society" (Hodgskin 1813, 57). Moreover, each monitoring apparatus has its costs—time and money that would be better used for other purposes.

As Hodgskin explains (1815b, 4):

> After men are impressed they are not immediately serviceable—they are not on board the very ships in which they are wanted to defend their country; they require in the first place gaols called guard ships, in which they may be secured, and in the next tenders, which are moving gaols to convey them to the vessels in which they are wanted to serve.

Impressment therefore appears as a gigantic waste of resources. And, for that reason, Hodgskin makes it the object of an astonishing comparison: the inefficiency of using forced labor on the one hand, and labor market efficiency on the other.

"It is a general fact ... that wherever food and employment can be procured, candidates to obtain them are always found." A shortage of seamen cannot therefore be regarded as a natural phenomenon, especially in light of the fact that there is "an abundance of men" who offer to perform "employments," such as working in mines, "more disagreeable, difficult and dangerous than the seamen's" with "their pecuniary rewards not greater—and their glory nothing." "Yet they get men without the aid either of press gangs or recruiting parties" (Hodgskin 1815d, 4). It was Adam Smith ([1776] 1981, I.10.5, 117) who explained that "wages of labour vary with the ease or hardship, the cleanliness or dirtiness, the honourableness or dishonourableness of the employment.[34] Why, then, was it so difficult to find candidates for a job that was not much harder than others, and far more honorable?

A possible answer to Hodgskin's question is that the demand of sailors for warships naturally follows a different path from that of other professions. It is fair to assume that the need to enroll sailors would dramatically increase at the start of a war and that, on the other hand, in time of peace it would be possible to conduct the routine operations of the Royal Navy with a smaller number of seamen. Yet to be a sailor requires a certain highly specific knowledge that cannot be learned overnight. Skilled sailors in wartime were thus particularly scarce and valuable: so much so that the private sector would swiftly drag them away from the navy. The debate we are examining took place in the early nineteenth century, well before the seemingly irreversible trend toward the growth of public expenditure and "stabilization" of the civil service, which is typical today.

Hodgskin's answer is that "if a voluntary service did not bring men fast enough, as many soldiers should be embarked" (1815e, 4). That is, if recruiting people who are not seamen cannot be avoided, then at least they should be recruited among army soldiers, for whom serving their homeland on the seas should be worth as much as doing it on dry land. But such a possibility would not solve the problem of recruiting experienced sailors.

An Essay on Naval Discipline opens with an examination of impressment because the presence of sailors who are forcibly enrolled leads to the regime of naval discipline, and most importantly, the frequent recourse to corporal punishment. As we know, Hodgskin himself had played a role in a terrible accident which had resulted in the loss of a young recruit's life. Hodgskin had direct experience, especially during his service under William Ferris, of the brutality that commanding officers imposed upon their subordinates.

"Punishment came in all shapes and sizes. But the word 'punishment' meant one thing: flogging. The cat-o'-nine-tails was the symbolic heart of discipline, and a formal flogging was *the* ceremony of power" (Neale 1985, 25). Flogging was extremely common: even worse was "starting," which was "one man beating another with a piece of rope as hard as he can hit him; the other being perfectly defenseless, and forbid even to look displeased, as that is contempt or disrespect" (Hodgskin 1813, 62).

Such brutality is conceivable only because forced laborers were its subject. "Seamen are not flogged to compel them to fight bravely, but to force them to be submissive.... We first violate the liberty of these men, and then we severely punish them for the feelings and actions necessarily resulting from so violent an outrage" (Hodgskin 1815a, 4).

Hodgskin (1813, 43) does not agree that flogging was necessary due to the understandable rebelliousness of seamen who were forcibly enrolled. Rather, he suggests that "as the real duties of a ship can never occupy the time of half of the men employed," the reasons why the sailors were flogged were whims, invented by the captains to "entertain" themselves and their subordinates.

Some of the iron allotted to a man to polish does not shine well; his hammock has not been clean scrubbed; his clues [sic] have not been blacked; his clothes have wanted mending; his shirt has been dirty; or, perhaps, he may have neglected the captain's stock, or the wardroom dinner: These, and a thousand similar trifles, are what seamen are flogged for, as neglect of duty. The captain's orders have made doing these things their dirt; and custom sanctions his inflicting flogging for their neglect.

As we have seen, Hodgskin always defends the innate sense of bravery and patriotism of the English people. When they are punished harshly, most of the time it is not because of negligence in battle or for endangering their shipmates but for failing to meet trivial or unreasonable requests born out of the whims of their commanding officers. "Another customary mode of forcing men's labour in men of war sometimes in use … was to flog the whole of the men stationed to perform a particular service, such as the main-topsail-yard men & c., if they were last at executing a part of their duty" (Hodgskin, 1813, 47). Every so often the officers in command simply punished with flogging those who would not pay them their respects ("in the navy, with many, [respect] is positive servility or unlimited obedience to any commands, however absurd; with others, it is simple obedience to positive and legal commands") or those who fought and caused disorders among the crew (56).

Boarded as slaves, seamen ended up being treated as such—puppets at the service of their officers.

The whip was also frequently used against drunkards. Hodgskin (1813, 49) agrees that alcohol abuse "can cause nothing less than destruction to every ennobling sentiment, of every regularity that can keep up order or preserve health." But it's clearly not enough reason to justify flogging or similarly cruel corporal punishments. In the *Essay*, Hodgskin compares the incidence of theft among all crimes in England as opposed to those committed in the navy. Since sailors are British, Hodgskin suggests, it would be logical to expect the same propensity to steal when they are on dry land as when they are at sea. But if not—and such was the case—this should suggest that the "system" of naval discipline encourages certain behaviors more than it curtails them.

Ultimately, every problem of life on board comes down to an *institutional* matter, related to political order and to the essentially tyrannical nature of the individual ships: "possessing power has ever led to oppression" (Hodgskin 1813, 144).

On ships, the role of captain combines totally heterogeneous functions: he is the chief executive but is also the sole judge of the behavior of his subordinates, and he only answers to the courts martial which are deaf, almost by definition, to the needs of sailors and devoted to consolidating existing customs of punishment. Captains "possess an unlimited and unrestrained power" (Hodgskin 1813, 68) and end up using that power in an entirely arbitrary way. It is then hardly surprising that, besides drunkenness, sailors could be flogged because of profanities or otherwise defined (or perhaps not defined at all) "bad behavior."

The criticism of naval discipline is therefore an indictment of the non-regulation of political power: arbitrary and cruel when it decides whom to submit to its command (through impressment), cruel and arbitrary when it makes use of the cat-o'-nine-tails to punish crimes without the slightest respect for the principle of proportionality.

It is certainly possible that a despot might be an enlightened one.[35] Hodgskin takes the opposite direction. He quotes William Paley (1743–1805), who remarked that "it is tyranny in the legislature leaving to magistrates the power of defining what the laws intended to punish" (Paley [1785] 2002, 3). Hodgskin (1813, 29–30) accuses "civilian" institutions of having allowed to consolidate upon the ship captains an authority that no one should ever possess:

> [O]ur legislature has left to the captains the power of punishing according to custom; has left them the power of making customs equal to laws; has made them, when they form courts martial, the only judges of these customs, and they have the power of condemning to punishment: in short, they are legislators, they are judges, they are juries, and they are very often parties and executioners.... The entrusting arbitrary power to any governor or governors is not less destructive of his or their happiness than it may be of all the men governed; that this unhappiness to both is the fruit of arbitrary power being in the possession of any men, experience must show to all; that its fruits are the same in the navy, I am convinced from experience; it is as pernicious to the happiness of officers, through making them distrustful and jealous, instead of their having confidence and attachment, as it is to the seamen's happiness, through the cruelty that is exercised upon them.

Thus, the system tends to appoint an absolute ruler for every ship. As such, those rulers are completely unrestrained in their behavior, their respect for their subordinates being discretionary and dependent, in essence, on individual attitudes. But, as a captain must have undergone all other steps of the hierarchical ladder, it is to be expected that the actions of those who preceded him in command would have had a strong influence over him. The system tends to produce officials groomed in the worship of a cruel discipline, distrustful of their men and fierce advocates of the omnipotence of the whip; what kind of consequence this has on their subordinates is easily imaginable.

The fact that officers were, on average, very poorly educated aggravated the problem—an issue, we know, to which Hodgskin was very sensitive due to his personal experience. However, although he disapproved of the centralization of power in the hands of the captains, he admitted without hesitation that a certain degree of discretion is simply necessary by the very nature of a warship command. Decisions must be taken quickly, the enemy must be met head-on, and much depends on the adaptability and flexibility of those in charge.

A different system of naval discipline—a purely voluntary Royal Navy, composed of sailors who have specifically chosen to be part of it—would also educate differently the officers groomed for command. But the sailors would have to be better educated themselves, better informed, and able to appreciate the fairness of the British system of institutions and the value of freedom.

If the navy must continue to embark 13-year-old boys, "their parents should wholly provide for them, and pay all the expenses of their education, till they were sixteen; and till that age, they should never be suffered to do any duty that in any way involved command" (Hodgskin 1813, 162).

Education, as Hodgskin (1813, 164) informs us, was "derided as useless, despised as superfluous, and treated with contempt as a hindrance to advancement." However, he hoped that "better days are coming, when officers themselves will be sensible of the value of knowledge." For this to happen, individual initiatives would not be sufficient, although he was very much committed to one: the institution of libraries "established at the different naval stations," with an active role and book contributions by the sailors themselves. "If these [libraries] were countenanced by government for us, if they would furnish the building, our own pecuniary means would do all the rest."

The issue was, however, systemic. The officers' education would not improve unless the rules for recruitment changed. Impressment was the source of the problems to which a cruel naval discipline tried to find (wrong) answers, and therefore only its abolition could begin a reform process. Only a genuinely voluntary system would provide an appropriate framework of incentives that would exploit in the most appropriate way the need to excel that Hodgskin (1813, 165) saw as the core of human nature:

> Nothing can so effectually make knowledge desirable, or be so strong a stimulus to its acquisition, as abolishing the compulsory mode of doing naval duties; then men will feel they will be respected, and willingly obeyed, in proportion as they merit it; the reputation of a smart officer will then, probably, depend upon a man's virtues, and then talents and abilities will not be deprived, as they now are, of their legitimate reward—*praise*.

It would not be possible to expect an improvement of the naval discipline otherwise, and certainly Hodgskin (1813, 30) never expected it to come from the judicial authorities: "Justice cannot be obtained at courts martial," he wrote, since these are path-dependent institutions. Their members had grown up in that specific culture and it is highly unlikely that they would stray from it. The point of view of military courts was pretty much the same as the commanding officers' and they would be deaf to any complaints that came from "a junior officer, or a common seaman." For Hodgskin (1813, 30–31), "it is as rational to expect justice from a court martial as from a Turkish Cadhi; both possess the same power, and both are subject to the influence of that power through their passions upon their judgment."

What he proposes is nothing less than a total rethinking of the system. Not only should inhumane and cruel punishments be outlawed but, simultaneously, the whole system centered upon impressment should be abolished. There is no possibility of any incremental change for the better if the evil that poisons the whole system of "naval discipline" is not eradicated. Such was the plea that the former sailor addressed to the civil authorities and, in a sense, it proposes a harmonization of the legal system, inside and outside the Royal Navy. The navy should not be allowed to remain an enclave of violence and totally arbitrary power. The constant reminder is to the effectiveness of the order of freedom, as it has been experienced "on dry land." Precisely because, more than any alternative, it would better guarantee happiness and progress, there is no reason for depriving it from those British citizens who have had the misfortune of being conscripted into the navy by a press gang.

Condemnation of the brutality of naval discipline is not universal. John Byrn Jr. (1989, 2) acknowledged that the abolition of impressment and the implementation of strict rules to limit the use of corporal punishments were reforms, the supporters of which "produced reams of propaganda promoting their adoption," and of which Hodgskin's book was a prime example. But Byrn argued that "the methods used to maintain harmony in the king's fleet were similar to those of the eighteenth-century English system of criminal justice. Indeed, within its own clearly defined jurisdiction, naval discipline was in many ways a microcosm of that system" (5). He maintained that corporal punishments had a sort of "ceremonial" nature that contributed to institutionalize them, making them mostly a symbolic ritual (77). N.A.M. Rodger (2006, 60), perhaps the most eminent historian of the Royal Navy, also maintains that discipline in the Royal Navy was "notably milder than that of the army."

While most well-advised scholars sought, as they should, to consider every phenomenon in the right context, aiming to understand before passing judgment, for our purposes Hodgskin's passionate criticism of naval discipline is crucial to better define the contours of his political sensitivity. Hodgskin was developing a form of liberalism that was both deeply humanitarian—striving for a tangible improvement of the living conditions of actual human beings—and absolutely distrustful of any coercive authority. His basic assumption was that it is highly unlikely that men can achieve happiness when they are not allowed to make independent choices. And, since the Creator cannot but wish happiness for human beings, freedom is necessarily the natural order. Hence, the natural order is an order devoid of coercion.

This belief in a coercion-free natural order will be the culmination of Hodgskin's reflections. Yet the crucial elements are already present, in a nutshell, in this first essay: the condemnation of arbitrary power; the belief that there is, instead, an "orderly liberty" that emerges spontaneously when men are free to follow their own volitions; confidence in the power of education to improve the conditions of those who pursue it; and the power of an informed public opinion to change, for the better, the course of things.

We have already mentioned how *An Essay on Naval Discipline* had made Hodgskin an interesting interlocutor in the eyes of Francis Place and, through him, of the English radical philosophers. These had in Jeremy Bentham their own ideal mentor. It was indeed the works of Bentham, as explained by Albert V. Dicey (1835–1922), that provided the intellectual trigger to the great season of reforms that was the British nineteenth century. Hodgskin's thoughts on natural order would lead him to distance himself quite considerably from Bentham, whom he soon came to regard as his intellectual adversary. In this first work, however, the outlines of a broader worldview are merely sketched while he drew a specific picture of how a crucial British institution—such as it was, at the time, the Royal Navy—needed to be reformed.

The contrast between British liberties and naval discipline called, indeed, for an adjustment of the discipline on board to the legal standards of civilian life: the reform of the Royal Navy into a professional military institution free from the stigma of coercion. It is easy to imagine how such a project could catch the attention of avid social reformers such as Francis Place and convince them that in Thomas Hodgskin they had stumbled upon a kindred spirit.

Notes

1 Applying political labels is always a dangerous exercise. However, as an introduction to modern libertarianism, see, *inter alia*, Gaus and Mack (2004); Boaz (2015); Barry (1987). The most relevant contemporary philosophical work on libertarianism is Huemer (2012).
2 Thomas was the fourth of six children; two of his sisters were born after the family moved to Sheerness in 1800, when Thomas was already at sea.
3 As an example, see the annotations "from personal experience" in Hodgskin (1827, 153–154) which support his vision on international exchange.
4 The famous library founded by the publisher Charles Mudie (1818–1890), who had the idea of lending books by an annual subscription of a guinea, dates only to 1842.
5 In his *Essay on Naval Discipline*, Hodgskin advocated the establishment of libraries in "different naval stations," suggesting that the government could just provide the locations and that "our own pecuniary means would do all the rest" (Hodgskin 1813, 164).
6 Hodgskin became a lieutenant at the age of 18; Royal Navy regulations prescribed that such promotion was possible only after the age of 20, but these standards were enforced rather flexibly (Hodgskin's case was no exception).
7 Information about Hodgskin's naval service is taken from Driver (n.d.) and Stack (1998).
8 He would later write about a captain under whom he served for a long time and who was "rightfully celebrated" for his accomplishments: "This captain was a religious man, and a man, whom I believe, most firmly thought himself conscientiously just, and that, in committing numberless cruelties, he was promoting the good of the service … . I have seen this captain flog, I think, twenty-six men, part of them by candle-light, at both gangways, because their hammocks were not properly cleaned" (Hodgskin 1813, 33).
9 In particular, Hodgskin chose not to attend any Greek and Latin courses. Stack (1998, 50) suggests that "he may have felt inferior to the younger boys who had been trained in Latin and Greek at their parish schools."
10 According to Place, his father had "no intention of causing harm to his family," but the means he chose to pursue his questionable ends left a lot to be desired: "he wished to do his duty towards his children and he thought he did do his duty. He had no notion of producing effects by advice, his passions were strong, and too little under control to permit him to produce effects by example" (Thale 1972, 61, 62).

11 Unlike other liberals, Hodgskin never supported the cause of free public education. In those years, he feared the inevitably ideological nature of direct public participation. In *Travels*, he describes the schools of Hanover, not without some praise, but he also notes that "national education ... is good inasmuch as it models the whole community according to the wish of the controllers. Where the nation is entirely excluded from communication with other nations, it produces a certain uniformity of manners, a quiet submission, and a most perfect contentment. But it almost excludes improvement in all the great arts of life, and limits the attainments of the society by the attainments of its rulers" (Hodgskin 1820, 258–259).
12 For a thorough account of the disagreement in question, see Stack (1998, 82–88).
13 On the role of the *Economist* as a propagator of economic ideas in Victorian England, see Gordon (1955).
14 To what extent Hodgskin, being older and wiser, might have influenced the development of the younger Spencer's ideas is a matter of speculation. In his majestic *Autobiography*, Spencer mentions Hodgskin without betraying any particular gratitude or affection. However, it must be noted that Spencer was always reluctant to acknowledge intellectual debts that could cast a shade of doubt on his absolute originality. See Spencer (1904, I) and the Conclusion of this book.
15 Hodgskin accused Wilson, who had become a Westbury parliamentarian in 1847, of being overly submissive to the Whigs. Hodgskin's daughter wrote to Halévy, "When Wilson desired the whole spirit of his articles changed, my Father ... simply refused to write anything contrary to his convictions and left the office" (Halévy [1903] 1956, 168^{fn}).
16 Halévy's statement is not entirely true. We know, for example, that a rather extensive obituary, although partly inaccurate with respect to Hodgskin's education, appeared on August 16, 1869, in the *Bath Chronicle and Weekly Gazette*, p. 6, among the "Deaths of Note." Other papers published obituaries, too, although they were succinct.
17 Ross Dancy has contested such estimates and argues for a much smaller figure. He states that "impressment accounted for 8 per cent of seamen during the first year of the war and grew to 27 per cent in 1801" (Dancy 2015, 146). While estimates of the dimensions of the phenomenon vary sharply, it is hard to maintain that it was a trivial one.
18 Dancy (2015, 149) points out that "the Royal Navy was not only pressing skilled sailors, but sailors who were also young. Working in the rigging, and being a topman, did not just involve skill, but also required the agility of youth," a point that is well epitomized by Billy Budd's story.
19 Hodgskin on impressment was actually a source Melville took advantage of for his 1850 novel *White Jacket* (Philbrick 1960).
20 In the opera *Billy Budd* by Benjamin Britten, Billy says goodbye to his old ship with an evocative "Farewell, Rights o' Man./Farewell, old Rights o' Man./Farewell to you for ever,/old Rights o' Man."
21 In 1824, Hodgskin (1824, 160) advanced similar estimates and then asked, "Why should they [the sailors] enter a service where only half price is offered for their labour? or can anything be more preposterous than for Government to go into a market, and, finding no supply can be got *under the market price*, immediately to seize on the commodity by force, throw down half its value in return, and justify the proceeding on the score of *necessity*?" Dancy (2015, 119) maintains that "merchant ship owners were forced to offer extraordinarily high pay to seamen, not because press gangs drained the maritime labor market dry, but because vast numbers of seamen volunteered for naval service during wartime.
22 Hodgskin (1815e, 4) himself notes that, with the abolition of impressment, "merchants will not have to give such high wages as they now do."

23 In reviewing some contemporary literature on impressment, Hodgskin (1824, 161) estimated that foreigners accounted for one-eighth of the navy's sailors during the Napoleonic wars. It should be noted that foreign prisoners of war were given the option to join the navy.
24 For an analysis of how impressment fed revolutionary sentiments, see Magra (2013).
25 In 1775, in the acts of the English Parliament that led to hostilities against the colonies, impressment emerges as a kind of strategic instrument, ironically defended by the British government as a humanitarian act: the humane alternative offered to American sailors was to work like slaves rather than face execution. See Ramsay ([1789] 1990, I, 266–267).
26 *Declaration of Independence*, July 4, 1776, Washington, D.C., National Archives, available at https://www.archives.gov/founding-docs/declaration-transcript.
27 The fact that the size of the Royal Navy, in terms of personnel, more than doubled during the Napoleonic wars is itself a meaningful gauge of the ratio between performance and number of recruits. As mentioned earlier, we are talking about the necessity of manning and maneuvering large sailing vessels, before the large steamships began to be used—indeed, a most labor-intensive task. Hodgskin, in contrast, appears on more than one occasion persuaded that there was an excess of manpower on the individual ships beyond actual needs.
28 It is not surprising that, in this respect, Hodgskin is fiercely opposed to the involvement of foreign sailors, such as "Africans, who had been stolen from Africa, taken to a slave ship, afterward cloathed, on board a guard-ship and, without being able to speak a word of English, sent to man the British fleet, to fight the battle of our country." The use of slave labor and the conscription of foreign convicts demeaned the naval service precisely in that "voluntaristic" dimension of moral commitment toward one's own political community that Hodgskin endorses. See Hodgskin (1813, 97–98).
29 A similar principle, but more extreme, is advocated by a young Herbert Spencer thirty years later, in his first work, the short pamphlet "The Proper Sphere of Government" ([1843] 1981). In the fifth of the letters that appeared in *The Nonconformist* (later collected and published in a single volume), Spencer argues that it is possible to imagine that active resistance against a hypothetical invader could be left to the spontaneous organization of society, without any coercion. The assumption that this could not happen appears to him as the product of "old knowledge" rather than reasonable belief. See Spencer ([1843] 1981, 210–217).
30 "It is the observation of some great man, that whenever a virtue is much wanted, it will be produced … . As courage and conduct in naval affairs and, as an attachment to the sea is absolutely necessary, in a large portion of the people, for the safety of the whole community, I have no doubt these virtues would always be produced if they were permitted" (Hodgskin 1813, 21–22).
31 See, *inter alia*, Broadie (2001).
32 For example, "the desire of praise is the remote cause of [the] greater part of the thieving in society" (Hodgskin 1813, 57).
33 "Many merchant ships built tiny secret hiding places where two or three valued men could try to evade the sharp-eyed press gang" (Pope 1987, 99).
34 Smith added that "Honour makes a great part of the reward of all honourable professions."
35 N.A.M. Rodger, for instance, goes as far as to argue that "good captains frequently backed their men's grievances against the Navy, especially over their pay," which may be perfectly true, but reasoning on the moral fiber of those who occupy a position of command may lead us far from thinking about the institutions that restrict their power—such is, instead, Hodgskin's intention (Rodger 2006, 134).

References

Barry, Norman. 1987. *On Classical Liberalism and Libertarianism*. London: Palgrave.
Bechervaise, John. 1847. *A Farewell to My Old Shipmates and Messmates*. Portsea: W. Woodward.
Boaz, David. 2015. *The Libertarian Mind: A Manifesto for Freedom*. New York: Simon & Schuster.
Borges, Jorge Luis. (1935) 1975. *A Universal History of Infamy*. Harmondsworth: Penguin Books.
Brake, Laurel and Marisa Demor, eds. 2009. *Dictionary of Nineteenth Century Journalism*. Ghent: Academia Press.
Broadie, Alexander. 2001. *The Scottish Enlightenment: The Historical Age of the Historical Nation*. Edinburgh: Birlinn.
Brunsman, Denver. 2013. *The Evil Necessity: British Naval Impressment in the Eighteenth-Century Atlantic World*. Charlottesville: University of Virginia Press.
Byrn Jr., John D. 1989. *Crime and Punishment in the Royal Navy: Discipline in the Leeward Islands Station 1784–1812*. Aldershot: Scholar Press.
Dancy, J. Ross. 2015. *The Myth of the Press Gang: Volunteers, Impressment and the Naval Manpower Problem in the Late Eighteenth Century*. Woodbridge: Boydell Press.
Declaration of Independence. 1776, July 4. Washington, D.C., National Archives, https://www.archives.gov/founding-docs/declaration-transcript.
Driver, Cecil Herbert. n.d. "Memorandum on the Life of Thomas Hodgskin (1787–1869)," in Thomas Hodgskin Papers, Yale University Library.
Dudley Edwards, Ruth. 1993. *The Pursuit of Reason: Economist 1843–1993*. London: Hamish Hamilton.
Ferguson, Adam. 1756. *Reflections previous to the Establishment of a Militia*. London: Dodsley.
Gaus, Gerald, and Chandran Kukathas, eds. 2004. *A Handbook of Political Theory*. London: Routledge.
Gaus, Gerald, and Eric Mack. 2004. "Libertarianism and Classical Liberalism," in *A Handbook of Political Theory*. Edited by Gerald Gaus and Chandran Kukathas. 2004. London: Routledge, 15–129.
Gordon, Scott. 1955. "The London Economist and the High Tide of Laissez Faire." *Journal of Political Economy* 63 (6): 461–488, https://doi.org/10.1086/257722.
Halévy, Élie. (1903) 1956. *Thomas Hodgskin*. Edited in translation with an introduction by A. J. Taylor. London: Ernst Benn.
Halifax, Lord-Savile, George Savile. (1692) 1700. "A Rough Deal of a New Model at Sea." In *Halifax, Miscellanies*, edited by the Right Noble Lord, the Late Lord Marquess of Halifax. London: Mtt. Gillyflower.
Hilton, Boyd. (2006) 2013. *A Mad, Bad, & Dangerous People? England, 1783–1846*. Oxford: Oxford University Press.
Hodgskin, Thomas. 1813. *An Essay on Naval Discipline, Shewing Part of its Evil Effects on the Minds of the Officers, on the Minds of the Men, and on the Community; with an Amended System, by which Pressing May Be Immediately Abolished*. London: Printed for the Author by C. Squire.
Hodgskin, Thomas. 1815a. "On Impressment. Letter V." *Morning Chronicle*, November 22.
Hodgskin, Thomas. 1815b. "On Impressment. Letter VII." *Morning Chronicle*, December 1.

Hodgskin, Thomas. 1815c. "On Impressment. Letter IX." *Morning Chronicle*, December 12.

Hodgskin, Thomas. 1815d. "On Impressment. Letter X." *Morning Chronicle*, December 16.

Hodgskin, Thomas. 1815e. "On Impressment. Letter XI." *Morning Chronicle*, December 23.

Hodgskin, Thomas to Place, Francis, June 29, 1817.

Hodgskin, Thomas. 1820. *Travels in the North of Germany. Describing the Present State of the Social and Political Institutions, the Agriculture, Manufacture, Commerce, Education, Arts and Manners in That Country, Particularly in the Kingdom of Hannover*. 2 vols. Edinburgh: Archibald Constable.

Hodgskin, Thomas. 1824. "Abolition of Impressment." *Edinburgh Review* 41 (October): 154–181.

Hodgskin, Thomas. 1827. *Popular Political Economy: Four Lectures Delivered at the Mechanics' Institution*. London: Tait.

Hodgskin, Thomas. 1832. *The Natural and Artificial Right of Property*. London: Steil.

Huemer, Michael. 2012. *The Problem of Political Authority: An Examination of the Right to Coerce and the Duty to Obey*. London: Palgrave.

Hume, David. (1752) 1987. "Of Some Remarkable Customs." In *Hume, Essays Moral, Politi-cal and Literary*. Edited by Eugene F. Miller, 366–376. Indianapolis, IN: Liberty Fund.

James, William. 1837. *The Naval History of Great Britain, from the Declaration of War by France in 1793 to the Accession of George IV*, Vol. V. London: Richard Bentley.

Keegan, John. 1993. *A History of Warfare*. New York: Vintage Books.

Knollenberg, Bernhard. (1960) 2003. *Origin of the American Revolution: 1759–1766*. Indianapolis, IN: Liberty Fund.

Lilburne, John. (1648) 2017. "The Petition of 11 September 1648: To the Right Honourable, the Commons of England In Parliament Assembled. The humble Petition of divers wel affected Persons inhabiting the City of London, Westminster, the Borough of South-wark, Hamblets, and places adjacent. Whereunto is annexed, The humble desires of the said Petitioners for the Houses resolution thereon, before they proceed with the personal Treaty." In *Tracts on Liberty by the Levellers and their Critics (1638–1660)*. Edited by David M.Hart and Ross Kenyon, Vol. V. Indianapolis, IN: Liberty Fund.

Mackay, Charles. 1887. *Through the Long Day: Memorial of a Literary Life During Half a Century*, Vol. I. London: Allen.

MacLeod, Christine. (2007) 2010. *Heroes of Invention: Technology, Liberalism and British Identity, 1750–1914*. Cambridge: Cambridge University Press.

Magra, Christopher P. 2013. "Anti-Impressment Riots and the Origins of the Age of Revolution." *International Review of Social History* 58, S21 (December): 131–151, https://doi.org/10.1017/S0020859013000291.

Neale, Jonathan. 1985. *The Cutlass & the Lash: Mutiny and Discipline in Nelson's Navy*. London: Pluto Press.

O'Meara, Barry. (1822) 1888. *Napoleon at St. Helena*. London: Bentley.

Overton, Richard, and William Walwyn. (1646) 1998. "A Remonstrance of Many Thousand Citizens and Other Freeborn People of England to Their House of Commons." In *The English Levellers*. Edited by Andrew Sharp, 33–53. Cambridge: Cambridge University Press.

Paley, William (1785) 2002. *The Principles of Moral and Political Philosophy.* Indianapolis, IN: Liberty Fund.

Pettegree, Andrew. 2014. *The Invention of News: How the World Came to Know About Itself.* New Haven: Yale University Press.

Philbrick, Thomas. 1960. "Melville's 'Best Authorities.'" *Nineteenth-Century Fiction* 15 (2): 171–179, https://doi.org/10.2307/2932454.

Pope, Dudley. 1987. *Life in Nelson's Navy.* London: Unwin.

Prince, Kathryn. 2009. "Shakespeare in the Early Working Class Press." In *The Working-class Intellectual in Eighteenth- and Nineteenth-Century Britain.* Edited by Aruna Krishnamurthy, 129–142. Farnham: Ashgate.

Ramsay, David. (1789) 1990. *The History of the American Revolution.* Edited by Lester H. Cohen, Vol. I. Indianapolis, IN: Liberty Fund.

Rodger, N.A.M. 2006. *The Command of the Ocean: A Naval History of Britain, 1649–1815.* New York: W.W. Norton &Co.

Rogers, Nicholas. (1991) 1998. "Liberty Road: The Opposition to Impressment during the Mid-Georgian Era." In *Crowds, Culture, and Politics in Georgian Britain*, 85–121. Oxford: Clarendon Press.

Rogers, Nicholas. 2007. *The Press Gang: Naval Impressment and its Opponents in Georgian Britain.* New York: Continuum.

Rose, Jonathan. 2001. *The Intellectual Life of the British Working Classes.* New Haven: Yale University Press.

Smith, Adam. (1776) 1981. *An Inquiry into the Nature and Causes of the Wealth of Nations*, Vol. I, V. Edited by Roy H.Campbell and Andrew S.Skinner. Indianapolis, IN: Liberty Fund.

Spencer, Herbert. (1843) 1981. "The Proper Sphere of Government." Chapter 2 in *The Man Versus the State with Six Essays on Government, Society, and Freedom.* Indianapolis, IN: Liberty Fund.

Spencer, Herbert. 1851. "Social Statics; or, the Conditions Essential to Human Happiness Specified, and the First of them Developed." *Economist*, February 8.

Spencer, Herbert. 1904. *An Autobiography*, Vol. I. London: Williams and Norgate.

Stack, David. 1998. *Nature and Artifice: The Life and Thought of Thomas Hodgskin, 1787–1869.* Martlesham: Boydell & Brewer.

Thale, Margaret, ed. 1972. *The Autobiography of Francis Place.* Cambridge: Cambridge University Press.

Towers, Joseph. 1790. *Thoughts on the Commencement of a New Parliament with Re-marks on the Letter of the Right Hon. Edmund Burke on the Revolution in France.* London: Charles Dilly.

Wallas, Graham. (1898) 1925. *The Life of Francis Place 1771–1854.* London: Allen & Unwin.

2 Thomas Hodgskin's peculiar blend of "socialism"

Hodgskin: a Ricardian socialist?

Words, in politics, come and go—and so do their meanings. In endeavoring to understand thinkers who used a vocabulary that is now long past, it is wise to base our conclusions about their ideology on the ideas they expressed about specific issues, rather than rely on labels by others or even by themselves. This is what we will try to do as we deal with Thomas Hodgskin's understanding of the Industrial Revolution—an understanding that has often been misinterpreted. In this chapter, we will look primarily at his pamphlet *Labour Defended against the Claims of Capital*.

The most "dramatically revolutionary" (Cipolla 1973, 7) revolution in history was unfolding before Hodgskin's eyes. "In the short span of years between the accession of George III and that of his son, William IV, the face of England changed" (Ashton [1948] 1997, 1), to quote the very first lines of Thomas Ashton's (1889–1968) classic work on the subject. The Industrial Revolution would transform not only the economy but the whole of society. Its benefits, which include reduced mortality and better living conditions, which allowed the population to quadruple over the nineteenth century, were still not visible to many as early as the 1820s.

Major changes were happening and innovations appearing at a faster speed than ever before. It is certainly true, as Ashton ([1948] 1997, 2) notes, that "the system of human relationships that is sometimes called capitalism had its origins long before 1760, and attained its full development long after 1830." The market economy was not born in Lancashire—but its shape changed profoundly, spurring sometimes harsh reactions. Hodgskin is still considered one of the first anticapitalistic authors. He had great concern for the problems and demands of workers, with whom he sympathized profoundly. The sailor-turned-journalist signed himself "A Labourer." But his view of the great transformation was far more positive than most of his contemporaries.

He was a self-taught economist who did not spare his reader some high theoretical reasoning. Hodgskin lacked formal education, but not intellectual ambition. Thinkers usually belong to schools of thought, and if they do not, posterity will create some for them. At the end of the nineteenth century, he was thus labeled a Ricardian socialist, part of an uneven trio composed of Hodgskin, William Thompson (1775–1833), and John Gray (1799–1883). None of them ever identified himself as a socialist. The risk of anachronism is sometimes hard to avoid, particularly when dealing with a political doctrine. The word "socialist" was apparently used in English for the first time in 1827 in a working-class publication, the *Co-operative Magazine*, to mean co-operation as opposed to competition (Claeys 1987, 83).[1] Yet this does not necessarily mean that the concept was not already there.

Socialism's history is sharply divided into two ages: the one that preceded Karl Marx, and the one that followed him. Before Marx, to borrow his friend Engels' words, socialism was "Utopian"; then it became "Scientific." As Engels ([1880] 1908, 47) explained: "Modern Socialism is, in its essence, the direct product of the recognition, on the one hand, of the class antagonisms existing in the society of today between proprietors and non-proprietors, between capitalists and wage-workers; on the other hand, of the anarchy existing in production." Utopian socialists, from Charles Fourier (1772–1837) to Robert Owen (1771–1858), thought that the cure for all the wrongs in society was to "discover a new and more perfect system of social order and to impose this upon society from without" (58). At that time, the idea that workers could associate and thus simply acquire "capital for themselves" (Mill [1848] 2006, III, 775) often went hand in hand with a belief that "laisser-faire should be the general practice; every departure from it, unless required by some great good, is a certain evil" (995).[2] This was, for example, the case of John Stuart Mill (1806–1873), who favored a market economy and yet hoped for workers' associations to overcome conflictual relationships between holders of capital and their work-force. Things changed when the "anarchy existing in production" became a more central concern and, eventually, Marx came to decipher the laws of historical developments.

Behind the label of "Ricardian socialism" lay an attempt to retrieve a British lineage for Karl Marx (1818–1883), whom Sidney Webb (1859–1947) and Beatrice Webb (1858–1943) praised as "Hodgskin's illustrious disciple" ([1894] 1929, 162). Such exploration of Marx's pedigree chart was attempted by H.S. Foxwell (1849–1936) in his introduction to the English translation of Anton Menger's (1841–1906) famous essay (Menger [1886] 1899). That particular work glued the name of David Ricardo (1772–1823) to socialism: according to Foxwell (1899, xl), Menger demonstrated that "it was Ricardo's crude generalisations which gave modern socialism its fancied scientific basis, and provoked, if they did not justify, its revolutionary form."[3] Marx himself read Hodgskin as a follow-up and a "complement" to Ricardo. However, as we shall see, the most observant scholars noticed quite soon that placing Hodgskin within the socialist currents was to some extent a stretch that required caveats and clarifications.[4] While Foxwell maintained that "Hodgskin, more than any other individual, may claim to have originated Ricardian socialism," Élie Halévy ([1903] 1956, 135) on the contrary realized that he "remained the determined opponent to Ricardo's system." More recently, Noel W. Thompson (1984, 82–110) emphasized that Hodgskin fits squarely in the camp of the followers of Smith, not of Ricardo.

Yet there was ground for this interpretive tradition to develop. Indeed, as Bertrand Russell (1872–1970) pointed out, Hodgskin enjoyed "the rare distinction of being quoted with respect by Marx" (Russell [1934] 2001, 199), who was rather parsimonious with praise. And it is indisputable that *Labour Defended against the Claims of Capital* (1825)—according to Marx, an "admirable work" ([1871] 1906, 390^{fn}) and a "remarkable product of English political economy" ([1862–1863] 1971, 263)—is by far the best known among Hodgskin's works. The title suggests Hodgskin's proximity to the workers' movement, thus his supposed anticapitalism. He published it under the pseudonym "A Labourer," which he frequently used. The title alludes to James Mill's *Commerce Defended: An Answer to the Arguments by which Mr. Spence, Mr. Cobbett, and Others, have attempted to Prove that Commerce is not a source of National Wealth* (1808). Mill's goal was to eradicate the risk that protectionist ideas might influence the decisions of lawmakers:[5]

> ... should the legislature become influenced by a theory hostile to commerce, at a time when other circumstances conspire against it, the affairs of the nation might easily receive a turn, which would soon terminate her grandeur as the mistress of trade.
>
> (J. Mill 1808, 3)

"The main purpose" of Hodgskin's pamphlet was to provide "some argument in defence of Labour and against capital" so that it becomes ammunition for the workers "to be able to compel those owners to make concessions" (Hodgskin [1825] 1964, 22). The context is, however, crucial for better understanding this goal. In 1824 the Combination Laws were abolished; enacted in 1799, they forbade workers to establish associations for trade union purposes.[6] Their repeal was greeted with a wave of strikes, by the same principle as when a cork pops and the champagne pours out. To put an end to these purported abuses, in 1825 a new Combination of Workmen Act—which regulated anew the labourers' newly found freedom of association—became law. Such freedom, Hodgskin maintained, should in no way be considered as opposing the basic principles of a free society. "Combination in itself is no crime; on the contrary, it is the principle on which societies are held together" (23).

If Mill's *Commerce Defended* aimed at preventing the inclusion of certain ideas in the parliamentary debate, Hodgskin's *Labour Defended* sought to disavow an entire policy of controlling workers, although often disguised as the pursuit of the good common. He reasoned that such erosion of the workers' freedom to associate was correlated with the fact that Parliament was composed solely of capitalists and landowners. For most of his journalistic career, Hodgskin had followed the proceedings of Parliament as a parliamentary reporter, in the 1820s and 1830s for the *Morning Chronicle*. Those who know how laws and sausages are made will hardly be able to love them.

Therefore, Hodgskin's starting point is a defense of the freedom to form associations, whether by workers or employers. In developing his argument, he tries to set up conditions for a rebalancing between remuneration of capital and remuneration of labor. In Hodgskin's view, the prejudices of the day allowed an excessive remuneration of the "less useful" part of the social role, "while other parts are criticised by stigma." The most political conclusion of Hodgskin's pamphlet is, and not by accident, the defense of the workers' right of association and, consequently, of the use of whatever means available to the unions to achieve a role in political life.

Ideas were thus ammunition in a specific political battle. Hodgskin's fight against combination laws is consistent with the classical liberal tradition, which emphasizes freedom of association. Adam Smith ([1776] 1981, I.8.12, 68) noted that "we have no act of Parliament against combining to lower the price of work; but many against combining to raise it." It is against this "advantage through legislation" of capital holders that Hodgskin took a stand. He is not shocked by the factory system, so often considered as embodying a new organization of slave labour.[7]

Compared with the relative obscurity Hodgskin lived in for most of his life, the pamphlet was a success. In August 1825, two publications started publishing a long review of *Labour Defended* in multiple instalments, quoting a significant amount of the original text. These were *Trades' Newspaper* and *Mechanics' Weekly Journal*, the newspaper of "organised trades" which marks a "breakpoint between middle class utilitarianism ... and the nascent trade unionist theory"; it was edited by the same Robertson with whom Hodgskin had worked at the *Mechanics' Magazine* (Thompson 1964, 778). If he observes that the radical press gave a "warm but not uncritical welcome" to the book, E.P. Thompson (1924–1993) suggests that "the trade unionists of London turned not to Place but to Thomas Hodgskin for a theoretical justification of their practices" (1964, 521). This should have greatly upset Place, who indeed "steadily fought" against the ideas of his former protégé, which were at odds with his own blend of utilitarian liberalism (Wallas [1898] 1925, 270). The old tailor was convinced that Hodgskin's work had a tremendous following among the working classes, leading them astray from the "right path" traced by James Mill and Ricardo.

A response to *Labour Defended* came six years after its publication, with *The Rights of Industry*. The anonymous author was the journalist and editor Charles Knight (1791–1873). Knight (1831, 9) set out to explain that "the interests of every member of society, properly understood, are one and the same." He wrote to reassert "the restraints of order" against riots and attempts to smash machinery and destroy capital, which happened when unenlightened workers followed "the blind guides that would break down the empire of property": "these ministers of desolation would be able to sing their triumphal song of 'Labour defended against the claims of capital,' amid the shriek of the jackal, and the howl of the wolf" (209, 211–212). Whatever Knight knew, we will see that Hodgskin was no friend to machine breakers. Yet Knight regarded

Hodgskin's *Popular Political Economy*—except for its claims about the uselessness of capital—as a "useful and instructive work" (57). David Stack (1998, 142) notes that the publication of Knight's attack paradoxically gave "Hodgskin's name and doctrines a greater currency with radicalism than they had previously enjoyed." As pamphleteers of all ages know well, the harsher the polemics, the more prominent the profile.

Capital and privilege

Though later in time the invisible hand, perhaps not the most felicitous of metaphors, came to be seen as giving a pass to employers, Adam Smith was perceived by his contemporaries as "a friend of the poor."[8] As is well known, he opposed "[w]hatever obstructs the free circulation of labour from one employment to another" ([1776] 1981, I.10.100, 151), considering the law of settlement and long apprenticeships inimical to those who must live by their labor. More generally, Smith equated the "nature and causes of the wealth of nations" with "the causes which affect the happiness and comfort of the lower orders of society, which in every nation form the most numerous class," as Rev. Thomas Robert Malthus (1766–1834) uttered somewhat critically ([1798] 1826, III.XIII.1, 211). Smith's social theory, in Biancamaria Fontana's synthesis, "rested on the assumption that modern commercial society, though characterised by great inequality in the distribution of resources, could still guarantee to all its members—and especially to the humblest of them—higher living standards than any primitive, more egalitarian community" (1985, 13).

Hodgskin never faltered in his admiration for Smith, and such admiration was by no means in tension with his own sympathy for the working classes. The two actually went well together. When it comes to the subject of labor combination or association, as mentioned before, the Scottish philosopher knew that many laws prohibited combining to raise the price of work, but none prohibited lowering it (Smith [1776] 1981, I.8.12, 84). It was easier for masters to conspire to keep the price of labor down because they were fewer in number, but also because of political interference. When confronted with a laborers' uprising, they "never cease to call aloud for the assistance of the civil magistrate, and the rigorous execution of those laws which have been enacted with so much severity against the combinations of servants, labourers, and journeymen" ([1776] 1981, I.8.13, 85). It is against such complicity of lawmakers and holders of capital that Hodgskin took a stand.

To take such a stand, however, Hodgskin returned to ambitious theoretical considerations. In particular, he expatiated on the nature of capital. Throughout his work, the concept of capital, which should belong to political economy, is intertwined with the concept of privilege, which belongs to politics. Even more than that, he argued that "one is almost tempted to believe that capital is a sort of cabalistic word, like Church or State or any other of those general terms which are invented by those who fleece the rest of mankind to conceal the hand that shears them" ([1825] 1964, 59). These are polemical words but they are revealing, too: they suggest that capital is such a monstrosity that it cannot be explained by mere economics.

His perspective was based on a kind of bafflement at how capital—i.e., a supply of goods resulting from previous production, not intended for consumption but, instead, to produce other goods—seems to almost magically generate an income for those who possess it. Hodgskin, furthermore, deemed the rate of return of capital to be disproportionately high, considering it the mysterious product of compound interest.

In his defense, it should be noted that classical economists in general never came to a clear and convincing definition of "capital." The root of the trouble is well known: capital resources are heterogeneous. Capital, as distinct from labour, lacks a "natural" unit of measurement. While we may add head to head … and acre to acre … we cannot add beer barrels to blast furnaces nor trucks to yards of telephone wire (Lachmann 1978, 2).

Capital takes shape in many ways: barns, machineries, factories are all capital. There is no "amount of capital" that can really be reduced to the number of workers, hours of work, or acres of land. Such "computational" problems made it particularly difficult to understand, first, what capital is and what it is not and, consequently, the specific role of capital itself. It was not until the late nineteenth century that this confusion dissipated, largely thanks to Eugen von Böhm-Bawerk (1851–1914), the great Austrian economist.[9]

In the first significant systematic work on the subject, *Capital and Interest* (1884), Böhm-Bawerk tried to bring order to what seemed like an accumulation of theoretical approaches, sometimes complementary and sometimes mutually exclusive. Böhm-Bawerk introduced a taxonomy of the theories of capital, divided into neutral theories: productivity theories (of which use theories are a subset), abstinence theories, and exploitation theories. Hodgskin's theory falls among the latter. Böhm-Bawerk ([1884] 1890, VI.I.10, 318) maintained that Hodgskin's works did not have "any extensive influence." He did think that the value of all goods ought to be "economically considered … exclusively the product of human labour" (VI.I.3, 316). The seeds of such ideas had been planted since "the time of Adam Smith" as "it was taught and believed that the value of all … is measured by the quantity of labour incorporated in them" (VI.I.4, 317).[10]

Böhm-Bawerk explained that many a theory of capital was de facto first advanced by Smith, who "has not overlooked the problem of interest" but had "a many-sided mind" allowing him to see "all the many different ways in which the problem can be put" and yet "lacking the control which the possession of a distinct theory gives" ([1884] 1890, I.IV.3, 70). Not surprisingly, then, while Adam Smith "has not laid down any distinct theory of interest, the germs of almost all the later and conflicting theories are to be found, with more or less distinctness, in his scattered observations" (I.IV.3, 70–71).

In building his theory Hodgskin fancied himself in continuity with Smith. Indeed, he shared with him the theory of labor value—hardly an original point at the time. For Hodgskin (1827, 219) there is a "natural price" which is based upon "the whole quantity of labour nature requires from man, that he may produce any commodity." This is precisely the way Smith ([1776] 1981, I.8.2, 82) described natural price in relation to primitive societies (before capital accumulation and land appropriation): "In that original state of things, which precedes both the appropriation of land and the accumulation of stock, the whole produce of labour belongs to the labourer."

Yet in real-world economic life in a civilized society prices are not "natural prices" in this sense: we do not actually exchange the product of someone's labor with some else's. Hodgskin points to the "social price," which is the "natural price enhanced by social regulations." So, if in ancient times the natural price coincided with labor, in a civilized society it is determined instead by the need to pay for the other production factors as well; i.e., it has to "become" salary, income and profit (Hunt 1977, 337).[11] Hodgskin does not believe that labor, "crystallised" into an asset, determines the asset's value. He believes, instead, that a price is the sum of the labor needed to produce an asset plus the taxes paid for socially determined unjust income.

In Hodgkin's view, unjust social regulations allow income and capital to be remunerated in addition to labor. By "[t]he law-giver and the capitalist ... we are instantly condemned as insolent and ungrateful if we ask for more than was enjoyed by the slave of former times ... By our increased skill and knowledge, labour is now probably ten times more productive than it was two hundred years ago ... All the advantages of our improvements go to the capitalist and the landlord" ([1825] 1964, 22–23).

And yet when it comes to fixed capital (spaces, machinery, tools of the trade) Hodgskin ([1825] 1964, 52) does not deny its beneficial impact on productivity; on the contrary, he admits that by using these tools "man adds wonderfully to his power." You will never find in Hodgskin the hypothesis of a conflict— even latent—between machinery and human labor.

Machines are of course themselves just a product of labour. If machine tools are but a product of human labour, however, they do not produce benefits by virtue of such "past" labour: "Whether an instrument shall be regarded as productive capital or not depends entirely on its being used, or not, by some productive labourer. The most perfect instruments ever made by labour require, as in the case of a timepiece, a peculiar skill to render them productive (Hodgskin [1825] 1964, 57).

Resorting to past and present labor in order to subject the notion of fixed capital to criticism is the equivalent of Hodgskin's device concerning circulating capital: that is, reducing it to mere "co-existing labour." His ambition is to explain that there is no inherent property of capital that can disregard labor: both past labor, which builds the machinery that makes production more efficient and smoother, and present labor, which operates the machinery. For Hodgskin, the fact that fixed capital is both made and empowered by the workers' exertion reinforces the assumption that there is no other factor of production than labor.

Such a misconception may be understandable in Hodgskin's times. Let us consider the following comment by Edwin Cannan (1861–1935) on Adam Smith's own understanding of capital:

> If Adam Smith had been asked what is the function or use of 'capital', he would probably have answered in the first place, 'To yield a profit'; And, doubtless, to each individual capitalist this appears to be the principal use of his capital. But the yielding of a profit is a distributive, and not a productive function.
>
> (Cannan 1903, 79)

When talking about the nature of capital, what Hodgskin sees is precisely its "distributive" element: capital becomes the instrument originating an income which he considers absolutely illegitimate since the instrument itself is, in his opinion, the outcome of a different, much more hard-working factor of production, i.e., labor.[12]

On top of that, as we have already pointed out, for Hodgskin "capital" is not relevant as a factor of production, but as a means of consolidating particular power relations. Indeed, capital is a social relationship, a political one. According to John Lalor (1814–1856), Hodgskin expressed "the first clear conception of capital as power distinct from the possession of commodities" (Lalor 1852, xxiv). Capital is considered the by-product of power. The privileged position of the capitalists, as well as that of the landowners, is nothing more than a consequence of laws and norms tailor-made to their benefit by a Parliament in which they enjoy an exclusive representation.[13]

The crucial issue therefore appears to be the legislative domination by those whom Hodgskin considers "idle," not "productive," classes, as they live off private income. These privileged positions are not a natural consequence of the social division of labor; they are, in fact, parasitical to the division of labor. They "make the laws which both calumniate and oppress us" (Hodgskin [1825] 1964, 29). Leo Valiani (1909–1999) has perceptively argued that: "'Although Hodgskin has not adhered to any form of socialism, his conception of spontaneous economic and social development—which is more important than any government measure—and his appeal to the resistance of labour to capital, imply a concept of class struggle" (Valiani 1951, 39–40).[14]

Such a view of class struggle resonates with what has been called the "classical liberal exploitation theory." This set of ideas about class relationships, which foreshadow Marx's class theory, was based upon the view that "exploitation of and parasitism" are "attributes of the non-market classes, of the classes that stood outside the production process" (Raico 1977, 180).[15] In this framework, then, class membership is not predicated on the relationship to the means of production, but rather by one's relationship to political power. It is not the ownership status but political power that confers privileges.

Indeed, Hodgskin's class struggle is going on between those bereft of any power and the wealthy and lawmakers, the "legislating" classes, who in fact are the same people. If the economy does apparently work to the benefit of the powerful, it is because its "natural" working has been jeopardized by legislative meddling: exploitation is possible only if we deviate from a true market system.[16] And indeed what is the reduction of the laborers' negotiating freedom—the *casus belli* that occasioned the invective of *Labour Defended*—if not an intervention of politics to determine the outcome of economic competition, hindering those who cannot oppose it because they are not represented?

For Hodgskin points out that "no other combination seems unjust or mischievous, in the view of Government" except combining laborers.

> It is a heinous crime in the eyes of a legislature, composed exclusively of capitalists and landlords, and representing no other interests than their own, for us to try, by any means, to obtain for ourselves and for the comfortable subsistence of our families, a larger share of our own produce than these our masters choose to allow us. All the moral evils that ever plagued a society have been anticipated by the ministers from our persevering in our claims. To put down combinations they have departed from principles held sacred for upwards of two hundred years.
>
> (Hodgskin [1825] 1964, 24)

This may be a more forceful statement of Adam Smith's own point, quoted on p.36.

If all of the above may bring us to rank Hodgskin with the anarchists, does it account for his purported socialism? If the anachronistic aim of labelling him a "Ricardian socialist" was to produce a narrative of Marxian ideas being first generated in England rather than by a German refugee, how successful can such an attempt be?

In actual fact, Hodgskin does not even flirt with the idea of overcoming "the anarchy of production." He does not want to emend a "directionless" economy based on private property and hence on decentralized production decisions; if anything, he is convinced that it is wrong to associate what is good in it—i.e., a great increase in productivity and, consequently, an increased availability of goods—with the concept of capital.

A letter from Hodgskin to Francis Place (1820), in which he reports his reaction upon reading Ricardo, is revealing. On the one hand, Hodgskin challenges Ricardo's differential yield theory, which is based on the idea of differential soil productivity, because it is human labor that makes the soil productive. On the other hand, he rejects the idea of a tendency for the rate of profit to decrease (Ginzburg 1976, 297–308). Ricardo argued that "The natural tendency of profits then is to fall; for in the progress of society and wealth, the additional quantity of food required is obtained by the sacrifice of more and more labour" (Ricardo [1821] 2015, 120). Such a principle is incomprehensible to Hodgskin, for whom in as much as the capital employed by an ingenious and industrious man produces more than the capital consumed or employed by an ignorant or idle man, in so much "the Capital of the ingenious and industrious inhabitants of modern Europe be returned to them with a greater increase than the capital of ignorant and lazy barbarians. The natural profits, therefore, of capital constantly increase with the ingenuity of our species" (Hodgskin to Place 1820).[17]

Hodgskin's problem is not the role played in a modern economy by what we call "capital" (machinery, production plants, etc.). It is, instead, the fact that it derives, to some extent, from "past labor": in the extreme case of land rent, from past slave labor.

This might be seen as an anticipation of Marx's peculiar understanding of primitive accumulation. By stressing that holders of capital and lawmakers are basically the same persons, he can be seen as suggesting that the great fortunes of today are founded upon the great pillages of yesterday.

But industrial progress and the injustices against which Hodgskin thinks he is fighting so that laborers will finally receive their due are analytically separable. On the one hand, he denounces the injustice of a past of violence and abuse: plundering that reverberates on the riches and privileges of the old abusers. On the other, he does not want to do away with its products.

Nor is Hodgskin making his understanding of exploitation the gist of a new "science." Friedrich Engels (1820–1895) remarked that socialism was "made scientific" by "the materialistic conception of history and the revelation of the secret of capitalistic production through surplus-value, we owe to Marx." Such secret was "that the appropriation of unpaid labor is the basis of the capitalist mode of production and of the exploitation of the worker that occurs under it" (Engels [1880] 1908, 92–93). Scientific socialism aims to reveal the historicity of capitalism and upon this assumption claims to predict its next steps, namely a simultaneous concentration of wealth and misery at the two poles of society. This is the framework in which "the historic role of capitalism is that it creates the economic preconditions of socialism" (Sowell 1985, 71).

Hodgskin's forceful denunciation of lawmakers' taking advantage of laborers does not make him wish to "reform" economics. He considers economics a science that ventures to discover the natural laws "regulating and determining the production of wealth" (Hodgskin 1827, xx). These natural laws are not for man or government to change, and the only rule they provide governments with is to abstain from meddling. By appealing to natural laws, Hodgskin postulates harmony between interests, which is unsettled only by "social institutions," that is, political action.

Böhm-Bawerk ([1884] 1890, I.IV.19, 75) maintained that interest in the issue of capital "exploded" when the Industrial Revolution hit with full force, and the age of machinery truly began. David Landes (1924–2013) remarked that "[i]n the eighteenth century, a series of inventions transformed the manufacture of cotton in England and gave rise to a new mode of production—the factory system" ([1969] 2003, 41). New machines opened the door to growing productivity and to a form of organizing labor that seemed ghastly to many. Hodgskin saw this tumultuous change unfolding under his eyes, and he believed that the working classes should not resist it but indeed welcome it. His uneasiness with "capital" stemmed from the fact he did not understand why a role must be acknowledged for tyranny of the past.[18]

But Hodgskin ([1825] 1964, 83) did understand that in a complex division of labor "almost any product of art and skill is the result of joint and combined labour." Once more a thorough Smithian, he embraced his great master's understanding of the division of labor as an irrepressible force for progress. He saw no inhumane aspects in the division of labor, but, rather, the blossoming of cooperation and increased production. There is no man who is solely responsible for the production of a single artifact; on the contrary, the realization of virtually any good is the result of very complex cooperation chains. Such cooperation involves different kinds of labor, which include "the knowledge and skill of the master manufacturer, or of the man who plans and arranges a productive operation, who must know the state of the markets and the qualities of different materials, and who has some tact in buying and selling." All these kinds of labor "are just as necessary for the complete success of any complicated operation as the skill of the workmen whose hands actually alter the shape and fashion of these materials" (88). The division of labor witnesses "a wonderful co-operation of different classes of labourers to produce a common result" (25). If such cooperation is beneficial, then the struggle between classes is clearly a political, not an economic, phenomenon. In the economic realm Hodgskin saw harmony, in politics conflict.

This understanding of the division of labor differs sharply from the one shared by most advocates of socialism. After fiercely criticizing the way capital exploits labor, Hodgskin proposes nothing less than the market system as a model for obtaining the right remuneration for labor itself in a context freed from the unjust political privileges of capital. There is no "right" principle, he says, for the remuneration of labor:[19]

> I know no way of deciding this but by leaving it to be settled by the unfettered judgments [sic] of the labourers themselves. If all kinds of labour were perfectly free, if no unfounded prejudice invested some parts, and perhaps the least useful, of the social task with great honour, while other parts are very improperly branded with disgrace, there would be no difficulty on this point, and the wages of individual labour would be justly settled by what Dr. Smith calls the 'higgling of the market'.
> (Hodgskin [1825] 1964, 85–86)

The importance of this passage can hardly be overstated. An author intending to defend "labour against the claims of capital," who thinks that the role of the latter is essentially parasitic, and that such parasitism is possible due to unconscionable political interferences, proposes market negotiations as a system for governing the remuneration of laborers.[20]

In *Labour Defended*, Hodgskin essentially pursues the reduction of all production factors to one: labor. He criticizes interest on capital because it arises exclusively from past circumstances. Yet he does not reject the price system, which he maintains to be the right regulator of individual wages. E.P. Thompson (1964, 778) noted that "Hodgskin does not propose an alternative system." Indeed, Hodgskin is not interested in subverting the market economy; he was instead "primarily concerned with removing those malignly created obstructions which caused the market economy to malfunction" (N. Thompson 1984, 98). He does not at all reject capital's achievements, nor the idea that there is a specific function of the capitalist that is also useful for the laborers. This is a key point if we are to better understand his view of the Industrial Revolution.

The issue of machinery

So Hodgskin rejects the concept of capital but accepts the "outputs," so to speak, of capital. The fact that Hodgskin does not aspire to defend laborers from mechanization is perhaps more relevant than any other aspect of *Labour Defended*. It underlines a central element of his thought. Hodgskin's defense of labor is a defense of *divided* labor: what enables him to consider labor tantamount to the only factor of production is his understanding of the division of labor as central to economic progress.

This is by no means a marginal issue. To explain why the reflection on capital had, at some point, become a central theoretical elaboration of economists (and, conversely, why it had not appeared crucial to Adam Smith), Böhm-Bawerk points out that:

> This very introduction of machinery had begun to reveal an opposition which was forced on economic life with the development of capital, and daily grew in importance, —the opposition between capital and labour… Those machines which bore golden fruit to the capitalist undertaker had, on their introduction, deprived thousands of workers of their bread.
> ([1884] 1890, I.IV.20, 75)

Of crucial importance in the opposition between labor and capital was Ricardo's work. As is well known, Ricardo had several hesitations over this subject. In the first two editions of the *Principles*, he claimed that the use of machinery, by increasing labor productivity, would benefit all, including the working classes. But in the third edition he changed his mind and argued that "the substitution of machinery for human labour is often very injurious to the interests of the class of labourers" (Ricardo [1821] 2015, 388). These words suggest that an increase in wages pushes holders of capital to replace laborers with machines, and vice versa. Therefore, it is ultimately the wage test that determines the return on capital. It is not surprising that the assumption has fueled a sense of the inevitability of a stark, inexorable conflict between workers and capitalists. That this conflict could have originated precisely from the "issue of machinery" was a consideration entirely plausible in light of the strikes, boycotts, and sabotage that had already taken place at the dawn of the industrial age.

The Industrial Revolution indeed saw a gradual replacement of home work with factory work. "Mechanization" turned into a serialized, fragmented process of work in what had been a few years earlier the domain of skilled craftsmen (thus making possible a level of output that was unimaginable until then).[21] It was perhaps this change to machinery that most strikes observers.[22] Marx wrote:

> The machine, which is the starting point of the industrial revolution, supersedes the workman, who handles a single tool, by a mechanism operating with a number of similar tools, and set in motion by a single motive power, whatever the form of that power may be.
>
> ([1871] 1906, 410)

"The history of the proletariat," announce the opening words of a celebrated essay by Friedrich Engels ([1845] 1969, 2), "begins ... with the invention of the steam-engine and of machinery for working cotton." One by one, "handworkers have been driven by machinery from one position after another" (6); it is, therefore, the machinery that "calls to life" the proletariat.[23]

The debate over the reasons for the emergence of the factory system, and whether or not a more hierarchical arrangement of production was necessary to technological innovation, goes far beyond what is desirable to deal with here.[24] But the factory system and technological innovation marched together and together provoked a reaction. It was "the fear of the factory and of the destruction of those modes of production which enabled labour to exercise autonomy per work" (Randall 1991, 45).

Industrial sabotage was "a significant, widespread form of industrial relations in Britain for a century," long before the Luddite riots (Horn 2003, 138–152). To mention a single episode, when James Hargreaves (1720–1778) invented the multi-spindle spinning machine (spinning jenny) in 1764, he had to face two violent protests (in 1767 and 1769), which resulted in the destruction of the machines and his having to leave Lancashire for Nottingham. The diffusion of machinery and inventions was not instantaneous and progressed at different speeds in different industries and territories. But indeed "the Industrial Revolution meant ... the ever-growing physical separation of the unit of consumption (household) from the unit of production (plant)" (Mokyr 2001, 1).

The system of cottage industry has been considered, perhaps with the benefit of hindsight, as balancing the need for bigger industries while still allowing for decentralized household work.[25] The experience of the factory was new and often shocking and helps explain why concern for the "Age of Machinery" (Carlyle ([1829] 2007, 31–50) was one of the dominant passions of the time, and certainly a passion of the emerging socialist movement. Mechanization was accused of reducing the remuneration of labor and changing its nature. Better technological instruments enabled the transition toward the factory system and out of cottage industries. As David Landes (1924–2013) has summarized it:

The machine imposed a new discipline. No longer could the spinner turn her wheel and the weaver throw his shuttle at home, free of supervision, both in their own good time. Now the work had to be done in a factory, at a pace set by tireless, inanimate equipment, as a part of a large team that had to begin, pause, and stop in unison ... The factory was a new kind of prison; the clock a new kind of jailer.

([1969] 2003, 43)

For Marx ([1847] 1956, 140fn), machinery played such a central role in the development of capitalism that it made possible a growing, fully international, truly "soil-less" division of labor—but also made it possible to enroll children and women in factories, even though they had far less muscle power than men.[26]

This hostility toward machinery was deep-rooted—and, to a certain extent, still informs our understanding of what the "great transformation" of the Industrial Revolution implied. While in Germany, Hodgskin (1820, I, 56) found himself repeatedly trying to "resist the prejudice" that "all the evil came from machinery," a prejudice "stronger in Germany than anywhere else." In a letter to the *Trades' Newspaper and Mechanics' Weekly Journal* in 1825, he remarked that it was the engineer who worked, not the engine:[27] thus, by destroying the very instruments other workers used to work, machine breakers were in fact damaging the "talent" and "knowledge" of their fellow men. "Those persons who occasionally set about destroying instruments and machines of different descriptions, would have paused before they had come to the resolution of extirpating the skill and suppressing the knowledge of their brother workmen" (Hodgskin, 1825b).

In his perspective, thus, machines are the result of the division of labor as well as an enabling actor of it. Hodgskin takes a position against machine-breakers and Luddites, not viewing their strategy as a way to get more out of employers. But he takes a different route from Pierre-Joseph Proudhon (1809–1865), who opposed the division of labor as the "primary cause of intellectual degeneracy and ... civilized misery" (Proudhon [1847] 1888, III.1) but considered "the incessant appearance of machinery" as "the antithesis, the inverse formula, of the division of labor; it is the protest of the industrial genius against parcellaire and homicidal labor." Machinery was for Proudhon (IV.1) "a method of reuniting diverse particles of labor which division had separated," not the result of such divided labor.

E.P. Thompson (1964, 552) pointed out that the Luddites' demands "looked forwards, as much as backwards." Marx and Engels were well aware of the role of mechanization in the Industrial Revolution. And yet they would have readily recognized that machinery (and the bourgeoisie) had "greatly increased the urban population as compared with the rural, and has thus rescued a considerable part of the population from the idiocy of rural life" (Marx and Engels [1848] 2007, 13). On the other hand, there was indeed a conservative stream in the emerging socialist movement, one that looked backwards to a mythical Arcadia. Right from the beginning, the world of factories, watches, machinery, and female employment was contrasted with a mythical age of rustic happiness.

In *The Effects of Civilization on the People in European States* (1805), Charles Hall (1740–1825) argued that "however much civilisation ... may have been of advantage to a privileged minority, it has depressed and rendered miserable the bulk of humanity."[28] Maxine Berg pointed out that for Robert Owen's followers it was essential to "bring the introduction of machinery under cooperative control as a measure to increase leisure time, and not one for reducing wages and raising unemployment" (1980, 275).

Instead, "the division of labour and the introduction of machinery were neither to be stopped nor tempered in Hodgskin's system" (Berg 1980, 172). Hodgskin seemed impervious to the argument that machines were substituting for human labor—because he saw machine tools as both the embodiment of people's labor and a device for enhancing other individuals' labor.

Hodgskin's position is, in fact, perfectly consistent with Adam Smith's ideas about the nature of the division of labor and his understanding of workers being a driving force for innovation. "Mechanized" production and a more complex division of labour are linked. Not that Hodgskin concurred with the prophecy that exerting oneself in a series of simple operations, repeated continuously, would have made people "as stupid and ignorant as it is possible for a human creature to become" (Smith [1776] 1981, V.1.178, 782).[29] He instead took far more seriously the broad section of the first book of his masterpiece, where Smith links technological developments and division of labor. For Smith, laborers are anything but victims of the introduction of machinery: in fact, machinery is a consequence of that refining process of their skill which takes place as the division of labor is perfected.

Smith ([1776] 1981, I.1.5, 17) considered the invention of a great number of new machines among the causes of that "great increase of the quantity of work which, in consequence of the division of labour, the same number of people are capable of performing." Such inventions were often dependent on laborers' own needs and intuitions:

> It is naturally to be expected ... that some one or other of those who are employed in each particular branch of labour should soon find out easier and readier methods of performing their own particular work, wherever the nature of it admits of such improvement. A great part of the machines made use of in those manufactures in which labour is most subdivided, were originally the inventions of common workmen, who, being each of them employed in some very simple operation, naturally turned their thoughts towards finding out easier and readier methods of performing it. Whoever has been much accustomed to visit such manufactures, must frequently have been shewn very pretty machines, which were the inventions of such workmen, in order to facilitate and quicken their own particular part of the work.
>
> (I.1.8, 20)

Improvements can be due also to "the ingenuity of the makers of the machines" or to "those who are called philosophers or men of speculation"

(Smith [1776] 1981, I.1.9, 21) but the division of labor plays a role in this case, too: you need specialization for the making of the machines to become a job, and the same for philosophical speculation too.

Hodgskin is certainly indebted to Smith's understanding of the division of labor ubiquitously breeding new inventions. As we have already seen, for Hodgskin a capital good both results from labor and needs to be activated by labor. Labor consists, in fact, in applying a certain "skill": knowledge of how to perform a specific task.

> By the skill acquired during many years' experience, and by much labour guided by this skill, a ship is built. It would trouble me to enumerate the various species of industry which are necessary to prepare her for sea. There is the skill and labour of the draughtsman, of the working shipwright, of the carpenter, the mast maker, the sail maker, the cooper, the founder, the smith, the coppersmith, the compass maker, etc., etc., but there is nothing necessary more than the skill and labour of these different persons ... She is then, however, of no use unless there are seamen to manage her. To conduct her safely from port to port ... a great deal of knowledge of the winds and tides, of the phenomena of the heavens, and of the laws which prevail on the surface of the earth, is necessary; and only when this knowledge is united with great skill, and carried into effect by labour, can a ship be safely conducted through the multitudes of dangers which beset her course. To have and to use this fixed capital, knowledge, labour and skill are necessary.
>
> (Hodgskin [1825] 1964, 58–59)

Similarly, the "vast utility" of the steam engine "does not depend on stored up iron and wood, but on that practical and living knowledge of the powers of nature which enables some men to construct, and others to guide it" (Hodgskin [1825] 1964, 61). In short, economic progress rests always on human knowledge and ingenuity, which come to life in the division of labor. For Hodgskin, the secret of the great enrichment indeed lay in a growing division of labor:

> The discoveries made in London, Manchester, or Glasgow, are known in either of these other towns, and are spread over the whole island, in a few days. Numbers of minds are instantly set to work even by a hint; and every discovery is instantly appreciated, and almost as instantaneously improved. The chances of improvement, it is plain, are great in proportion as the persons are multiplied whose attention is devoted to any particular subject. It appears to me, therefore, that an increase in the number of persons produces the same effect as communication; for the latter only operates by bringing numbers to think on the same subject.
>
> (Hodgskin 1827, 94–95)

On that intuition, Hodgskin built a whole theory in his later *Popular Political Economy*, a collection of lectures he gave at the London Mechanics' Institute, which sum up his economic views, as we will see in more detail in the next chapter.

If Hodgskin considered himself a champion of the working classes, he was not, for the most part, speaking to the vast number of unskilled workers. He was primarily addressing an audience made up of specialized laborers who were most likely aware, in turn, of being more skilled and better trained than the previous generations. The Industrial Revolution created the demand for a highly specialized job force, precisely because the mechanized management of production brought with it a greater degree of complexity.

Two historians describe the evolution of demand for skills in these terms:

> The tremendous growth of the Lancashire cotton industry, from about 1770 onward, based on the mechanical inventions of Hargreaves, Arkwright, Crompton and Cartwright, powered by water wheels and steam engine, gave rise to an equally rapid development of mechanical engineering. Lancashire soon came to manufacture not only cotton, but also cotton machinery, steam engines, boilers, machine tools and, later on, railways locomotives, iron bridges, gasworks plant, and a vast range of other engineering products.
>
> (Musson and Robinson 1960, 209–210)

This kind of labor, characterized by a high level of specialized skills and expertise, increased with the Industrial Revolution. In short, it led to "new opportunities for growing numbers amongst the poor to acquire the skills, and with them the advantages—above all more work and better-paid work—that artisans had always enjoyed" (Griffin 2013, 31).

Such was the audience to which Hodgskin, as a writer, appealed. In talking to this particular audience, he downplayed the danger of machines stealing people's jobs to sing the praise of innovation, including labor-saving innovation, which was indeed the main trade of such group of tinkerers and specialized workers. Theirs was a growing society, in which was evident the "utility of all our boasted improvements" precisely because "the same quantity of labour which at any former period produced 100 quarters of wheat and 100 steam engines will now produce somewhat more" (Hodgskin [1825] 1964, 79). Such society was growing also in terms of population, thereby confirming Hodgskin's opinion that "[t]he foundation of all national greatness is the increase of the people" (1827, 26). It was not the powers of the soil that produced food, but labor and ingenuity, which grew as mankind increased in number. In the modern world, a growing population is not "a drag or burden on economic growth" but "quite the opposite. More people means more demand and stimulates productive economic activity in response" (Davies 2019, 15).

Hodgskin, unlike most contemporary socialists, grasped well ahead of his contemporaries the fact that living standards were improving. Nowhere was he to deny the considerable hardship endured by workers. But he foresaw clearly that their situation was improving, not getting worse, in the greater scheme of things. Indeed, as time went by Hodgskin became so aware of "the impressive increase of material wealth" happening on his own watch that, according to a commentator, he arrived at the point of forgetting "that there would always be the rich and the poor ... even in the days to come" (Stark 1943, 102).

The lower costs of living and higher living standards were more widely perceived in the later part of the 1800s than at Hodgskin's time.[30] The debate over the improvement of living standards has tantalized historians. Charles Feinstein (1932–2004) argued that for the majority of the working class almost a century of hard times passed by before they could begin grasping the fruits of the new industrial economy (1998, 625–658). It was all toil and sweat for quite a long time, before eventually income went up across the board. Yet the picture was not homogenous among different trades and different locations. A prominent historian, more or less a century ago, already pointed out that wages went up markedly: they "had risen more than 40 per cent" for London bricklayers or compositors and other "fortunate classes" of workers in 1790–1850 and "for urban and industrial workers in the mass ... perhaps about 40 per cent" (Clapham [1926] 1950, 561). Thomas Ashton (1954, 33–63) maintained that improvement began to spread around the 1820s. John Hicks (1904–1989) explained that capital accumulation in the nineteenth century worked largely to the benefit of the poor, highlighting that "the things whose production has been facilitated [by capital accumulation]" were articles of mass consumption, thereby benefiting the working classes (1946, 292). Indeed it is hard to imagine such a long-lasting economic expansion like the Industrial Revolution without a growing demand, which was unlikely to be confined to better carriages for the grand and mighty.

Differences, of course, were paramount. As Emma Griffin (2018, 84) points out, "farm-workers in the 1840s were spending 75 per cent of their income on food, miners were spending 58 per cent of their income on food, and only 40 per cent of their food expenditure was on bread. The total proportion of their income devoted to this staple was about 25 per cent—less than half the proportion paid by agricultural labourers. Among the factory workers, 60 per cent of income was spent on food, and of this 36 per cent was spent on bread. The overall proportion of family income that was spent on bread was 23 per cent." This is an important consideration, since percentage of income allocated for food purchases tends to decrease as income rises (contemporary Westerners, the richest lot that ever walked on earth, spend less than 10 per cent of their income on food). Griffin cautions that early industrial Britain was halved into a dynamic, urban, industrial one and a stagnant, rural one. Incomes rose in the latter.

Hodgskin's "constituency," so to speak, was composed of skilled urban workers. They were artisans, men of a trade, working masters included. He could then envision the importance of the emergence of a stronger and independent middling rank:

> [A] large middle class, completely emancipated from the bondage and destitution which the law, by fixing the rate both of wages and interest, sought to perpetuate, has grown up in every part of Europe, uniting in their own persons the character both of labourers and capitalists. They are fast increasing in numbers; and we may hope, as the beautiful inventions of art gradually supersede unskilled labour, that they, reducing the whole society to equal and free men, will gradually extinguish all that yet remains of slavery and oppression.
>
> (Hodgskin 1832, 102)

The great lever of such progress was innovation: "it is probable that since Mr. Watt's improvements on the steam engine one man can perform as much work with these instruments as ten men did before" (Hodgskin [1825] 1964, 68).

A theorist of human capital?

A contemporary reader is likely to think that, given his conclusions, Hodgskin attacked capital with a zeal worthy of a better cause; convinced as he was of demolishing it, today he mostly gives the impression of not having understood its nature. And he certainly was not the only one among his contemporaries.

Unlike many of them, however, he understood something else, something relevant, about the great change that he was able to observe and on which he decided to write. Building on Smith, he saw that machines, which he thought by and large the result of the contrivances and ingenuity of workers, would "facilitate and abridge labour, and enable one man to do the work of many" (Smith [1776] 1981, I.1.5, 17). This was the crucial one: the extraordinary productivity growth was due to the availability of machinery that, up to just a few years earlier, was unimaginable. It is the "'wave of gadgets,'", to quote T.S. Ashton ([1948] 1997, 59), that swept all of England.

The rapid spread of innovation, whether it was motivated by a will to increase production or by the necessity to compress wages that were much higher than in the rest of Europe, was possible only through major investments. These, in turn, were possible only thanks to the accumulation of capital that took place in England during the previous centuries (by virtue of enclosures or thanks to relatively stable government institutions). But can a transformation as extraordinary as the one that took place in those years be explained only by virtue of the accumulation of capital? Deirdre McCloskey (2010, 134, 136) thinks otherwise:

> The supply of saving to one region such as Lancashire or one country such as Britain — even economically bulky Britain around 1840 — came at a fixed rate of interest, 4 or 6 percent. What made for the demand for saving was the usefulness of a loan to build a barn or a machine, a usefulness which economists call the "marginal product of capital." Piling brick on brick, however, or even machine or machine, led to rapidly diminishing

returns. Think of a ditch digger oversupplied with shovels, or a 100-acre farm with six tractors and only one worker. ... innovation prevented the return to capital from declining ... better machine tools and innovative construction techniques and a thousand other fruits of resourcefulness made people richer, and incidentally kept investment profitable ... If investment and saving were crucial to economic growth, then Britain with its low rates of investment would not have been the leader in industrialisation. Rates of investment and saving rose as a result of innovation. They did not cause it. What was indeed "crucial" was innovation itself, the steam engines and the steel ships.

McCloskey reports that "from 1770 to 1839, Britain was the most innovative economy on earth ... and yet savings/investment rates in Britain were lower than in most of other countries." The "exorbitance of compound interest" could not thus be the deciding factor in explaining why the Industrial Revolution happened and, specifically, why it happened in England. "The fact that, after 1870, the economy could finance both increasing industrialisation and a large war expenditure without serious inflation confirms this view that the capital needs of early industrialisation were modest" (Hartwell 1965, 172).

According to McCloskey (2010, 25), what happened was a "cultural" revolution: a growing social appreciation for jobs that were previously considered trivial (jobs for men "of iron and bronze") gradually led to the emergence, in England and the Netherlands, of a social situation where producing and innovating became socially valued activities. This particular event, or rather series of events—a cultural shift—can explain changes of too great a magnitude and radical nature to be exclusively the consequence of capital accumulation: "the historically unique economic growth on the order of a factor of ten or sixteen or higher ... depended on ideas more than on economics."

This does not mean that capital accumulation was irrelevant. More capital eased work and made production plentiful. This is what typically happens if capital is wisely employed. Those scholars who emphasize the importance of the relative political stability enjoyed by England from the Glorious Revolution onwards, or those instead who highlight the role played by the enclosures or the British thriving international trade, and even those who suggest that industrialization in England benefited from an infrastructural network (roads, canals, etc.) quite developed for the time are basically affirming the importance of the accumulation of capital for the purposes of industrial development. That capital played a role is not in question: it was the crucial factor for the sudden transformation of England into the world's first modern economy. But does not the fact that the accumulation of capital takes the form of productive investment rather than goods conservatively stocked in aristocratic mansions reflect a cultural shift as well?

If this framing of the issue appears plausible, it is because the new social appreciation for "bourgeois" professions went along with a more granular spreading of a scientific mind-set. Joel Mokyr called it "Industrial Enlightenment": what made the wave of gadgets that swept England at the end of the eighteenth century possible was, in part, the scientific advancement of the previous century. But such advancement was not the product of the sort of big research lab we know today, nor was it due exclusively to theorists. The thousands of microinventions that spurred Britain's spectacular success depended, for the most part, on newly acquired knowledge, beyond the direct involvement of scientists in the industrial activity. "Most of the foremost inventor-entrepreneurs of the Industrial Revolution were of rather modest, artisanal origin" (Ó Gráda 2014, 8). At the same time, the demand for highly skilled laborers increased. Those workers were "the top 3–5 percent of the labor force in terms of skills: engineers, mechanics, millwrights, chemists, clock and instrument makers, skilled carpenters and metal workers, wheelwrights and similar workmen" (Meisenzahl and Mokyr 2012, 447).

Is it possible to consider Hodgskin a contemporary who in some ways anticipated this later understanding of the cultural determinants of the Industrial Revolution that was happening before his very eyes?

Hodgskin was constantly aware of the increase in importance of what today we would call human capital. His appreciation was theoretical as much as practical. He invested his time and passion hoping to help the betterment of skills and knowledge on the part of labourers. He strove for the establishment of the London's Mechanics' Institute, he collaborated with the *Mechanics' Magazine*, and was editor-in-chief of its sister publication *The Chemist*. These journals tried to acquaint their readers with novel techniques, hoping in this way to contribute to their adroitness.

Hodgskin clearly considered that emancipation for the lower classes would come from education and acted to make such education available and widespread. Better education had both a "political" intent, i.e., putting workers on the political map because they could read, write, and agitate, and also a practical one. It was extremely clear to Hodgskin that the revolution that was shaping up, in labor and daily practices, was a revolution of knowledge. Joel Mokyr (2009, 238) argues that "Hodgskin ... without using the term, came closer than anyone to realising the central role of human capital in economic growth."

Hodgskin ([1825] 1964, 88) strongly criticized capital and yet, by reducing all factors of production to one—labor—, he ended up acknowledging that entrepreneurs are laborers too. As we saw, "labor" includes what today we would refer to as the businessman's job: "The knowledge and skill of the master manufacturer, or of the man who plans and arranges a productive operation, who must know the state of the markets and the qualities of different materials, and who has some tact in buying and selling, are just as necessary for the complete success of any complicated operation as the skill of the workmen whose hands actually alter the shape and fashion of these materials." Note the dual reference to both the managerial duties of the master manufacturer and his ability to know "the state of the markets."

The capitalist's remuneration can be analytically distinguished between capital interest (the remuneration of capital in a stricter sense) and entrepreneurial profit (that is, the entrepreneur's specific contribution to managerial innovations, for example).[31] For Hodgskin ([1825] 1964, 89) "the wages of the master, employer or contriver has [sic] been blended with the profit of the capitalists.[32] The author of *Labour Defended* puts himself in a difficult position:

> Masters ... are labourers as well as their journeymen. In this character their interest is precisely the same as that of their men. But they are also either capitalist, or the agents of the capitalist, and in this respect their interest is decidedly opposed to the interest of their workmen. As the contrivers and enterprising undertakers of new works, they may be called employers as well as labourers, and they deserve the respect of the labourer. As capitalist, and as the agents of the capitalist, they are merely middlemen, oppressing the labourer, and deserving of anything but his respect.
> (Hodgskin ([1825] 1964, 90–91)

How can we distinguish the one from the other? How can we take and use the entrepreneur's talent without yielding to the interest of the capitalist? The answers to these questions are sought in vain in Hodgskin's work; in fact, he announces the good news that laborers should be entitled to their whole product, but then he includes among the laborers those who manage the laborers' work. Hodgskin's theory fits into Böhm-Bawerk's category of theories of capital as exploitation. And yet he defends the usefulness of the function performed by the exploiters! To the point of arguing that:

> If by combining the journeymen were to drive masters, who are a useful class of labourers, out of the country, if they were to force abroad the skill and ingenuity which contrive, severing them from the hands which execute, they would do themselves and the remaining inhabitants considerable mischief.
> (Hodgskin ([1825] 1964, 91)

The "capitalists," as in the holders of inherited wealth who sit in the Parliament, are the object of his criticism. But to the "entrepreneurs" Hodgskin acknowledges a fundamental role, perhaps more so than most of his contemporaries.

Such a view stayed with him for all his life. Much later, in an 1858 letter, he exalted "trade without capital," those "pure entrepreneurs" who enter the market without a big starting capital (not unlike today's garage start-ups). "The success of many little traders excites the envy and abuse of certain great and leading capitalists, who expected to enjoy a monopoly, and having found themselves distanced in the race by cleverer, poorer, and more observing men, sound a great alarm" (Hodgskin 1858).

It should not come as a surprise, then, that as a journalist at *The Chemist*, young Hodgskin offered his support to the public petition for a monument to James Watt (1736–1819). The Scottish instrument maker and inventor was a larger-than-life figure for contemporaries, as he is to posterity. He substantially improved the steam engine developed by Thomas Newcomen (1664–1729), using a separate chamber to condense steam without cooling the rest of the engine. With the separate condenser, much waste of energy was avoided and thus the power, efficiency, and cost-effectiveness of steam engines were greatly improved. Eventually Watt adapted his engine to produce rotary motion, widening its use beyond pumping water and paving the way for future appliances, including motive steam power. That Watt's importance in the history of mankind exceeds that of many a sovereign is undoubted. But it took political courage to celebrate it with a public monument.

Indeed, this initiative was part of a phenomenon studied by Christine MacLeod (2010): an attempt to "glorify" the entrepreneur and inventor for political ends. In the early nineteenth century, statues and public portraits were almost exclusively the privilege of the aristocracy: they celebrated Lord Nelson (1758–1805), the Duke of Wellington (1769–1852), the military victories, the aristocrat spirit. Even today, one can hardly ride around in any major European cities without inadvertently paying tribute to some mass slaughterers when seeking directions. The emerging classes, which provided a great contribution to the national welfare, sought both parliamentary and symbolic representation. It was indeed the "productive classes" seeking recognition equal to that of the law-making ones.

As McCloskey puts it:

> Without liberty and dignity for ordinary people the anxious elite would have suppressed commercial improvements, such as Wedgwood's pottery (Wedgwood despised patents, and only had one) or Edison's movie camera (his patent on movies, among the fully 1093 he acquired, was overturned only in 1902, partly, and for good in 1917), which in the event were brought within the reach of factory girls in return for steadily decreasing amounts of effort.
>
> (2016, 39–40)

Therefore, the institutions in themselves (even a regime of strong property rights protection) would not be enough to safeguard the improvements contributed by the entrepreneurial class from political predation: it took a different, widespread culture.

Hodgskin, who considered public opinion to be the true sovereign of mankind,[33] participates enthusiastically in that symbolic battle. He commends Watt (who is credited with "bestowing almost immeasurable benefits on the whole human race") precisely as an entrepreneur, depositary of "practical" knowledge, and oriented to the pursuit of profit:

> He was not bred a philosopher but a man of business, having his way to make in the world; and it deserves to be remarked that the guiding motive for his exertions was a clear view of his own interest.
>
> (Hodgskin 1824b)

The pursuit of his own interest does not demean Watt and does not make his accomplishments less extraordinary. In another article in *The Chemist*, Hodgskin embarks on a eulogy for the passion for wealth and distinction, reprising a theme that he touched upon in the *Essay on Naval Discipline*, [34] "much stigmatized by those moralists, who notice only the deviations from the general and regular course of nature."

> [T]he thirst for wealth and distinction is the source of almost every improvement in the condition of man. It strengthens the love of liberty, and kindles the spirit of invention. By it the tooling mechanic is kept steady to his task, and the adventurous seaman induced to brave all the dangers of the ocean; spreading not only the different product of the globe more equally over every party, but also everywhere diffusing knowledge and civilization, as to bind the whole human race in one general community, having a common interest and a common fate.
> (Hodgskin 1824a)[35]

The entrepreneur is then vindicated not only as a vessel of knowledge useful to the organization of labor, but also because, in some manner, he is honoring the all-too-human thirst for distinction from a very different standpoint than did the aristocrats of the past. The entrepreneur's profit, in this perspective, is a particular case of a more generic premise of Hodgskin's: the equivalence between manual and intellectual work.[36]

The "disposition to restrict the term labour to the operation of the hands" (Hodgskin ([1825] 1964, 91) is an unfortunate misconception. Even if you think of the mechanical and repetitive actions performed by a manual worker, in the context of a highly branched division of labor the way he has learned how to perform such labor is the result of a mental effort. Such disposition, no matter how well meaning, may end up trivializing labor, missing its true nature. It is obvious that Hodgskin has in mind a very loose definition of intellectual work; he does not refer only to his own, as a journalist and thinker, nor to that of a university lecturer (which he also desired to be). There is, in Hodgskin, the idea that knowledge is dispersed and multiform.

Knowledge is the true heart of economic life:

> For a nation to have fixed capital, then, and to make a good use of it, three things, and only three things, seem to me to be requisite. First, knowledge and ingenuity for inventing machines. No labourer would, I am sure, be disposed to deny to these their reward. But no subject of complaint is more general or more just than that the inventor of any machine does not reap the benefit of it. Of all the immense number of persons who have acquired large fortunes by the modern improvements in steam engines and cotton mills, Mr Watt and Mr Arkwright are the only two, I believe, who have been distinguished for their inventions ... Thousands of capitalists have been enriched by inventions and discoveries

> of which they were not the authors, and capital, by robbing the inventor of his just reward, is guilty of stifling genius. The second requisite for having fixed capital is the manual skill and dexterity for carrying these inventions into execution. The third requisite is the skill and labour to use these instruments after they are made. Without knowledge they could not be invented, without manual skill and dexterity they could not be made, and without skill and labour they could not be productively used. But there is nothing more than the knowledge, skill and labour requisite on which the capitalist can found a claim to any share of the produce.
>
> (Hodgskin ([1825] 1964, 63–64)[37]

Hodgskin admired Watt but was very careful never to embrace any sort of "great man theory of history," to use the words that Thomas Carlyle (1795–1881) would make popular in a few years. On the contrary, Hodgskin emphasized the ubiquity of knowledge in the division of labor, pointing out that Watt's achievements had been possible precisely because of other people's skills. Mr. Watt "must have met with a vast deal of practical manual skill ready formed to his hands, which needed only some peculiar direction, or he could not have succeeded in manufacturing his own inventions. In addition, therefore, to the commercial demand for means of abridging labour, which was felt in this country, there also existed a great degree of manual dexterity among workmen; or a considerable number of skilful millwrights, founders, smiths, and carpenters, were ready formed, by whose assistance Mr. Watt was enabled to realize his conceptions" (Hodgskin 1827, 94–95). Individuals can make remarkable contributions to increase our stock of knowledge, but it nonetheless remains a collective enterprise. Truly remarkable contributions would not go very far, indeed, if they could not rely on other people's provisions. Once again, Hodgskin sees harmony in economic life, if unhampered by politics.

Nowadays, among economists, it has become rather common to point out, as Gary S. Becker (1930–2014) stated, that

> tangible forms of capital are not the only type of capital. Schooling, a computer training course, expenditures on medical care, and lectures on the virtues of punctuality and honesty are also capital. That is because they raise earnings, improve health, or add to a person's good habits over much of his lifetime. Therefore, economists regard expenditures on education, training, medical care, and so on as investments in human capital. They are called human capital because people cannot be separated from their knowledge, skills, health, or values in the way they can be separated from their financial and physical assets.
>
> (Becker [1993] 2008)

That certainly was not the case during Hodgskin's times. Since capital was such a muddy concept, hinting at human "capital" would have been surreal.

In the same encyclopedia entry we just quoted, Becker, who first pioneered the concept, maintains that "[t]he continuing growth in per capita incomes of many countries during the nineteenth and twentieth centuries is partly due to the expansion of scientific and technical knowledge that raises the productivity of labor and other inputs in production" (Becker [1993] 2008, 248). That too, appears as a self-evident truth today. It was not so in 1825.

It is easy to imagine a different interpretation than the one I have so far provided. When he advocates freedom of association for laborers, Hodgskin could be a "proto-reformist" of sorts—that is, a thinker who accepts an economy based on the division of labor, but corrected by strong representative institutions of the employees pushing to balance to some extent their contractual freedom against that of their employers. Rather than being a "Ricardian socialist," in the sense of a forerunner of Marx, Hodgskin may well have been a representative figure of the British workers' movement, of the sort that can put together some rambunctious language with a dedicated attention to real improvements in the real world.

The problem with this narrative is Hodgskin's unfaltering opposition to politics as such. In one of his last articles, Hodgskin vehemently attacks "political organisations" because each of them can create privilege to the advantage of its own members: "Each political organisation may give a great temporary advantage to the organisers, promoting some special purpose, and obtaining for them some special objects; but to all the rest of society it is injurious" (Hodgskin, 1867). This description of "political organisations" overtly includes trade unions that "make, by organisation, their power unpleasantly felt by employers and others." Indeed the unions "as they get organised, impose their power in a rather unpleasant way on the employers and the others." The workers' associations that Hodgskin declared himself in favor of in 1825 were quite different from the organized movement that would take hold later in the century, and that he did not support.

Any exploration of *Labour Defended against the Claims of Capital* cannot but conclude that it is a contradictory work, as we have repeatedly emphasized, and Hodgskin certainly did not propel the economic sciences further by understanding the nature of "capital." Instead, he fetishizes it, though he ultimately grasps that its detrimental effect could be "eliminated by purging the exchange process from its pathological characteristics" (Thompson 1984, 99). But there is something in this work other than Hodgskin's rumbling and ranting at capital, something which has not been made irrelevant by subsequent economic theory. *Labour Defended* can be read as an essay of remarkable lucidity when it comes to its portrayal of the unfolding of the Industrial Revolution.

Although lacking as a theoretical text, *Labour Defended* is extraordinarily interesting as a testimony about industrialization. Hodgskin's ultra-laborism in this essay seems prodromic to the formulation of a vision of the economy deeply rooted in the concept of knowledge, and that is precisely what Hodgskin tried to leave us, with his *Popular Political Economy* two years later.

Even in the 1820s, gloom and doom were more easily sold than "rational optimism," and the socialist movement was predicated upon such prophecies. Engels' picture of doom and destitution in filthy urban life became a cliché of the Industrial Revolution (Engels [1845] 1969). Machine-breaking became a foundational myth of socialism all through the world. Hodgskin's understanding of machinery creating prosperity for the masses was less of a blockbuster, but more accurate.

Notes

1. On the word "individualism, which was imported" in the 1840s, see Lukes (1971).
2. The debate over John Stuart Mill's "socialism" is long and complex. See, *inter alia*, Stafford (1998).
3. Gregory Claeys (1986, xxiii) has pointed out how, under the label of "Ricardian socialism," very heterogeneous thinkers are clumped together, although there does not seem to be a place for Hodgskin's "semi-anarchic liberalism." Noel Thompson (1984, 105) has polemically observed how the only real Ricardian socialist was Karl Marx.
4. Terence W. Hutchinson (1978, 242^{fn}) observed that "in the Marxist version of the history of political economy a rather important niche is assigned to Thomas Hodgskin, on the basis of a somewhat erroneous interpretation of his doctrines." An exception is an important essay by E.K. Hunt (1977), written precisely with the goal of "de-homogenizing" Hodgskin and Marx.
5. One of the main targets of Mill's criticism was William Spence (1783–1860), the entomologist and economist who despised industrialization to the extent of claiming that, in 1806/1807 the British should not care about Napoleon's blockade because the only source of wealth was to be found in agriculture.
6. It is important not to underestimate the brutality of the enforcement of these norms or their pervasiveness. In the post-war period, Habeas Corpus was suspended (in 1817) and meetings of more than fifty people were forbidden without prior notice. "They have made also a law handing us over to the magistrates like vagabonds and thieves, and we are to be condemned almost unheard, and without the privilege and formality of a public trial" (Hodgskin [1825] 1964, 24).
7. It needs to be pointed out, however, that "Even as large factories became a familiar sight in the early nineteenth century, they were not the most common mode of production in the British textile industry. Nonfactory production, far from disappearing, continued end even grew in various sectors of the industry. As late as the mid-nineteenth century, many textile manufacturers had both factories for spinning and weaving and networks of domestic hand weavers" (Freeman 2018, 9).
8. There was some debate over his lending a helping hand to those in need. For an uncompromising exposition of the argument, see, *inter alia*, McLean (2006). For an acute review that puts McLean's book in perspective, see Den Uyl (2007).
9. Böhm-Bawerk ([1884] 1890) is the starting point of such a new perspective.
10. Indeed, as Böhm-Bawerk himself stresses, there is also in Smith, at its larval stage, the idea that "future profit" is privileged by the capitalist over "present enjoyment." Such a conception informs another category of theories of capital as understood by Böhm-Bawerk, the so-called abstinence theories: it is the present abstinence of the capitalist that constitutes the justification of his expectation of remuneration. Such view is perhaps the most striking antithesis of the theory of capital as exploitation.
11. Screpanti and Zamagni ([2004] 2005, 141) note that, concerning pricing, Hodgskin "in particular had a deep understanding of how the problem arose with Smith and the reasons for his analytical difficulties, and proposed a solution which could be considered as beyond criticism."

12 In *Popular Political Economy*, Hodgskin (1827, 241) refers precisely to the passage by Smith quoted by Cannan to argue that capital is "part of the national wealth employed, to use the language of Dr. Smith, to procure its owner a revenue."
13 Although public spending was incomparably lower than current values, the possibility of getting commissions and particular privileges could make the fortune of entire families. During the many years when trading activities were considered somewhat unbecoming, there was a sort of "intergenerational alternation" between business and politics. Namier ([1929] 1968, 47, 48–49) explains that "Government contracts were usually held with a seat in the House of Commons, while baronetcies, the crest over the profits, had to be gained by service in the House; and a generation or two later, provided the money was preserved, the trade discontinued, and a seat in the House retained, a coronet was within the reach of the children or grandchildren of the successful Government contractors… In 1761, fifty merchants were returned to Parliament, and of these at least thirty-seven can be proved to have had extensive business dealings with the Government."
14 De Vivo (1988, 185) argued that Hodgskin's reasoning ought to be considered "Ricardian" since "strictly woven in it is the point that profits are made at the expense of wages." It needs however to be pointed out that, unlike Marx, Hodgskin makes no attempt to link the level of wages to the rhythm of capital accumulation.
15 For an overview of this tradition, including Hodgskin, see Hart, Chartier, Kenyon Miller and Long (2018).
16 Noel Thompson (1984, 106–107) considers Hodgskin as holding what he calls a "Smithian" conception of exploitation. Even stronger was perhaps the influence on Hodgskin from J.B. Say, whom Raico (1992) credits for distinguishing between anti-productive and productive classes, which informed classical liberal class theory.
17 Hodgskin (1832, 66) applied the same principles to land: "[A]s agriculture is improved, the quantity of land necessary to supply each individual with the means of subsistence diminishes. As mankind have multiplied, and as time has flowed on, knowledge has been extended, and the arts improved. Agriculture sharing the general fate, has also been improved, and is continually improving; so that a less and less quantity of land gradually suffices for the maintenance of individuals."
18 What Hodgskin perhaps did not have time to appreciate is that if it is true that capital "produces" capital, it is also true that "[c]apitalistic accumulation does not consist mainly in adding new layers of capital to those already created, but in replacing those already created with new layers of greater value" (Ricossa 1995, 29).
19 It seems therefore rather bizarre that, in his monumental *History of Economic Analysis*, Joseph Schumpeter ([1954] 1986, 454), after crediting Hodgskin with "traces of genuinely analytic intention," comments, "It should be observed that as soon as an author combines the idea that labor is the only source of wealth and that the values of all commodities can be represented in terms of labor hours with the idea that labor itself is a commodity, he is inevitably drawn to the conclusion that the market mechanism robs the workman of the difference between the labor value of 'his' product and the labor value of the amount of work invested in that product."
20 Those who rushed to celebrate Hodgskin as the "discoverer of surplus value" often faced a rude awakening when realizing that, in their own intellectual framework, his conclusions must be deemed "inaccurate." See Osier (1976, 82).
21 It is worth mentioning that this process went on by degrees, and that the prominence of factories over individual manufacturing only dates back to the middle of the nineteenth century. For example, the "number of blacksmiths (112,000), in '51, was still higher than the number of workers employed in basic steel industrial processes (79,590)" (Bianco and Grendi 1970, xviii).
22 A particularly interesting case is Robert Owen, for whom the introduction of machinery represented a watershed in history. For a review of the ambiguity and evolution of Owen's analysis of mechanization, see Claeys (1987, 34–66).

23 The most recent researches seem to indicate that the "mechanization" of the British economy, in fact, required a substantial increase in skilled laborers. See Van der Beek (2015).

24 The claim that such phenomena coincided with general impoverishment of the humbler classes is rather difficult to support today with solid historiographic arguments. In an interesting review of working-class literature, Emma Griffin (2013, 16) noted that, in claiming that the Industrial Revolution impoverished the masses, "the only difficulty is that autobiographies, those rare and unique records in which the laboring poor retold their stories, refuse to cooperate ... it is not possible to frame the autobiographical literature within the dark interpretation without imposing a wilful distortion upon the messages our writers are seeking to communicate."

25 The drive toward factory organization was almost irresistible as "the opportunity cost of many ... potential factory employees was set by what they could earn in cottage industry. This alternative declined rapidly and by 1850 was, in most cases, no longer available" (Mokyr 2001, 9).

26 For workers, women and children were competitors who could lower their wages. Hodgskin (1825a) suggested "to my workers brothers" that they prohibit their wives and children from working, as the better means to keep their wages up.

27 Likewise, in *Popular Political Economy* Hodgskin (1827, 151) reasoned:

> We speak, for example, in a vague manner, of a windmill grinding corn, and of steam engines doing the work of several millions of people. This gives a very incorrect view of the phenomena. It is not the instruments which grind corn, and spin cotton, but the labour of those who make, and the labour of those who use them. The co-operating labours of the millwright, for example, and the almost numberless other workmen who prepare his tools and the materials, of which the mill is fabricated, or who bring them from remote parts of the earth,—they themselves using very complicated machines for this purpose, which are prepared by the combined labour of a vast number of persons—in the first instance construct the mill; and then the labour of the miller, assisted also by various instruments, millstones, sieves, sacks, &c. which are made by some other labourers, profiting by the force of the wind, and the natural hardness of the stones, as compared to the hardness of corn, grinds it, sifts it, and prepares it for the use of the baker. So the united labours of the miner, the smelter, the smith, the engineer, the stoker, and of numberless other persons, and not the lifeless machines perform whatever is done by steam engines.

28 As quoted in Gray (1946, 263). Marx and Engels notwithstanding, in Hall's view, as Gray explains, "no sane man would ever voluntarily abandon the land for any other occupation."

29
> In the progress of the division of labour, the employment of the far greater part of those who live by labour, that is, of the great body of the people, comes to be confined to a few very simple operations, frequently to one or two. But the understandings of the greater part of men are necessarily formed by their ordinary employments. The man whose whole life is spent in performing a few simple operations, of which the effects are perhaps always the same, or very nearly the same, has no occasion to exert his understanding or to exercise his invention in finding out expedients for removing difficulties which never occur. He naturally loses, therefore, the habit of such exertion, and generally becomes as stupid and ignorant as it is possible for a human creature to become.

On Adam Smith's "two visions of the division of labour" there has been an ample debate. See, *inter alia*, West (1964) and Rosenberg (1965). It did not escape Marx's attention that two visions of the division of labour coexist in Adam Smith. See Marx ([1871] 1906, 382–383[fn]).

30 I do not want to claim Hodgskin's farsightedness was unique. Howes (2019) has recently pointed to a speech by mathematician Olinthus Gregory (1774–1841), published indeed in the *Mechanics' Magazine*, who saw "new machines to advance our arts and facilitate labour; waste lands enclosed, roads improved, bridges erected, canals cut, tunnels excavated, marshes drained and cultivated, docks formed, ports enlarged" (Gregory 1826, 459) as proof of progress, and promise of further progress.
31 Obviously, the fact that one thing is analytically distinguishable from the other does not mean that making this distinction is easy in the real world with respect to real capitalist enterprises.
32 It is perhaps worth mentioning a comment by Say ([1803] 2002, 129^{fn}): "The term entrepreneur is difficult to render in English; the corresponding word, undertaker, being already appropriated to a limited sense. It signifies the master-manufacturer in manufacture, the farmer in agriculture, and the merchant in commerce; and generally in all three branches, the person who takes upon himself the immediate responsibility, risk, and conduct of a concern of industry, whether upon his own or a borrowed capital."
33 "All men are instinctively obedient to public opinion. The force of circumstances operates upon all mankind. It influences the sentiments, and even fashions the minds, of the most dignified members of the Bench and the Bar, as well of the meanest of our species" (Hodgskin 1832, 6).
34 For Hodgskin (1813, 18), the passion for distinction is "a general passion of our nature" that "will be stronger in our country than in any other; for it is one conspicuous effect of that liberty we enjoy to afford room for the gratification of, and consequently to excite, every human desire."
35 "Specifically," as Hodgskin (1824a) notes, all of us somehow contracted a debt with "the intense desire of wealth" of those "alchemists as such desire brought them to study chemical elements that they would have otherwise stayed away from" (because they appeared too dangerous or seemed repugnant).
36 For such equivalence, Hodgskin was strongly criticized by the Owenite William Thompson, who accused him of hypocrisy in effectively wanting to replace the "tax" workers needed to pay to capital with another tax to pay to "intellectual labourers" (Thompson 1827, 2–6).
37 Visiting Paris, Hodgskin attended lectures by J.B. Say. In *Popular Political Economy*, he explicitly mentions Say's *Treatise* as an influence on his understanding of the division of knowledge underpinning the division of labor (Hodgskin 1827, 96).

References

Ashton, Thomas S. (1948) 1997. *The Industrial Revolution, 1760–1830*. Oxford, UK: Oxford University Press.

Ashton, Thomas S. 1954. "The Treatment of Capitalism by Historians." In *Capitalism and the Historians*. Edited by F.A. Hayek. 33–63. Chicago: University of Chicago Press.

Becker, Gary. (1993) 2008. "Human Capital." In *The Concise Encyclopedia of Economics*. Edited by David R. Henderson. Indianapolis, IN: Liberty Fund.

Berg, Maxine. 1980. *The Machinery Question and the Making of Political Economy, 1815–1848*. Cambridge UK: University of Cambridge.

Bianco, Gino and Grendi, Edoardo, eds. 1970. "Introduzione." In *La tradizione socialista in Inghilterra* [*The English Socialist Tradition*], vii–cv. Torino: Einaudi.

Böhm-Bawerk, Eugen von. (1884) 1890. *Capital and Interest: A Critical History of Economic Theory*. Translated and edited by William A. Smart. London: Macmillan.

Cannan, Edwin. 1903. *A History of the Theories of Production and Distribution in English Political Economy, from 1776 to 1848*. London: P.S. King & Son.

Carlyle, Thomas. (1829) 2007. "Signs of Time." In *The Spirit of the Age: Victorian Essays*. Edited by Gertrude Himmelfarb. New Haven: Yale University Press, 31–50.

Cipolla, Carlo M., ed. 1973. *The Industrial Revolution 1700–1914*. Vol III of The Fontana Economic History of Europe. London: Collins.

Claeys, Gregory. 1987. *Machinery, Money and the Millennium: From Moral Economy to Socialism, 1815–1860*. Oxford UK: Polity Press.

Clapham, John. (1926) 1950. *An Economic History of Modern Britain: The Early Railway Age, 1820–1850*. Cambridge: Cambridge University Press.

Davies, Stephen. 2019. *The Wealth Explosion. The Nature and Origins of Modernity*. Brighton: Edward Everett Root.

De Vivo, Giancarlo. 1988. "Ricardo and His Disciples: Orthodoxy and Socialism." *History of European Ideas* 9(2): 183–189, https://doi.org/10.1016/0191-6599(88)90039-90033.

Den Uyl, Douglas J. 2007. "Adam Smith, Radical and Libertarian." *Journal of Scottish Philosophy* 5(2): 221–227.

Engels, Friedrich. (1880) 1908. *Socialism: Utopian and Scientific*. Chicago: Charles H. Kerr & Company.

Engels, Friedrich. (1845) 1969. *The Condition of the Working-class in England in 1844*. London: Panther Books.

Feinstein, Charles. 1998. "Pessimism Perpetuated: Real Wages and the Standard of Living in Britain during and after the Industrial Revolution." *Journal of Economic History* 3 (58): 625–658, https://doi.org/10.1017/S0022050700021100.

Fontana, Biancamaria. 1985. *Rethinking the Politics of Commercial Society: The Edinburgh Review 1802–1832*. Cambridge: Cambridge University Press.

Foxwell, H.S. 1899. Introduction. In Anton Menger, *The Right to the Whole Produce of Labour*. London: Macmillan, v–cx.

Freeman, Joshua B. 2018. *Behemoth: A History of the Factory and the Making of the Modern World*. New York: London.

Ginzburg, Andrea, ed. 1976. *I socialisti ricardiani*. Milano: ISEDI.

Gray, Alexander. 1946. *The Socialist Tradition: Moses to Lenin*. London: Greens.

Gregory, Olinthus. 1826. "Substance of the speech delivered at the first anniversary of the Deptford Mechanics' Institution, October 19, 1826 by Dr. Olinthus Gregory, President." *Mechanics' Magazine* 169, November 18.

Griffin, Emma. 2013. *Liberty's Dawn: A People's History of the Industrial Revolution*. New Haven: Yale University Press.

Griffin, Emma. 2018. "Diets, Hunger and Living Standards during the British Industrial Revolution." *Past and Present* 239 (1): 71–111, https://doi.org/10.1093/pastj/gtx061.

Halévy, Élie. (1903) 1956. *Thomas Hodgskin*. Edited in translation with an introduction by A.J. Taylor. London: Ernst Benn.

Hart, David M., Gary Chartier, Ross Kenyon Miller and Roderick T. Long, eds. 2018. *Social Class and State Power Exploring an Alternative Radical Tradition*. London: Palgrave Macmillan.

Hartwell, Ronald M. 1965. "The Causes of the Industrial Revolution: An Essay in Methodology." *Economic History Review* 1 (18): 164–182, https//:doi.org//10.2307/2591880.

Hicks, John. 1946. *Value and Capital: An Inquiry into Some Fundamental Principles of Economic Theory*. Oxford: Clarendon Press.

Hodgskin, Thomas. 1813. *An Essay on Naval Discipline, Shewing Part of its Evil Effects on the Minds of the Officers, on the Minds of the Men, and on the Community; with an Amended System, by which Pressing May Be Immediately Abolished*. London: Printed for the Author by C. Squire.

Hodgskin, Thomas, to Francis Place, May 28, 1820.

Hodgskin, Thomas. 1820. *Travels in the North of Germany. Describing the Present State of the Social and Political Institutions, the Agriculture, Manufacture, Commerce, Education, Arts and Manners in That Country, Particularly in the Kingdom of Hannover*. 2 Vols. Edinburgh: Archibald Constable.

Hodgskin, Thomas. 1824a. "Chemistry as a Science. Art. X. Phosphorus." *The Chemist*10 (May 15): 155–156.

Hodgskin, Thomas. 1824b. "Monument to Mr. Watt." *The Chemist*16 (June 28): 250–251.

Hodgskin, Thomas. 1825a. "How to Lessen the Number of Labourers." *The Trades' Newspaper and Mechanics' Weekly Journal*, October 16.

Hodgskin, Thomas. 1825b. "Is it Men or Engines that Work?" *The Trades' Newspaper and Mechanics' Weekly Journal*, September 25 (signed T.H.).

Hodgskin, Thomas. (1825) 1964. *Labour Defended Against the Claims of Capital*. London: Hammersmith Bookshop.

Hodgskin, Thomas. 1827. *Popular Political Economy: Four Lectures Delivered at the Mechanics' Institution*. London: Tait.

Hodgskin, Thomas. 1832. *The Natural and Artificial Right of Property Contrasted: A Series of Letters, addressed without permission to H. Brougham, Esq. M.P. F.R.S.* London: B. Steil.

Hodgskin, Thomas. 1858. "Trade Without Capital." *Morning Chronicle*, January 23 (signed T.H.).

Hodgskin, Thomas. 1867. "Political Organisation." *Brighton Guardian*, March 20.

Horn, Jeff. 2003. "Understanding Crowd Action: Machine-breaking in England and France, 1789–1817." *Journal of the Western Society for French History* 31 (2003): 138–152, http://hdl.handle.net/2027/spo.0642292.0031.009.

Howes, Anton. 2019. "Age of Invention: Improveable Beings." December 18. https://antonhowes.substack.com/p/age-of-invention-higher-perfection?r=2juq6&utm_campaign=post&utm_medium=email&utm_source=copy.

Hunt, Emery K. 1977. "Value Theory in the Writings of the Classical Economists, Thomas Hodgskin, and Karl Marx." *History of Political Economy* 9 (3): 322–345, https://doi.org/10.1215/00182702-9-3-322.

Hutchinson, Terence W. 1978. *On Revolutions and Progress in Economic Knowledge*. Cambridge: Cambridge University Press.

Knight, Charles. 1831. *The Rights of Industry: Addressed to the Working-Men of the United Kingdom*. London: Charles Knight.

Lachmann, Ludwig. 1978. *Capital and Its Structure*. Kansas City, MO: Sheer Andrews and McMeel.

Lalor, John. 1852. *Money and Morals: A Book for the Times*. London: Chapman.

Landes, David. (1969) 2003. *The Unbound Prometheus: Technological Change and Industrial Development in Western Europe from 1750 to the Present*. Cambridge: Cambridge University Press.

Lukes, Steven. 1971. "The Meaning of 'Individualism'." *Journal of the History of Ideas* 32 (1): 45–66.

MacLeod, Christine. 2010. *Heroes of Invention: Technology, Liberalism and British Identity, 1750–1914.* Cambridge: Cambridge University Press.

McCloskey, Deirdre. 2010. *Bourgeois Dignity: Why Economics Can't Explain the Modern World.* Chicago: University of Chicago Press.

McCloskey, Deirdre. 2016. *Bourgeois Equality: How Ideas, Not Capital or Institutions, Enriched the World.* Chicago: University of Chicago Press.

McLean, Iain. 2006. *Adam Smith, Radical and Egalitarian: An Interpretation for the Twenty-First Century.* Edinburgh: Edinburgh University Press.

Malthus, Thomas. (1798) 1826. *An Essay on the Principle of Population.* London: John Murray.

Marx, Karl. (1847) 1956. *The Poverty of Philosophy Answer to the Philosophy of Poverty by M. Proudhon.* Moscow: Foreign Languages Publishing House.

Marx, Karl. (1862–1863) 1971. *Theories of Surplus Value, Part III.* Moscow: Progress Publishers.

Marx, Karl. (1871) 1906. *Capital: A Critique of Political Economy.* New York: The Modern Library.

Marx, Karl, and Friedrich Engels. (1848) 2007. *Manifesto of the Communist Party.* New York, NY: International Publishers.

Meisenzahl, Ralf, and Joel Mokyr. 2012. "The Rate and Direction of Invention in the British Industrial Revolution: Incentives and Institutions." In *The Rate and Direction of Inventive Activity Revisited.* Edited by Josh Lerner and Scott Stern, 443–482. Chicago: University of Chicago Press.

Menger, Anton. (1886) 1899. *The Right to the Whole Produce of Labour.* London: Macmillan.

Mill, James. 1808. *Commerce Defended: An Answer to the Arguments by which Mr. Spence, Mr. Cobbett, and Others, have attempted to Prove that Commerce is not a source of National Wealth.* London: C. and R. Baldwin.

Mill, John Stuart. (1848) 2006. *Principles of Political Economy: The Collected Works of John Stuart Mill*, Vol. 3. Edited by J.M. Robson. Indianapolis, IN: Liberty Fund.

Mokyr, Joel. 2001. "The Rise and Fall of the Factory System: Technology, Firms, and Households since the Industrial Revolution." *Carnegie-Rochester Conference Series on Public Policy* 1 (55): 1–45, https://doi.org/10.1016/S0167-2231(01)00050-00051.

Mokyr, Joel. 2009. *The Enlightened Economy: Britain and the Industrial Revolution 1700–1850.* London: Penguin.

Musson, Albert E., and Eric Robinson. 1960. "The Origins of Engineering in Lancashire." *Journal of Economic History* 2 (20): 209–210, https://www.jstor.org/stable/2114855.

Namier, Lewis. (1929) 1968. *The Structure of Politics at the Accession of George III.* London: Macmillan.

Ó Gráda, Cormac. 2014. "Did Science Cause the Industrial Revolution?" University of Warwick Working Paper no. 205: 1–31, http://dx.doi.org/10.2139/ssrn.2523358.

Osier, Jean-Pierre 1976. *Thomas Hodgskin: Une critique prolétarienne de l'économie politique* [*Thomas Hodgskin: A Proletarian Review of Political Economy*]. Paris: Maspero.

Proudhon, Pierre-Joseph. (1847) 1888. *System of Economical Contradictions: or, The Philosophy of Poverty.* Translated and edited by Benjamin R. Tucker. Boston: Benjamin R. Tucker.

Raico, Ralph. 1977. "Classical Liberal Exploitation Theory: A Comment on Professor Liggio's Paper." *Journal of Libertarian Studies* 3 (1): 179–183, https://cdn.mises.org/1_3_2_0.pdf.

Raico, Ralph. 1992. "Classical Liberal Roots of the Marxist Doctrine of Classes." In *Requiem for Marx*. Edited by Yuri N. Maltsev, 189–220. Auburn, AL: Ludwig von Mises Institute.

Randall, Adrian. 1991. *Before the Luddites: Custom, Community and Machinery in the English Woollen Industry 1770–1809*. Cambridge: Cambridge University Press.

Ricardo, David. (1821) 2015. *The Works and Correspondence of David Ricardo. Vol. 1 of Principles of Political Economy and Taxation*. Edited by P. Sraffa with the collaboration of M.H. Dobb. Indianapolis, IN: Liberty Fund.

Ricossa, Sergio. 1995. *Passato e futuro del capitalismo* [*Capitalism: the Past and Future*]. Roma-Bari: Laterza.

Rosenberg, Nathan. 1965. "Adam Smith on the Division of Labour: Two Views or One?" *Economica* 126 (32): 127–139, https://doi.org/10.2307/2552544.

Russell, Bertrand. (1934) 2001. *Freedom and Organization, 1814–1914*. London: Routledge.

Say, Jean-Baptiste. (1803) 2002. *A Treatise on Political Economy*. Translated and edited by C.R. Prinsep. Kitchener: Batoche Books.

Schumpeter, Joseph. (1954) 1986. *A History of Economic Analysis*. London: Routledge.

Screpanti, Ernesto, and Stefano Zamagni. (2004) 2005. *An Outline of the History of Economic Thought*. Translated and edited by David Field and Lynn Kirby. New York: Oxford University Press.

Smith, Adam. (1776) 1981. *An Inquiry into the Nature and Causes of the Wealth of Nations*, Vol. I, V, edited by Roy H. Campbell and Andrew S. Skinner. Indianapolis, IN: Liberty Fund.

Sowell, Thomas. 1985. *Marxism: Philosophy and Economics*. London: Unwin.

Stack, David. 1998. *Nature and Artifice: The Life and Thought of Thomas Hodgskin, 1787–1869*. Martlesham: Boydell & Brewer.

Stark, Werner. 1943. *The Ideal Foundations of Economic Thought*. London: Routledge.

Stafford, William. 1998. "How Can a Paradigmatic Liberal Call Himself a Socialist? The Case of John Stuart Mill." *Journal of Political Ideologies*, 3 (3): 325–345, https://doi.org/10.1080/13569319808420784.

Thompson, Edward P. 1964. *The Making of the English Working Class*. New York: Vintage Books.

Thompson, Noel. 1984. *The People's Science: The Popular Political Economy of Exploitation and Crisis, 1816–1834*. Cambridge: Cambridge University Press.

Thompson, William. 1827. *Labour Rewarded: The Claims of Labour and Capital Conciliated*. London: Hunt and Clarke.

Valiani, Leo. 1951. *L'epoca della prima internazionale* [*The Days of the First International*]. Vol. I of *Storia del movimento socialista* [*A History of the Socialist Movement*]. Florence: La Nuova Italia.

Van der Beek, Karine. 2015. "England's Eighteenth-Century Demand for High-Quality Workmanship." In *Institutions, Innovation and Industrialization: Essays in Economic History and Development*. Edited by Avner Greif, Lynne Kiesling and John V.C. Nye. Princeton: Princeton University Press.

Wallas, Graham. (1898) 1925. *The Life of Francis Place 1771–1854*. London: Allen & Unwin.

Webb, Beatrice and Sidney Webb. (1894) 1929. *The History of Trade Unionism*. London: Longmans, Greens & Co.

West, E.G. 1964. "Adam Smith's Two Views of the Division of Labour." *Economica* 121 (31): 23–32, https://doi.org/10.2307/2550924.

3 Political economy and free trade

A defender of political economy

In the previous chapter, I argued that Hodgskin should not be considered a "socialist" in the contemporary meaning of this word. But can we consider him a *classical liberal* and an economist? I would dare to answer yes: we can consider him both an *economist* and a *classical liberal*. Hodgskin's blend of classical liberalism was, as we have seen, predicated on the idea that the removals of restraints and hindrances on free exchange will lead to greater prosperity. Such greater prosperity, as we have already seen, was to benefit first and foremost the working classes. Thus, Hodgskin felt no tension between his advocacy of *laissez-faire* and his view of himself as a partisan of the poor. If he thought free exchange was bound to foster a *harmonious* development, it was because he maintained it was the working class that would benefit most from innovation and unhampered competition.

Hodgskin had no formal education and made his living as a journalist, yet political economy remained a central concern from the very first to the very last of his writings, and political economy was the science he always looked to for guidance and enlightenment. A *particular version* of it, to be precise: he revered Adam Smith and strongly disapproved of a few contemporary economists (among others, Ricardo and McCulloch [1789–1864]), who he thought perverted the "simple and even sublime principles [of economics] to the bolstering up of monopolies, and to supporting some of the laws most hostile to its principles" (Hodgskin 1848a).

Hodgskin was so passionate about political economy that he did whatever he could to teach it at the London Mechanics' Institute. After their friendship ended, his old mentor, Francis Place, was reluctant to provide his former protégé with an outlet for spreading his ideas and thus opposed his teaching (Wallas [1898] 1925, 268[fn]). Hodgskin volunteered to hold twelve classes in 1825, but his offer was declined. Yet, as Hodgskin managed to maintain a friendly relationship with George Birkbeck, the patron of the Institute, he was able to lecture on the subject in September 1826. His lectures, presumably expanded, provided the foundation for *Popular Political Economy*. The first lecture, "The Influence of Knowledge," became the second and third chapters.

The second lecture, centered on the concept of the division of labor, informs chapters four through six. The seventh chapter, on exchange, coincides with the third lesson, while the fourth and last lecture occupies the rest of the volume, focused on currency and prices.[1]

These circumstances—the fact that the book is based on a series of lectures—should not be misleading. Hodgskin had high ambitions. The adjective "popular" in the title does not imply that it was addressed to a broad audience. The book indeed "makes no pretensions to be what is called practical." Instead, it focused on first principles. Though he lectured to classes composed of common people, craftsmen and skilled workers, his intent was not to write just a pamphlet.[2]

Rather, Hodgskin was aiming for a book on economics written "from the point of view of the people."

The adjective "popular" was chosen to mark his distance from Thomas Malthus. The latter's population theory quickly became part of the orthodox political economy of the time; Malthus was viewed as having conclusively demonstrated that a society's population tends to increase to the point of pressing hard against the means of subsistence. In a sense, Malthus (and, later, David Ricardo) put greater emphasis on the limits, rather than the potentialities, of economic life. Political economy acquired gloomier nuances than in Adam Smith's times, as scarcity took center stage. In contrast, Hodgskin thought that present limits on the supply of resources could be overcome: society could achieve abundance, provided that unnecessary government interventions were lifted. In this context, two different views of the people's contributions to the economy faced one another. If Malthus feared inordinate population growth, Hodgskin (1827a, 26) believed "the foundation of all national greatness is the increase of the people."[3]

Hodgskin (1827a, 452) thought we could rely on people's ingenuity and creativity. His version of political economy stood out because, on the normative side, he preached strict non-intervention. For him, political economy was a science that studies "the natural laws that govern the production and distribution of wealth." The economists, Hodgskin writes citing Dugald Stewart (1753–1828), are those philosophers who first found that social order is the outcome of nature's wisdom rather than human contrivances.[4] The study of natural laws calls for an attempt to *understand* them, and to avoid meddling with them.

This is how we may distinguish, according to Hodgskin, between "proper" political economy and its perverted degeneration: the proper one is an attempt to discover laws with a general character (natural laws); its corrupted version coincides with shrouding in a cloak of scientific rigor the pretenses of the paternal government. Hodgskin (1827a, 3) even resented the use of the adjective "political," for such an investigation ought to be helping us better understand laws that were *natural*; the "erroneous name" gave the impression we could replace them with *man-made ones*.

Hodgskin's treatise was published after the so-called panic of 1825. Recessions never help the popularity of the market economy; this was true back then as much as today.

In the context of a depressed economy, in January 1825 the *Trades' Newspaper*, "the only authentically working-class newspaper outside the co-operative press in the late 1820s" (N. Thompson 1984, 12), published a fierce invective against William Huskisson's (1770–1830) decision to end England's ban against importing foreign silk. The importation of processed silk had been prohibited in 1765, while from 1713 to 1765 it was burdened by heavy duties (Brady [1928] 1967, 96). William Huskisson was chairman of the Board of Trade after 1823 and in this capacity strove to steer England in a free-trade direction. Thanks to Huskisson, the ban was repealed but this move won him enemies. He also succeeded in abolishing the Spitalfields Acts, which had allowed weavers in Spitalfields, London, to set their wages as in modern collective agreements, insulating themselves from competition.[5] Huskisson's "assault on the prevailing silk duties, favoured child of the mercantilist system, provoked the ire of the industry and many within parliament" (Rowe 2018, 210).

Thus, in Asa Briggs' ([1959] 2000, 192) words, "when the great boom of 1825 collapsed, many people blamed Huskisson's 'theories' for the distress which followed. Bank failures, stock exchange collapse, and business bankruptcies in the autumn and winter of 1825 introduced a new phase in English politics." If the crisis had its epicenter in the banking sector (1825 saw widespread bankruptcies of banks), the subsequent boom was fueled by investment in the bonds of newly independent Latin American countries. Yet Huskisson's policies, as opposed to these less visible factors, were clear for all to see and came to be an easy target. In a parliamentary address, Huskisson himself lamented being singled out as the individual who had "thrown so many persons out of bread, in the trial of a rash experiment, and in the pursuit of a hollow theory."[6]

In the name of artisans and weavers, the *Trades' Newspaper* (January 22, 1826, 440–441) argued that the abolition of the ban "is producing at the offset, a vast deal of misery in the country." Free trade meant leaving to their own resources "thousands of industrious, harmless men."

> What is to men perishing for present want of food and raiment, that at some future period their country may be benefitted by that change of system of which they are victims?
> ... PERISH POLITICAL ECONOMY, BUT LET THE PEOPLE LIVE.

The argument was not all that different from many a polemic against free trade in the last two centuries: abolishing tariffs altogether did not allow for smooth adjustment.[7] That final statement, "perish political economy," sparked Hodgskin's reaction. Such an omen did not surprise him because he thought the *Trades' Newspaper* and its readers "probably understand by these terms [*political economy*], some prevalent theories influencing the decisions of statesmen, to the production of great present evil. Nor am I surprised that you should conceive of the science, because its professors have said of it, that it is to the 'state what domestic economy is to a family':[8] and the domestic economy of a family being always regulated by its head, it follows that political economy consists only of regulations established by the head or government of the state" (Hodgskin 1826c, 452).

Yet such an idea is incorrect—and dangerous too. Hodgskin calls on the authority of Jean-Baptiste Say, for whom "the science of political economy was not a branch of the science of the legislator" (Forget 1999, 112). Hodgskin likewise argued that political economy was not to be "a political science, prescribing regulations for society, or dictating duties to men ... It does not pretend to say what men will do, but it says the consequences of their actions, some of which it endeavours to trace, are inevitable" (1827a, 38–39). People, left to their own devices, could move beyond present living standards and achieve prosperity through economic growth. Such optimism was perhaps more evident in French economists like Frédéric Bastiat (1801–1850), whom, unsurprisingly, Hodgskin came to admire.

The economist should not, then, provide prescriptions.[9] He could not "inform us how the hand can be made skilful" but should limit himself to observe "the close connexion between individual gain and the general welfare." Neither should the economist "pretend to direct the operations of the merchant, the trader, or the farmer, any more than those of the engineer" (Hodgskin 1827a, 40). Economic science shall peruse "the circumstances which influence the productive power of labour, the prosperity or decay of nations, and, in a general sense, the opulence and poverty of individuals" (15). Such an approach was not meant as a condemnation of the modern business school, but of government aiming at *coercively* directing production.

This defense of economic science continued to be a theme of Hodgskin's writings. In an article published by the *Brighton Guardian* in 1863, thirty-eight years after the *Trades' Newspaper*'s article, Hodgskin blamed the economists who were too busy suggesting new laws, thus neglecting the advancement of science and "taking a wrong path"—Frédéric Bastiat being "the chief important exception." Too much emphasis on "administrative" measures, Hodgskin believed, went to the detriment of the true scope of the science— which he nonetheless continued to regard as the most "important and instructive" of all (Hodgskin 1863a, 2). Such a wholehearted defense of economic, "natural" laws was possible only because Hodgskin thought they freed people from intrusive government.

Labor, knowledge and a principle of population

So why is it necessary for economic development that people be free of intrusive government? As we have seen, Hodgskin's reliance on human ingenuity is crucial to his thinking. "Knowledge-guided labour" is the hero of his inquiry into the causes of the wealth of nations, the true engine of the economic world as it sees it. Economics is indeed the science that unveils this truth.

Ever an admirer of Adam Smith, Hodgskin criticizes him for not having given a central role to knowledge in his work. Hodgskin maintains that the division of labor has a cognitive dimension that he thinks was poorly investigated by Smith. Although there are in *The Wealth of Nations* "numberless scattered remarks, which show that Dr. Smith was aware of the influence of knowledge in adding to productive power; yet he has not dedicated any part of his book expressly to this subject" (Hodgskin 1827a, 53).

Certainly Smith articulated knowledge as a factor in the limitations of power, and Hodgskin acknowledged that.[10] Think of the famous passage of *The Theory of Moral Sentiments* dedicated to the man of system, who aims to arrange society as pieces on a chessboard, without understanding that each human being has his or her own will and intentions (Smith [1759] 1869, IV, II, 2), but also consider his skepticism toward government's farsightedness in directing business. In *The Wealth of Nations* he discharges the sovereign from "the duty of superintending the industry of private people, and of directing it towards the employments most suitable to the interest of the society," "the proper performance of which no human wisdom or knowledge could ever be sufficient" (Smith (1776) 1981, IV, IX, 51).

In Hodgskin's *Popular Political Economy* there is no shortage of remarks that sound very "Smithian"—about the *hubris* of the decision makers and the inevitable nefarious effects of public policies conceived in ignorance of natural laws. Hodgskin (1827a, 43) understood that Smith demonstrated that "the science which pretended ... to add to the wealth of the people through the instrumentality of government, had and could have no existence." But he wants to go further: he wants to explain the division of labor *as a consequence* of the progress of knowledge.

At the core of production lies the creative labor of man. Labor (both manual and intellectual) is knowledge-guided. Indeed, not even the simplest manual labor can be accomplished without first having acquired and applied some form of knowledge: every kind of activity is immersed in a flow of knowledge. This is more applicable to manufacture than agriculture, but the primary sector, too, provides "numerous examples of the hand of the labourer having been rendered productive by the observations of the philosopher" (55).[11]

Yet this comment is not concerned with the consequences of improved scientific knowledge only. When writing about knowledge, Hodgskin refers to a complex and vast array of notions, observations, ideas, *know-how* that can present itself in very different forms depending on different circumstances and places, and still find tangible application in man's labor. For this reason, indeed, an inquiry about the economy is by and large an inquiry about knowledge.

As in his discussion of James Watt, Hodgskin thinks of knowledge as a collective enterprise, built through the centuries, brick by brick. It has already been noted (see Jaffe 2000, 49–54) how Hodgskin's approach was strongly influenced by some of his epistemological reflections, contained in the short essay *The Word BELIEF Defined and Explained* (1827b). There Hodgskin built on the work of Thomas Brown (1778–1820). For Brown, there are intuitive beliefs, including the belief in regularity (Psillos 2011, 231),[12] that lay the foundation for our belief in the permanence of a natural order. Brown "suggested that all sensations, emotions and intellect were simply 'states of mind' whose relationship could be scientifically deduced through the analysis of the interplay between physical causes and mental effects" (Jaffe 2000, 50).

Likewise, for Hodgskin (1827b, 22) "bodily sensations, perceptions, remembered and imagined notions, with suggestions of the understanding and deductions of reason, our chief feelings, all produce actions, and are all equally believed in the philosophical sense of the term." This set of beliefs, elicited by the external reality, accumulates during time "increasing as it rolls onward" (32). True, human beings can have wrong perceptions or notions, "but the chances that the error will be detected are precisely in proportion to our knowledge" (31). Instinctive practices, in this context, have the same dignity as theoretical knowledge: and, being even more widespread, they are open to a process of continuous correction which the solitary speculations of philosophers do not enjoy. Such empiricist and "associationist" epistemology constitutes the background against which Hodgskin emphasizes the "cumulative" nature of the process of knowledge, which eventually manifests itself in industrial artifacts.[13]

This perspective has room for know-how, a form of knowledge that is transmitted with relative awareness between individuals and consists precisely in the ability and in the dexterity demonstrated in carrying out a certain task. Consider tools and instruments: "inside" each of them there is not only an in-depth knowledge of the particular kind of production they are needed for, but also all the information and technical experience related to their design, their construction, and the transformation of the raw materials needed to create them.[14]

Hodgskin seems to believe that know-how and formal knowledge stand in a sort of continuum. In 1823, as editor of *The Chemist*, he wrote a series of articles about the history of chemistry. In the first he commented that this science has gradually gone from being an art exercised in the exclusive interest of a few practitioners to a discipline that, besides its utility as a practical art, tries to explain the basic natural phenomena (Hodgskin 1824, 11): its ambitions and the knowledge that it conveys have increased with the passing of time.

The enterprise of knowledge is thus both a "collective" and a "spontaneous" endeavor. Collective because it is not the effort of an isolated person, even in the rare case that the person is a genius; on the contrary, everyone builds incessantly on the legacy of the research, notions and experiments of others. Spontaneous because it really is an "invisible hand" process: individuals each follow their own path and try to cope with their personal needs. The increase in the *stock* of available knowledge is an *externality*: people pursuing their own interest end up adding to common knowledge, without necessarily knowing or wanting to do so.

But what is the relationship between knowledge and the division of labor? For Smith, technological advances were the result of specialization. Hodgskin (1827a, 79) recognizes that "progress in knowledge, and division of labour, mutually promote each other" but he also maintains that knowledge "precedes" the division of labor, though it also contributes to extending it. The observation of the natural world and, consequently, the development of some strategy to deal with it ("easing" the burden of fatigue that we all share, just because we walk on this earth) logically precedes the division of labor. Each task "is now rendered easy of acquisition by the transmitted habits, knowledge, and skill of former generations" (48). His critique of Smith, therefore, does not concern the impact of the division of labor on the creation of knowledge (specialization also makes research and technical application more productive) but is, rather, a matter of logical priority:

> Undoubtedly they had learned to make bows and arrows, to catch animals and fish, to cultivate the ground and weave cloth, before some of them dedicated themselves exclusively to making these instruments, to hunting, fishing, agriculture, and weaving.
> (Hodgskin 1827a, 79)

For Hodgskin there is no problem in seeing it both ways, stating that "inventions always precede division of labour, *and extend it*, both by introducing new arts and by making commodities at a less cost" (1827a, 80, emphasis added).

Since the relationship between the increase of knowledge and the furthering of the division of labor went both ways, what could be seen as the spark which could light the fire of both?

The answer is an increase in population:

> the increase of population is the chief natural circumstance which promotes the increase of knowledge, and which extends division of labour; thus augmenting productive power, not merely in the simple ratio of the increase in the number of labourers, but in the compound ratio of this increase, multiplied by the effects of knowledge, and division of labour, whatever they may be, he will then perceive, that every improvement, which, like the introduction of potatoes into husbandry, augments the means of subsistence, is a cause, by increasing the number of people, of multiplying to an astonishing degree the productive power of our species.
> (Hodgskin 1827a, 59^{fn})

It is possible to catch, in such a statement, an echo of Say's law.[15] The law of markets is often expressed as "supply creates demand," but it would be perhaps more appropriate to say that "production is the only source of wealth." Rephrasing the concept, William H. Hutt (1899–1988) suggested that "all power to demand is derived from production and supply" (1974, 27). At any rate, its cornerstone is still the understanding of how money is but an intermediary through which all can turn what they produced into *means* for buying what others produce.

From the notion that production is the only source of wealth, Say ([1803] 2002, 102) infers that "to stimulate industry, mere consumption is not enough; it is necessary to promote the development of those tastes and needs that drive people to consumption; the same way as, to promote sales, it is necessary to help consumers to earn enough to be able to spend." The correspondence between demographic growth and "the amazing multiplication of the productive potential of our species" can then appear as a corollary of the law of markets. Say himself, although he subscribed to Malthus's principle of population,[16] noted that "if the annual products are prevented from multiplying, men are also prevented from being born and are killed, thus wasting capital, stifling the industry, exhausting the sources of production" (339^{fn}). Stack (1998, 80) suggests that Hodgskin conceived a refutation of Say's law.[17] But if the law of markets says that there's no way to get rich other than producing more, certainly the principle is there in the pages of *Popular Political Economy*. Net of this suggestion about the "reflection" of Say's law on Hodgskin's thesis on population, we should not underestimate the originality of the latter.

The concept that population growth was a marker of relative prosperity in a country was not exactly a new notion. Skeptical as he was with the claim that the ancient world was more populous, David Hume ([1777] 1987) repeatedly associated populousness with wealth.[18] Paley ([1785] 2002, 420) had noted how "a competition can seldom arise between the advancement of population and any measure of sober utility; because, in the ordinary progress of human affairs, whatever, in any way, contributes to make a people happier, tends to render them more numerous." Hodgskin, however, puts the issue in quite different terms: population growth is considered not as evidence of the wisdom of an enlightened government, but as the single factor that most facilitates economic progress. Close to Hodgskin's stance appears to be the American ambassador to the Hague at that time, Alexander Hill Everett (1790–1847), who, as an answer to Malthus, pointed out that "It is sufficiently notorious, that an increase of population on a given territory is followed immediately by a division of labor; which produces in its turn the invention of new machines, an improvement of methods in all the departments of industry, and a rapid progress in the various branches of art and science" (1823, 26).

Hodgskin expressed the same concept, somewhat more rigorously:

> The chances of improvement … are great in proportion as the persons are multiplied whose attention is devoted to any particular subject … an increase in the number of persons produces the same effect as communication [on longer distance]; for the latter only operates by bringing numbers to think on the same subject … Almost all discoveries and improvements have been made in crowded cities and in densely peopled countries.
>
> (1827a, 93–95)

In fact, the difference between more advanced and less advanced societies is read by Hodgskin through the lens of the population growth rate.[19] As noted by a contemporary historian, "the rate of inventions is determined by the supply of inventors as well as by the demand for new products and processes" (Allen 2009, 238). Hodgskin finds the increase of the population to be a "stimulus" to innovation, because it increases the demand for goods and services and the probability of the demand itself, simply because with the availability of human beings, so to speak, the availability also rises of that peculiarly human product that are ideas. "The chances of improvement ... are great in proportion as the *persons are multiplied* whose attention is devoted to any particular subject. ... an increase in the number of persons produces the same effect as communication; for the latter only operates by bringing numbers to think on the same subject" (Hodgskin 1827a, 36). It is worth noting that Hodgskin defends population expansion of *human beings as they are*. If William Godwin held that as men and women people became better off, their higher natures would become more developed and they would have less interest in sex, and if he later contested Malthus's empirics in his *On Population*, Hodgskin was making a wholly different point.[20]

For Hodgskin, the increase of available knowledge *depends* on population growth: more people create more knowledge.[21] This is based upon a peculiar version of the principle of population pressure: "independent of all governments and of all their regulations, there is in the universal necessity to labour a universal stimulus for all men to exert those natural faculties with which all are endowed." Thus "this stimulus is at all times the cause of observation, and that observation brings knowledge" (Hodgskin 1827a, 96–97).

The principle of population was to dominate the century: Malthus's *Essay on Population* was to lead Charles Darwin (1809–1882) to develop his evolutionary theory. Likewise, population was central in the thought of Herbert Spencer (1852, 498–499), who tried to interpret Malthus's notion of the pressure of want over population as "an increasing stimulus to better the modes of producing food and other necessaries."[22]

Hodgskin ends up formulating a population principle which is the opposite of the Malthusian one. His political economy can indeed be seen as "a Malthusian inversion driven by demand-side stimuli and founded upon human cognitive ability" (Jaffe 1995, 507).

Hodgskin's population principle is also a progress principle. He is trying to update Smith's claim that "the division of labour is limited by the extent of the market." Ultimately, "the irresistible principle of population ... causes what is called an extension of the market, which continually extends therefore division of labour, and forces into existence those new arts such as banking, printing, journalism, engineering, photography, &c &c" (Hodgskin 1862a, 2). References to the "market extension" usually emphasize the spatial and geographic dimension, while for Hodgskin the crucial element is the number of participants in the game of the market itself. A more populous country, therefore, by definition implies a more branched division of labor.

As we saw in the preceding chapter, Hodgskin—in a personal interpretation of Smith—distinguishes between natural and social price. The natural price measures the amount of labor needed to produce a certain good. The "social" price, on the other hand, "is the natural price increased by social regulations" and, therefore, the actual price paid for the purchase of a particular good in the "real world," affected by regulations, taxes, and the intervention of politics. The social price forces the laborers to pay more or, better, since every cost is an opportunity, "to provide more work" than would be required in the absence of regulations (Hodgskin 1827a, 220). The system of land rent, import duties, and monopolies on the sovereign's license is what entitles some to demand a "social" price higher than the "natural" one. The artificial protection from the rules of competition, as economists know, leads to an increase in prices. In Hodgskin's perspective, the "natural price" is a sort of "minimum market price" around which a certain good would gravitate in a competitive economy. Therefore, there is a mechanism endogenous to the market that produces a reduction in prices: competition.

In Hodgskin's (1827a, 233) words, "Over natural price, the relation of the demand to supply, which is frequently said to regulate price, seems in the long run to have a tendency to lower it. The ingenuity of man being necessarily first and chiefly directed towards supplying his more urgent wants, the labour employed in supplying necessaries will be most improved." According to Malthus, the growth of population causes an increase in the cost of life and in prices. In the theories of Malthus and Ricardo, a pivotal role is played by the differential rent, the consequence of which is that the rent that can be derived from cultivation varies with the different fertility of soils. For Hodgskin, on the other hand, agriculture too is permeable to technological innovation.[23] If this is the case, it is obvious how the natural "fertility" of one soil in relation to another can be overcome thanks to new tools and techniques.

> The opinion that the natural price of food lessens rather than increases in the progress of society, seems borne out by facts … . if we observe how the proportion of persons who raise no raw produce,—including not only those who do not labour at all, but also those who are engaged in the various departments of manufactures and trade, as well as all the officers, dependents, and servants of government,—continually increases, forming, as I have already mentioned, five-sixths of this community,—we must be convinced, that in the progress of society food is obtained by less and less labour. When we look also at the various improvements continually made in the arts, most of which tend, in some way or other, to diminish the labour necessary to prepare bread and procure meat, we must come, I think, to the same conclusion.

Whoever "embraced the opposite opinion" was misled by a short-term analysis: that is, by the fact that when the demand grows—because the number of "bread eaters" grows—in the short term the prices climb too. The rise in the price of wheat in England in the early nineteenth century was conditioned by the Napoleonic wars first, and then by political interference. "But if we extend our observations over a longer period, we shall find no proof of a gradual and general rise in the price of corn as population increases" (Hodgskin 1827a, 226–227).[24]

On this point, he one day happily realized that his outlook was proven right. In an article from 1863, he remarked how "the population of Great Britain is more than doubled since the beginning of the century" and, along with it, the living conditions had also improved. Hodgskin (1863b, 2) felt vindicated against the Malthusian assertion that "fancied" between the "tendency in the food of mankind" and "the tendency of the population to increase an unfavourable discrepancy."

History did not contradict Hodgskin. The British population grew strongly in the course of the nineteenth century: about 1 percent per year between 1780 and 1900: at the beginning of the twentieth century it was four times as much as it had been in the mid-eighteenth century (see Vernon 2014). Urban population increased too, going from 1 percent in 1750 to 25 percent in 1801 to about 60 percent around 1850 (O'Brien and Engerman 1981, 164). Real salaries were growing "at a yearly rate of around 1,1% (with per capita income growing at a yearly rate of 1,3%)" between 1800 and 1840 with a "surge" after the end of the Napoleonic wars thanks to the lowering of prices that followed the end of the hostilities (170). All of this suggests that there was very little utopia in Hodgskin's vision. On the contrary, he comes off as a sharp observer, capable of inferring general rules from the reality that he sees with his own eyes.[25]

Hodgskin's view on population growth is consistent with his understanding of the Industrial Revolution. Among his contemporaries, the idea that the Industrial Revolution had *worsened* the living conditions of the population, and of the workers in particular, was quite widespread. The statistical work of J.H. Clapham (1873–1946), one century later, challenges this point of view.[26]

Perhaps Hodgskin was able to see, earlier and better than other authors, the remarkable improvement in living conditions that was taking place in those years. It is because of his life experience that Hodgskin (1862b, 2) considers progress "the natural law of society," "one continual stream of improvement."

A long-time opposition to the corn laws

In spite of his vigorous anti-statism, Hodgskin is not remembered as a central figure in England's most important economic policy discussion of the first half of the 1800s—the battle over the corn laws. Yet he did his best to take part in that debate and offer a distinctive contribution. He interacted with the Anti-Corn Law League led by Richard Cobden (1804–1865) and had a great deal of sympathy for the movement. His attempt to influence the events of that movement is essentially tied to a public lecture of 1843. Before detailing that lecture, we shall look at his positions on the theme of international exchange as they emerge from some earlier writings.

We have already said that Hodgskin's argument for population growth can be seen as an extension of Smith's idea that "the division of labour is limited by the extent of the market": a wider market allows for a growing specialization and, therefore, an increase in productivity. His defense of free trade should be understood in this framework.

The center of Hodgskin's reasoning is always *knowledge-guided* labour, and economics, as we have seen, was the science that unveiled its power. For this reason, he argues for free trade by going beyond "the immediate pecuniary advantages which accrue to all the parties concerned, in exchanging the products favoured by one climate, for those favoured by another," to identify the effect that a wider, indeed international, division of labor may exert on knowledge-guided labor.

> The mutual exchange of the products of different climates, is a great means, therefore, of promoting civilization. It offers additional enjoyments, and *to procure them it incites to additional exertions*. It is the parent, consequently, of much of our skill. To obtain its gratifications, gives a perpetual but gentle stimulus to our passions, saving us both from the weariness of idleness, and from those violent emotions which are followed by painful lassitude, and end in speedy when not self-destruction. A number of innocent desires fill up, with an equable flow of happiness, the time of our existence; and foreign trade is even a greater good by the stimulus it gives to thought and exertion, than by the enjoyments it immediately bestows.
> (Hodgskin 1827a, 156, emphasis added)

Trade has thus a beneficent effect on *human nature* itself: men would drown into "inglorious idleness" if they limited themselves to pursuing self-sufficiency. "The skill and knowledge requisite at any time to provide for our animal wants, must be small, and did not some other stimulus intervene, all the ingenuity and faculties of civilized man would remain dormant, or be much limited." Life in the smaller group, in face-to-face societies that aim to be self-sufficient, if not short is certainly nasty. It is by exchanging with others, in bigger and bigger groups, that "the utility of some wealth-creating arts" and "the enjoyment of some new productions of human skill" become, among others, driving forces of human toil. This way, "after our mere animal wants are gratified, we still labour, and are happy when labouring, to obtain some other, and generally foreign productions" (Hodgskin 1827a, 164).

This is not a novel argument. Razeen Sally emphasizes how David Hume and Adam Smith focused on the dynamic benefits of commerce, even more than the static ones.

> David Hume's comprehensive evaluation of commercial society takes in the psychology of an increasingly active human disposition—a 'spirit of industry'—that surges forward in tandem with the rise of commerce and manufacturers, the cultivation of the arts and sciences, the institutional

refinement of politics, increasingly influenced by an emergent middle class, and the establishment of stable, regular and equal laws of justice to protect property and contract.

(Sally 1998, 41)

And that trade is the midwife of the spirit of industry is precisely Hodgskin's view.

In his 1820 *Travels in the North of Germany* Hodgskin (446) had already shown a strong appreciation for international trade. He considered British prosperity a consequence of it: wealth had been, in fact, "diffused in our country by commerce," thanks to comparatively fewer protectionist restrictions. In Germany's case, alas, "the same freedom has not been left to its trade as to that of Britain" and thus "the diminution of its commerce has been caused by impolitic regulations."

The central issue in the debate between protectionists and free trade supporters was, at the time, the duties on wheat: the corn laws. They were hardly a new device: in some form or another, corn laws had existed since the Middle Ages and were meant to ensure self-sufficiency in England. A system of import duties and export subsidies of mercantilist design was in place to ensure that landowners would continue to produce wheat in the British Isles. In the last decade of the 1700s, however, "the increase in population caused Britain to become a net importer" (Hilton 2006, 264), and thus things began to change. "All corn laws from 1773 to 1804 had imposed prohibitory duties at low prices and nominal duties at high, with just a very small mezzanine stage between the two. The new bill merely abandoned the mezzanine and substituted statutory for virtual prohibition at one time, and perfect freedom for minimal restraint at another" (Hilton [1977] 1980, 13).

The Napoleonic wars postponed the day of reckoning. During the war years, importation of grains was prohibited. The system of protectionist duties took shape in the post-war period: in 1815, imports of wheat were completely forbidden until the price of domestic wheat had reached 80 shillings per quarter (a unit of measure roughly equivalent to 12 kilograms or 8 bushels). Similar thresholds had been set for other kinds of cereals—while, at a lower threshold, it became possible to use grains from the colonies.

Bread was indeed central to anybody's life—and among the most humble classes the substitution of potatoes for bread or oatmeal was considered a sign of degradation. This explains why the Corn Law of 1815 was deemed "one of the most naked pieces of class legislation in English history" (Blake [1970] 2010, 15). "When the Corn Laws were passed in 1815, the House of Parliament had to be defended from the populace by troops. 'NO CORN LAWS' was prominent among the banners at Peterloo, and remained so … until the anti-Corn Laws agitation of the 1840s" (E.P. Thompson 1964, 315).

On the other hand, landowners "regarded the new Corn Law as a permanent (or at least long-term) endeavor to maintain prices" (Hilton [1977] 1980, 15). Not only the Tories but the Parliament as well came to be seen—and, for sure, by and large were—an expression of the "landowning class."

In the following years, however, "extensive decultivation and an appalling catalogue of arrears, quittals and bloody riots" (Hilton 2006, 266) were noticed in the countryside. The price of bread tended to rise. For the free-trade supporters, this demonstrated the illusory nature of the grain autarky, while the protectionists saw in the phenomenon the need for greater support for agriculture.

Adjustments were introduced, by and large thanks to William Huskisson.

> Ever conscious of economic realities, Huskisson's views on corn underwent a volte-face as overproduction, stimulated by protectionist measures, brought about economic ruin for agriculturists ... He further cautioned that the 1815 law had created an artificial, and erroneous, expectation that corn would fetch 80s a quarter, disproved by subsequent events. By 1821 Huskisson was beginning to favour an open trade in corn, with a permanent fixed duty.
>
> (Rowe 2018, 211)

So, step by step, the Tory governments tried to mediate between the "principles of true political economy" and the interests of their constituencies. In 1822 there was a first revision of the Corn Law, which nonetheless maintained outright prohibition of imports when prices were above 80s, while in 1828 Parliament replaced the previous system with a "scale" of protected tariffs, with a fixed duty once prices reached a certain level, designed to guarantee producers a remunerative price but, at the same time, to allow the influx of foreign foodstuffs.

In 1839, a sharp worsening of the trade balance and a bad harvest began to build a climate hostile to the corn laws—a climate that would be exacerbated by the depression of 1840–1842. The duties were abolished only in 1846, after the great Irish famine triggered by the spread of potato blight.

Hodgskin was a staunch opponent of the duties on wheat. In the introduction to *Popular Political Economy*, he puts the corn laws among the (evil) social regulations that "also influence the production and distribution of wealth." Not only do "commercial prohibitions compel us to employ more labour than is necessary to obtain the prohibited commodity," but they also "curb the spirit of enterprise, and impede production, by checking the progress of knowledge and the acquirement of skill." On the duties on wheat in particular, he wrote:

> The corn laws of this country—to take an example of a social regulation influencing both production and distribution—compel all those who eat bread to give a greater quantity of labour to obtain it than nature requires; or they make us pay from fifteen to twenty shillings more for a quarter of wheat, than would otherwise be necessary; and they alter distribution, by putting, (through the medium of exchange, it must be remarked,) a part of the sum thus abstracted from the consumers into the pockets of the landlords.
>
> (Hodgskin 1827a, 34)

Further on, in the concluding note of Chapter 8 of *Popular Political Economy*, Hodgskin mentions William Huskisson's unsuccessful attempt to amend the tariffs on grains, linking it to his straying from the "free-trade" path in the issue of bank policies. In Chapter 9 he names the duties on grains as the foremost cause of the high prices of food staples. In Chapter 10 he compares them for their injuriousness to the Combination Laws, "our monstrous system of taxation ..., and church establishment, and our West and East India monopolies" (Hodgskin 1827a, 253).

One year after *Labour Defended* and one year before *Popular Political Economy*, Hodgskin wrote an article for *The Trades' Newspaper* on the possible effects of the corn laws' abolition, an essay already mentioned for its psychological insights on entrepreneurial behavior. There Hodgskin maintains that free trade advocates generally tend to "overlook the immense power which the capitalist has over the labourer" and criticizes as naive the idea that free trade will have only a positive impact on workers. He indeed points out that some mischief would be occasioned by repeal. While he joins the abolitionist camp, he claims that adjustment after the repeal of tariffs will not be automatic. Abolishing the corn laws would lower demand for agricultural labor in England. However, though "I take it that the principal commodities with which we shall pay for foreign corn will be cotton and woollen cloths, and hardware," Hodgskin doubts that increasing demand for industrial labor will occur correspondingly overnight (Hodgskin 1826a, 487–488). Well, it does not take a protectionist to realize that reactions of economic actors are not instantaneous (even when the "unbalancing" action of the public intervention does not take place).

In his assessment of the psychological effect of political announcements, Hodgskin fears that the prospect of abolition ("speeches and writings" on the part of government officials talking about "removing restrictions and prohibitions from our commerce") may "have flattered the cupidity and stimulated the enterprise of our manufacturers and merchants," thereby encouraging malinvestment. And yet he comes out clearly in favor of abolition:

> these laws levy a tax on the consumers of corn to the amount of TWENTY-FOUR MILLIONS OF POUNDS STERLING PER YEAR, about five of which go to the landlord, the other nineteen being completely lost. That is, we are obliged to give a greater quantity of labour, equal to 24 millions, to produce, in the geographical spot called Great Britain, that quantity of corn we required, than we should have to give if we bought it by our manufactures in other countries, and five millions only of this sum go to the landlords. The continuance of the law therefore plainly causes a vast deal more mischief than its repeal would occasion.
>
> (Hodgskin 1826a, 487)

In 1848, two years after the abolition, Hodgskin would summarize his pondering of the issue by comparing "what was said of the corn law" with "all this forced appropriation of the labourer's produce—it destroys as much, or more, than it appropriates. There is no tax levied which does not hamper industry as well as appropriates its produce" (Hodgskin 1848b).

Hodgskin, Cobden, and the League

The revolt against the corn laws remains a perhaps unique example of how an idea whose time has come may shape political decision making. The idea in question was free trade: beyond economics, it was meant as a weapon against the landed aristocracy and the necessary precondition for international brotherhood. In but a few years, the Anti-Corn Law League, established in 1838, succeeded in convincing Parliament to abolish tariffs on grains, seen as the paramount example of "class legislation" forged by the landed classes to their own benefit. In a handful of years, in 1846, Robert Peel's government signed the abolition, opening an era of freer trade in Britain and, subsequently, throughout Europe.

While trade liberalization is an object sought after by economists, it would be a mistake to assume that the League was an economists' movement. Its campaigns "lacked what one would have expected most—namely, the enthusiastic support and participation of the economists themselves. The actual leaders of the agitation, in fact, sought to dissociate themselves from the leading economists" (Langer 1987, 192), who tended to favor a gradualist approach rather than repeal. Later on, of course, the League became a genuine point of reference, inspiring economists throughout Europe.[27]

The League was not supported by scholars, but by practical men, which made it more attractive to Hodgskin. It embodied a sort of political awakening of the middle classes, who were eventually to challenge aristocracy. The League's members were radicals and non-conformists coming from the new bourgeois class, when both the Whig and Tory parties were an expression of the same aristocratic milieu. The League was "a new phenomenon in British history, a middle-class organization that neither sought nor needed upper-class patronage" (Longmate 1984, 19). The man who rapidly rose to the leadership of the League, Richard Cobden, was a "self-made" entrepreneur coming from the calico printing trade. He then became a passionate politician, agitating until his death for free trade and peace.

The League was made up of practical men, but practical men can be *idealists*, too. The abolition of grain duties was regarded by Cobden as the tipping point of a broader process, which included an overall downsizing of public expenditure, the shrinking of the powers of landed gentry, and a foreign policy based on the principles of non-intervention. Indeed, Cobden argued not in the language of economics, but of morals.[28] For Cobden, trade is a pedagogy of peace: by practicing exchange, peoples of different cultures and history will learn to depend on each other.

There was a strong class element in the agitation. As Anthony Howe (1997, 30) reminds us, the slogan "of 'the people versus the aristocracy' remained the most obvious rallying cry for the League, despite the growing adherence of aristocratic politicians to its cause." Still, although its fundamental goal was "cheap bread," the League did not always have a linear and easy relationship with the working classes.

It was the Chartists, named after the "People's Charter" drafted by William Lovett (1800–1877), which sought parliamentary reform and wider representation, who were winning support among workers and artisans. In a sort of competition for the allegiance of the working classes, the Chartists guarded their pool of consensus against the free traders: they[29] insisted that "it was machinery, not agricultural protection, which caused the impoverishment of the working class" (Grampp 1960, 73). With the lexicon of class conflict, the indictment was soon set: the Chartists claimed that the industrialists wished to abolish the duties and lower the price of bread, but only as a way to further cut wages.[30]

Thus the Chartist movement "began a long course of violent hostility by trying at the very outset of the agitation to break up a meeting at Leeds, insisting that the movement was a cheat put on the work-people of the country by cunning and rapacious employers" (Morley [1879] 1903, 156). Attempts by figures such as Francis Place and Samuel Smiles (1812–1904) to promote a dialogue between Chartists and free-trade supporters were frustrated.

It was perhaps a similar attempt to encourage dialogue between the Anti-Corn Law League and the workers that convinced Hodgskin, in 1843, to hold a conference on *"free trade in connection with the Corn Laws"* at the White Conduit House in Islington, on January 31. After publishing *The Natural and Artificial Right of Property Contrasted* in 1832, Hodgskin had not published any pamphlet under his name for eleven years; he was doing anonymous journalism.

Hodgskin's lecture was held two years before the repeal and in the midst of the agitation. He wanted to support the League but also to reassure workers. Hodgskin felt the urge to clarify that "if I had the shadow of a shade of a suspicion that it would lower wages, diminish employment, delay the progress of freedom or retard for one hour the emancipation of the masses, I should belie my whole life if I undertook its advocacy" (Hodgskin 1843, 4–5). Hodgskin wanted to use his own reputation as a champion of the laboring classes (earned when he wrote *Labour Defended* under the *nom de plume* "A Labourer") to build bridges between the Chartists and the Anti-Corn Law League.[31]

Why? Was Hodgskin, in 1843, really a good candidate for the job?

On Hodgskin's motivations for supporting the League, I offer two speculations. One may be that he simply wanted to be helpful to Richard Cobden, with whom he must have had some intellectual sympathy. Another possibility, assuming a grander ambition on Hodgskin's part, is that he may have been attempting to feed the free traders with his own ideas.

An industrialist turned agitator and then member of the House of Commons, Cobden may have found value in a connection with Hodgskin, because of the latter's parliamentary journalism. At the same time, Cobden's tendency to see the issue of trade as a matter of justice and peace more than of efficiency may have made him a very attractive public figure to Hodgskin, always a radical at heart. There is limited evidence of the relationship between the two, but there is some. We should not be deceived by the bibliographic addendum to the English translation of Halévy's book (Halévy [1903] 1956); an 1848 open letter addressed by Hodgskin to the leader of the League is mentioned, concerning "free trade and the issue of slaves"; however, it is actually a letter from the coeval Thomas Hodgkin (1798–1866), minus the "s," an illustrious physician and activist against slavery.[32]

Nevertheless, there was a certain familiarity between "our" Hodgskin and Cobden. In the summer of 1842, Cobden wrote to Hodgskin to seek his help. At that time, England was being swept by a wave of strikes. The unrest had started, Wendy Hinde (1987, 110) writes, when "colliers at Longton in Staffordshire, faced with a sudden cut in wages, stopped work and began marching from colliery to colliery throughout the Potteries, enforcing closure by raking out boiler fires and drawing boiler blues (Hence the name Plug Plot given to these disturbances)."

The "Plug Plot" was considered as having been caused by the League. According to some, social discontent had arisen due to the reduction in wages demanded by the pro-free trade industrialists.[33] According to others, the League was an accomplice of the Chartists, who had declared a series of strikes mainly in the Manchester area, with the city institutions (allies of the free-trade supporters) refusing to take tough measures. "The protectionists everywhere in the country charged that a few employers provoked the strike and that others urged their men to join it. The employers' purpose, it was asserted, was to give the workers' discontent a forcible expression and to turn it against the government in order to force the repeal of the corn laws" (Grampp 1960, 68).

Cobden fiercely denied that the League was in any way involved with the protest. Addressing Hodgskin with apparent familiarity (Cobden [1842] 2007, 287), he begs him to not leave "the defence of your old friends of the League entirely in the hands of the *Globe Chronicle* & other 'strangers.'" Hodgskin was then writing mostly for the *Evening Chronicle*, which actually defended the League. From their correspondence, it seems clear that Cobden considered Hodgskin certainly by then (one year before Hodgskin's *Lecture*) a friendly voice, to whom he did not fear to turn in a delicate instance.

An exchange with Charles Dickens—at the time editor-in-chief of the *Daily News*, where Hodgskin was a columnist—suggests another occasion when he might have wanted to support Cobden in the press. On January 31, 1846, the *Daily News* published a "Letter from Mr. Cobden to the Tenant Farmer of England" (Cobden 1846, 5) in which the leader of the League claimed that, for the masses of farmers who farmed rented plots, the immediate abolition of grain duties would protect their income better than a gradual reduction for three years until their cancellation, due to the current conditions of the food market. On February 2, Cobden's letter was commented on, and quite favourably, in an anonymous article by John Towne Danson (1817–1898), who wrote about economic and financial issues for the newspaper. Hodgskin wanted to offer a comment himself and was offended that Danson's was preferred.[34]

In 1848, when he came back from his European tour, Cobden was faced with a panic over a possible French invasion, which began with a letter by the Duke of Wellington published in the *Morning Chronicle*. Cobden reacted strongly and among other things pointed out, in a speech in Manchester, that the Duke's fears might be the result of senility. Immediately Hodgskin took Cobden's side in the columns of the *London Telegraph*, of which he was editor-in-chief at the time.[35]

The relationship between Hodgskin and Cobden was therefore amicable. The two corresponded also on the occasion of Hodgskin's leaving the *Economist*. In this exchange, Cobden told Hodgskin (1857a) that he was unaware of his working for the *Economist* (which Cobden claimed he did not read) and subsequently sent him a long letter criticizing anonymity in journalism as unaccountable and therefore dangerous (1857b). Thinking of Hodgskin's fondness for distinction and presuming anonymity to be discouraging for a man of ideas, this may have been also a gesture of fondness toward an old friend who thought life did not sufficiently recognize his work.

In a Ph.D. dissertation, Peter Nelson Farrar suggests that Cobden was actually influenced by Hodgskin's thinking. In 1857 Cobden described Hodgskin as "an old literary acquaintance of mine" and wrote that they had known each other "since 1828–30." According to Farrar, "some of Hodgskin's ideas were regarded as dangerous by the propertied class ... despite his belief in private property legitimately acquired ... there is nothing strange in the fact that Cobden did not refer to Hodgskin's ideas in public" (1987, 36). Alas, we'll never know.

Hodgskin's free trade manifesto

His friendship with Cobden may help explain why Hodgskin attempted to come back on the public stage with his lecture in Islington in 1843. It is likely that his lecture was regarded, as I have already written, as an attempt to mend the gap between the free trade movement and the working classes.

Let us give the text a closer look. When it comes to the supposed aim of "reconciling" the working-class movement with the corn law agitation, Hodgskin's lecture seems poorly fit to fulfil the object. It did not compete with pamphlets such as *Anti-Bread Tax Tracts for the People* (1841), which explained the ideas of free trade in comprehensible terms to a larger audience, using everyday life examples.

Hodgskin does not reflect specifically on the damages that tariffs inflict on workers. The lecture begins as a refutation of the very idea that the abolition of grain duties can have redistributive effects adverse to the "working classes," whom here he champions as never before. Middle classes, farmers, laborers: they are all really in the same boat. It is interesting to note how, for once,

Hodgskin is attempting an exercise in social algebra: he wants to prove that grain duties do not even benefit those who seem to obtain advantage from them. Even the clergy and landowners, if it is true that they would pay a price in the short term, in the long term would certainly benefit from an environment more consistently open to the market. Removing the duties would, in itself, contribute to a better allocation of resources.[36] It is really a matter of general interest: to reduce it to a dispute between "landowners and entrepreneurs,"[37] to consider it "a question of pounds, shillings and pence," means not having understood its importance. At stake "is a question of morals and general legislation, not limited to that object, food, to which it is nominally confined" (Hodgskin 1843, 4).

Yet Hodgskin tried to reconcile the working-class radical movement of people like the Chartists to free trade, presenting a classic account of the harmony of interests model and its corollary, which is complete free exchange. The working classes could look to the future with optimism, because unhampered competition would work in their favor as it meant the liberation of the economy from the nefarious influence of privilege.

In so doing, Hodgskin hoped that he could push the League's own arguments a bit further, suggesting that a revolt against the corn law should extend to all the other social regulations that he deemed dangerous and illiberal. The doctrine of free exchange should not stop at any door. He notes how "every prohibition abolished and every duty lowered have contributed to increase employment, to extend the national resources, and arrest the mischievous consequences of excessive taxation and of the prohibitions and restrictions that are still suffered to remain on the statute-book" (Hodgskin 1843, 6). The conclusion is thus quintessentially political: "every law is a restraint on freedom, and per se mischievous, though this truth is continually lost sight of." The burden of proof must be on those who propose an interference with the spontaneous order determined by the exchanges between people: it is up to them to demonstrate the effectiveness of their actions.

In this lecture, Hodgskin raises—perhaps with more clarity than elsewhere—a non-secondary problem in its perspective: if indeed the British Isles pay the toll for such arbitrary and capricious rules, how come their performance seems to be better than the continental states?

While Hodgskin maintains that "pauperism and crime are rapidly increasing,"[38] at the same time he is willing to admit that England is in a good position: "In skill and industry lie all the sources of wealth; and with these, Nature has bounteously endowed our people" (Hodgskin 1843, 9).

For once, Hodgskin seems willing to give the British government system some credit. He admits that "to the energy and courage of our forefathers manfully resisting the peculiar oppressions of their rulers and their times, we are indebted for a tolerable degree of political security" (Hodgskin 1843, 9). In other words, the British institutions reflect the experience of a long struggle for the rights of individuals.[39] In England, the people's freedom of movement and freedom of conscience are "not much tyrannized over."

One rhetorical artifice Hodgskin frequently used (as early as in his *Essay on Naval Discipline*) was to compare the *promise* of liberty that is the heritage of all Englishmen, and the infringements upon their freedom the government commits. In his *Lecture on Free Trade* he claims that "we have achieved personal freedom—we have nearly conquered freedom of conscience; the press is almost free, but we have yet to conquer freedom for industry" (Hodgskin 1843, 7). What Hodgskin was thinking of was the abolition of the Combination Act in 1824, the emancipation of Catholics in 1829, and the Reform Act of 1832. Why not "liberate" trade as well?

The core argument of the lecture is a comparison between *internal* and *foreign* trade. Hodgskin emphasizes the asymmetry. Nobody denies the baker or the greengrocer the right to purchase his stock from the cheapest suppliers and he who does not do it is soon branded as an injudicious merchant. The freedom of looking for the best bargains, explains Hodgskin, guarantees not only what we would style today as greater allocative efficiency, but also the very life in society. The lack of the simple opportunity of exchanging with other individuals within the same country would cause "dissatisfaction, discontent, and collision" (Hodgskin 1843, 10).

This freedom of exchange within the borders of one nation is one of Britain's great advantages, whereas on the Continent the territories of Italy and Spain are still beset by multifarious custom barriers, and no wares are immune to duties and customs officers. The same, however, cannot be said of the "freedom of trade between individuals living under different governments" which, "though fools or presumptuous madmen cramp and prohibit it, is as much a part of the system of nature as trade between the subjects of the same government, which statesmen at length universally admit cannot be restricted." No real conceptual difference separates those transactions that are concluded between English subjects, and those between Britons and citizens of foreign countries. Both are part of the same natural system: "man is created free to buy and sell with whom, when, and where he likes, and legislators are bound to prove such freedom a great public injury, and that they are wiser than nature, before they venture in any case to restrain it" (Hodgskin 1843, 11). Richard Cobden would have probably endorsed such an argument. In a similar fashion, he argued that "Free trade, in the widest definition of the term, means only the division of labour by which the productive powers of the whole earth are brought into mutual co-operation" (Cobden [1862] 1903, II, 389).

Hodgskin also suggests looking at the restrictions on economic activity as artificial constraints placed on the ability of everyone to develop a particular exchange. Thus, regulations on trade can be seen as equivalent to taxation. He sees laws that obstruct the potential use of someone's property as comparable to a direct violation of his or her property rights. Property is thus violated whenever any regulation is made to force an individual to employ his labor or capital in a particular way. An artificial increase in the price of bread is logically equivalent to the forcible seizure of the greater amount of bread that would have been available in the absence of the duty. It is "in principle as great a violation of the right of property to prevent Mr Cobden importing corn, as it is to take away the Duke of Buckingham's estate."[40]

Grain duties are then truly "direct violations of liberty which is every man's natural right" (Hodgskin 1843, 13). An artificial increase in the price of bread is logically the confiscation of how much more bread could be had in the absence of duties. Although Hodgskin began his lecture by seeking to address the representatives of all social classes, he then converges on the usual anti-aristocratic polemic, condemning the corn laws as "a great robbery solemnly decreed by the owners of the rent, on all other classes, in which, like all other robberies, a vast deal more property is wasted and destroyed than is transferred and enjoyed" (Hodgskin 1843, 13).

On grain duties too, Hodgskin found himself on the side opposite from Malthus. Malthus defended the grain duties.[41] If, in *Observations on the Effects of the Corn Laws* (1814), he reviewed arguments for and against, in his *Grounds of an Opinion on the Policy of Restricting the Importation of Foreign Corn* (1815) Malthus pronounced in favor of the tariffs. He did so in the name of the productivity of the soil (by guaranteeing a greater income to the owners, the duties would "stimulate" the investments)[42] and for "food security": the need not to depend on imports of a commodity as important as grains. In turn, some of Malthus's disciples were watching with concern the progress of the Anti-Corn Law League, which, with its promise of cheap bread, they believed guilty of diverting attention from the issue of demographic control of the humblest classes (see McLaren 1978, 48–49).

In his lecture, Hodgskin goes so far as to accuse the defenders of the corn laws of acting on the basis of the worst and most ruthless form of "Malthusianism":

> It is, indeed, said, those who passed the Corn Laws, alarmed at the increase of a town population, deliberately limited the supply of food, that they might, in direct contravention both of the revealed and discovered laws of God, prevent the multiplication of the people. Knowing not that population carries with it its own laws, extending civilization and improving morality as it increases—they were afraid of God's creatures, and they secretly attempted to starve them down to a manageable number. We must be slow to believe that such diabolical intentions were ever entertained by those who ask and obtain the confidence of the people in order to protect them. No such motive was avowed in 1815; but when we recollect their regardlessness of the lives of the people, such an intention is not very foreign to their habits.
>
> (Hodgskin 1843, 17–18)

In a text that is quite a heartfelt denunciation of the system of duties, Hodgskin showed only support for the Anti-Corn Law League. As we have seen, the League was indeed *not* an economists' movement. For Hodgskin, this was a title of merit. The likes of Ricardo and Malthus, who emphasized scarcity more than the potential of economic development once restraints were removed, had little to do with the Cobdenites. Thus Hodgskin praised the League exactly because "is no knot of theorists, proposing some Frenchified police as the means of promoting security, or borrowing from that and other despotic lands a centralized system of providing for the people ... nor does it propose some Prussian scheme of drilling mankind into order" (Hodgskin 1843, 21).

The industrial entrepreneurs who "seek only freedom for buying and selling" (Hodgskin 1843, 21) earn Hodgskin's respect because such freedom openly promotes the repeal of a norm, and not some "Prussian system" or a "French-style police." The motives of the free trade supporters are practical: they want nothing more than the freedom to buy and sell whatever they please, grains included. But such practical need of practical men is perfectly in tune with a basic principle of justice: "They do not go to the legislature to demand cheapness or even abundance, though both, they believe, will be the consequence of the repeal. They ask no favour, they barely demand justice" (Hodgskin 1843, 21–22).

With his lecture of 1843, therefore, Hodgskin tries to rejuvenate the message of *Popular Political Economy*, by hopping on the most promising bandwagon in circulation at the time: indeed the text "prompts one to the speculation that he was trying to attach himself to the free-trade movement,"[43] In all likelihood, his attempt was not successful, simply because it could not be. Hodgskin complained that the League did not draw all the proper conclusions from its own principles. If its goals were "fair," yet "it does not go far and fast enough, and does not carry out the principles it advocates to their proper conclusions" (Hodgskin 1843, 22).

It must be said that it is hard to imagine an Anti-Corn Law League ready to follow Hodgskin's suggestion: to become, in other words, not a pressure group aimed at a single objective, but a real political movement.[44] In a sense, the decline of the great champions of free trade in British politics was possibly propitiated exactly by the closest thing they did to following Hodgskin's desires, that is by their adherence to a policy of pacifism (Grampp 1960, 116–132).

And yet, it must be said that of all the political movements of his time, there was not one that was more akin to Hodgskin's ideas and sensibilities than the free trade movement. Between the disciples "of Adam Smith first, and then Bentham" and the disciples "of Bentham first and then Adam Smith" (Hirst 1903, xi), Hodgskin had no doubts.

It is difficult to gauge in what measure in turn he was read and appreciated within the Anti-Corn Law League. It is probably not devoid of significance that the Anti-Corn Law League "poet" Ebenezer Elliott (1781–1849) dedicated his *Corn-Law Hymns* to "Mr Thomas Hodgskin, author of 'Popular Political Economy' ... with many thanks for his masterly work." Hodgskin, in turn, admired this poet whose "most remarkable trait is the fierce indignation he shows towards political oppression" (Elliot 1840, 167).[45] In the obituary in the *Economist*, it was most likely Hodgskin—who was in charge of books and reviews—who wrote that "with Ebenezer Elliot the people have lost a genuine and enlightened poet, whose mind was entirely dedicated to promoting their best interests" (Hodgskin 1850, 128–129).

Notes

1 These are all themes that will recur later, with slight variations, in Hodgskin's subsequent writing, including his late articles in the *Brighton Guardian*.
2 He explained feeling that "it was a perilous undertaking" to instruct the students of the Mechanics' Institute "on a subject, generally considered dry and repulsive" but "had, moreover, the satisfaction of observing, that there was nothing in the subject which the audience could not comprehend; and there was much in which they took a lively interest" (Hodgskin 1827a, vii–viii).
3 The controversy over Malthus' theses obviously did not involve just Hodgskin. See, *inter alia*, Kenneth Smith ([1951] 2006).
4 "Adam Smith was clearly of the same opinion" (Hodgskin 1827a, 24–25).
5 Spitalfields, in London's West End, had sheltered the Huguenot silk weavers who had fled from France. The Act of 1773 allowed judges to set the wages of the weavers. In practice, this worked like a modern collective bargaining agreement, with the judges (who had no particular skills that would allow them to determine what price was "fair") ratifying a price consensually agreed upon or, in the event of stalling negotiations, pronouncing in favor of one of the parts: most typically, the weavers. In a system of cottage industry, this meant that the pieces produced were all paid for at the same rate. So, any improvement in the machines and tools employed could not result in lower prices: de facto the act established a system of price controls. See Clapham (1916).
6 Quoted in Gordon (1979, 99). Huskisson was indeed strongly identified with the cause of free trade. After his death Ebenezer Elliot, the free trade poet, composed an "Elegy" for him: "O Huskisson, our friend in vain!/Where now are hope and liberty? Thou should'st have lived, if with thee dies/The poor man's hope of better days… . Our hope is gone! why didst thou go?" (Elliot 1840b, 103).
7 Another argument by opponents of the abolition reminds us of more contemporaneous polemics over protectionism: as free trade did not extend to all businesses, "given the ruinous nature of partial competition, it was imperative that Parliament pass or retain on the statute books legislation that would allow the control of product prices and hence the earnings" of producers (N. Thompson 1984, 37).
8 This is likely to be a reference to James Steuart (1712–1780), who maintained that "What oeconomy is in a family, political oeconomy is in a state" (Steuart [1767] 1966, 16). Say ([1803] 2002, 43) thought that Steuart "may be looked upon as the leading advocate of the exclusive system, the system founded on the maxim, that the wealth of one set of men is derived from the impoverishment of another." See also Anderson and Tollison (1984). Hirschman (1977, 81–87) offered a rather different interpretation of Steuart.
9 Similarly, in his correspondence with Malthus, Say (1820, 72) argued that

> nothing prevents the historian to love humanity, and to feel painful musings on the unfairness of politicians flood his heart. But history is not made of these remote associations, aphorisms and admonitions. Moreover, I do believe that neither political economy is made of such things. It is our duty to tell the public how and why one fact is the consequence of another. Whether they like such consequence or not, it is their judgement. How to behave, it is up to

them to decide. We are not preachers. Therefore, I better refrain from preaching frugality, like Adam Smith did; and you, sir, from praising squandering, like Lauderdale did. Let us be content with clarifying the facts and connections of the accumulation of capital.

10 Smith's attention lingers on what, along with James Otteson, we could call the "great mind fallacy." See Otteson (2010).
11 Likewise, however, "without practical manual skill, the most elaborate learning may be of no use" and "without dexterous workmen, the most ingenious contrivances must be classed merely as visionary dreams" (Hodgskin 1827a, 91).
12 Christopher Berry (2015, 97) pointed out that "It is one of the Scots' contribution to the history of the social sciences that they effectively write a history of belief: the history of what Hume himself calls 'the minds of men.'"
13 The emphasis on the advancement of knowledge as a determinant of the improvement of society's conditions is reminiscent of another "Scottish" influence on Hodgskin, notably Dugald Stewart. See Collini, Winch and Burrow (1983, 38–42).
14 This point was not lost on Adam Smith. Smith ([1767] 1985, 223), discussing the "simplification" of language, notes that:

> It is in this manner that language becomes more simple in its rudiments and principles, just in proportion as it grows more complex in its composition, and the same thing has happened in it, which commonly happens with regard to mechanical engines. All machines are generally, when first invented, extremely complex in their principles, and there is often a particular principle of motion for every particular movement which it is intended they should perform. Succeeding improvers observe, that one principle may be so applied as to produce several of those movements; and thus the machine becomes gradually more and more simple, and produces its effects with fewer wheels, and fewer principles of motion.

This remark about the progressive simplification of the way in which machines operate appears to us to be truly extraordinarily illuminating, in the light of the technological advances of the last century.

15 Literature on the "law of markets" is extensive. For an overview of the controversy it raised in the nineteenth and twentieth century, see Sowell (1972).
16 It is, indeed, a more nuanced issue than one would suspect. According to Say ([1803] 2002, 307):

> If population depends on the amount of product, the number of births is a very imperfect criterion, by which to measure it. When industry and produce are increasing, births are multiplied disproportionately to the existing population, so as to swell the estimate; on the contrary, in the declining state of national wealth, the actual population exceeds the average ratio to the births.

17 Stack is referring to the first of a series of articles about the Spitalfields Acts published on the *Mechanics' Magazine* in 1823. The article is anonymous but attributed to Hodgskin. It says:

> It is a maxim with political economists, that products always create their own market; but this maxim is derived from the supposition that no man produces but with the intention of selling or enjoying, and it does not therefore hold good with our laborers who are compelled to produce but are not permitted to enjoy.
>
> (Hodgskin 1823, 21)

If it is true that the article postulates a form of overproduction due to the excess of working hours, however, it seems difficult to consider the aforementioned passage a "refutation" of Say's principle.
18 Though without explicitly mentioning Hume, Hodgskin (1863b) builds on this essay.
19 "Among savages all the men and women labour; their labour barely supplies the necessaries of life, and they increase very slowly, if at all, in numbers; while in civilized society the labour of only a small part of the people supplies numerous conveniences and luxuries, and the society grows in population and power" (Hodgskin 1827a, 14). As an exception to this possible rule, Ireland comes to mind: "one of the most densely peopled countries of Europe, and that one in which population has made the most astonishing progress, yet Ireland is at this time conspicuous for the ignorance and poverty of the mass of its people" (122). Hodgskin, however, points out that in reality Ireland has had an extraordinary development since the days of Elizabeth I and therefore he does not consider the miserable state of the green island a counter-argument to his thesis. The famine that developed, twenty years after this essay by Hodgskin, with the outbreak of the Great Blight and, more generally, the poverty of the green island were, according to Joel Mokyr, one of the main reasons that induced economic science to abandon the principles of *laissez-faire*. However, he also maintains that the contention that the misery of the Irish was due to overpopulation is not supported by empirical evidence. See Mokyr (1983, 278).
20 On the Godwin-Malthus debate, see, *inter alia*, Petersen (1971).
21 This way, the reason behind Place's strong hostility toward Hodgskin is better understood. The only book written by Place, *Illustrations and Proofs of the Principle of Population*, was precisely an attempt to popularize Malthus's ideas. Wallas ([1898] 1925, 166) writes that Place "was to the end a disciple rather than a maker, and a disciple who accepted without reserve the one doctrine from which the classical political economy followed as a series of corollaries, Malthus' celebrated "Principle of Population." In his work he tried "to separate the harsh principle of population, which he believed in, from the harsh treatment of the poor by the rich, which he regarded as irrelevant to this principle" (James 1979, 385).
22 Spencer's article is notable because he argued that the greater the complexity of the social organism was to be, the fewer the number of offspring. Hence, today it may be read as a prophecy.
23 With regard to British agriculture in the eighteenth century, important changes were observed from the technological and organizational point of view (territorial specialization, crop rotation, crop adjustment speed to match market demand). According to E.L. Jones, "the landed estate system was nicely adapted to ensure the diffusion of new ideas" (Jones 1981, 82).
24 In this case too there is a considerable distance from Malthus who, in the first edition of his *Essay*, questioned the Smithian idea that the British economy had seen a general improvement of the living conditions of the population since the Glorious Revolution. According to Malthus, the concentration of investments in trades and manufacturing meant that wealth had grown faster than the actual funds for the sustenance of the labor power. The lower classes "have not, I believe, a greater command of the necessaries and conveniences of life; and a much greater proportion of them, than at the period of the revolution, is employed in manufactures, and crowded together in close and unwholesome rooms" (Malthus 1798, 98–99).
25 It is true that the causes of the increase in population are still debated but "it is doubtful that these changes were unrelated to improvements in potential living standards" (O'Brien and Engerman 1981, 177).

26   the crude birth rate fell a little after 1790 being about 2 per 1000 less between 1811 and 1831 than it had been in the decade 1781–90. The conquest of small-pox, the curtailment of agueish disorders through swamp drainage, the disappearance of scurvy as a disease of the land, improvements in obstetrics leading to a reduction in the losses both of infant and of maternal life in childbed, the spreading of hospitals, dispensaries and medical schools, all had helped to save life.

(Clapham [1926] 1950, 55)

27. Probably more relevant is the influence exerted *ex post* by the abolition of grain duties. The journalistic activity of Frédéric Bastiat and the French liberals comes to mind. Likewise, when the *Società Adamo Smith* (the Adam Smith Society) was founded in Florence in 1848 by the initiative of Francesco Ferrara, its magazine was naturally christened *L'economista* [The Economist], in explicit reference to the newspaper inspired by the Anti-Corn Law League. Vilfredo Pareto (1848–1923) remembered that at the beginning of his career he thought that "political economy, as it was established by the so-called classical economists, was a perfect, or almost-perfect, science; [what only remained was] to put into practice its principles." That required imitating Cobden's League, the most fruitful and loftiest example for mankind in centuries (Pareto [1907] 1974, 809).
28. Indeed, Cobden often employed "evangelical language" (Hollis 1974, 11).
29. In the first phase of the Chartist movement, the goal was to have workers and middle classes converge on the same platform. Such stance, however, was soon overcome.
30. Engels ([1845] 1969, 223) maintained that "the Anti-Corn Law League has used the most despicable falsehoods and tricks to win the support of the workers." For Marx (1848), the apparent humanitarianism of the holders of the means of production would only serve to reduce the wages that they had to pay to the workers. A more intense international competition could only exacerbate the competition among the available workforce, to the benefit of the owners of the means of production.
31. In the first months of 1842, Joseph Sturge established the Birmingham Complete Suffrage Union, which aimed at forging an alliance between Chartists and the League. Sturge had been trying to push Cobden to embrace the idea of complete franchise for years, but Cobden considered it impractical at that moment to abandon the single-issue nature of the League.
32. Stack (1998, 219) also adds the letter in a "Nota Bene" at the end of his Hodgskin bibliography.
33. "The Manchester Courier, anti-League paper, quoted an employer as saying he would go on cutting wages until his men had not 'a cabbage a day' to live on" (Grampp 1960, 68).
34. See Dickens ([1846] 1977). Dickens himself was in favor of the immediate abolition of grain duties. See Drew and Slater (2011).
35.   Mr Cobden referred to the great age of the Duke, and we think justly referred, as explaining in one sentence why his authority, great on many questions, is on the question of invasion, not be relied on. For nearly FIFTY years the Duke has made war his profession. His whole being, totally foreign to that of peaceful industrious men continually intent on serving others and themselves, is moulded on war. ... He knows nothing of the mutual good offices and kindly feelings that the mutual services of industrious men generate. ... The Duke is biased by his profession; and it is not blaming him or throwing any shade on the illustrious name he won in past times, to indicate that his feelings and his knowledge are those of the passing or past generation.

(Hodgskin 1848a, 2)

36 A similar thesis was argued by James Wilson—who would later be Hodgskin's employer and editor-in-chief at the *Economist*—in his *Influences of the Corn Law*, an essay with a strongly empirical character, scrupulous in referring to the (few) statistics then available. The first of the "effects" that Wilson examines is "that the influence of protective duties must always be to induce a great excess of capital and labour to be for a time employed in the cultivation of grain." Wilson's argument was, in short, that the duties interfered to such an extent with the adjustment of supply and demand, that removing them would have made it easier to reach a balanced price. This would have left no room for uncertainty. See Wilson (1840, 27–28). Stack (1998, 163) somehow alludes to the possibility that Hodgskin's *Lecture on Free Trade* was useful in placing him on friendly terms with James Wilson, since he "had deployed many of the same arguments as Wilson's anti-corn law pamphlet, *Influences of the Corn Laws, as affecting all classes of the community, and particularly the landed interests*." As already mentioned, Dudley Edwards (1993, 127) suggests that the relationship between Hodgskin and Wilson "worked well." Yet, the two parted ways in 1857. Hodgskin seemed to have been increasingly turned off by the *Economist*'s inclining toward supporting the government, as a by-product of Wilson's political career.
37 Further ahead, Hodgskin (1843, 4) points out:

> Among them are skillful and painstaking manufacturers, long thoughted merchants, and enterprising inventors—men who are ever planning, some new combinations to enrich themselves. I admit, but which in the end confer benefit to the public. If they should reap advantage from the abolition as well as the labourers, that would be a strong recommendation of the measure; but they are comparatively so few in number, that it is no justification of a law merely to say that it adds to the wealth and power of capitalists.

38 The topic anticipates Hodgskin's 1856 lectures on crime.
39 The notion of a progressive refinement of the degree of freedom enjoyed by the people is a recurring topic in Hodgskin's work. Two different tendencies always coexist in his analysis: on the one hand, the conviction that freedom is consistent with a natural order, compromised by the very existence of any coercive apparatus. On the other hand, it is precisely the historical development, in particular the technological development that followed the Industrial Revolution, which ushers in a fuller enjoyment of freedom.
40 In making thus argument, Hodgskin quotes McCulloch, who was actually one of his targets (the other happened to be James Mill) in *Labour Defended*. This may suggest a change in tone from the 1820s pamphlets. Yet there are multiple references to McCulloch in *Popular Political Economy* and they are not by all means all negative.
41 For a synthetic discussion, see Mayhew (2014, 118–120). For some context on the dispute between Malthus and Ricardo over the corn laws, see Salvadori and Signorino (2013).
42 Fay ([1932] 2017, 139) also noted how he "believed still that high rents were a sign of prosperity."
43 This is also the thesis of Gordon (1955, 474).
44 In an article for the *New York Daily Tribune*, Marx ([1852] 1979, 334) mocked the failure of the League and, more generally, of the British bourgeoisie, in being truly revolutionary. "Having obtained, in 1846, a grand victory over the landed aristocracy by the repeal of the Corn Laws, they were satisfied with following up the material advantages of this victory, while they neglected to draw the necessary political and economical conclusions from it."

45 The premise affixed by Elliot to his *Hymns* (1840b), in which he complains about the pernicious influence of Malthus's ideas and spurs the public opinion and the middle classes to awaken from apathy, actually allows us to assume that he might have been indeed familiar with Hodgskin's work. The bard of Free Trade was a metals dealer from Sheffield. On Elliott, see Briggs ([1950] 1985) and Neilson (1951).

References

Allen, Robert C. 2009. *The British Industrial Revolution in Global Perspective*. Cambridge: Cambridge University Press.

Anderson, Gary M., and Robert D. Tollison. 1984. "Sir James Steuart as the Apotheosis of Mercantilism and His Relation to Adam Smith." *Southern Economic Journal* 51 (2): 456–468, https://doi.org./10.2307/1057824.

Berry, Christopher. 2015. *The Idea of Commercial Society in the Scottish Enlightenment*. Edinburgh: Edinburgh University Press.

Blake, Robert. (1970) 2010. *The Conservative Party from Peel to Major*. London: Faber and Faber.

Brady, Alexander. (1928) 1967. *William Huskisson and Liberal Reform*. London: Cass.

Briggs, Asa. (1959) 2000. *The Age of Improvement, 1783–1867*. New York: Routledge.

Briggs, Asa. (1950) 1985. "Ebenezer Elliott, The Corn Law Rhymer." In *The Collected Essays of Asa Briggs*, Vol. 2, *Images, Problems, Standpoints, Forecasts*. Chicago: University of Illinois Press.

Clapham, John Harold. 1916. "The Spitalfields Acts, 1773–1824." *Economic Journal* 26 (104): 459, https://doi.org/10.2307/2221846.

Clapham, John Harold. (1926) 1950. *An Economic History of Modern Britain: The Early Railway Age 1820–1850*. Cambridge: Cambridge University Press.

Cobden, Richard. 1842. "Richard Cobden to Hodgskin, 17 August 1842." In *The Letters of Richard Cobden*, Vol. I: 1815–1847. Edited by Anthony Howe. Oxford: Oxford University Press.

Cobden, Richard. 1846. "To the Farming Tenantry of the United Kingdom." *London Daily News*, January 31.

Cobden, Richard. 1857a. Richard Cobden to Thomas Hodgskin, May 20.

Cobden, Richard. 1857b. Richard Cobden to Thomas Hodgskin, October 14.

Cobden, Richard. (1862) 1903. "Richard Cobden, Letter to Mr Henry Ashworth, Esq, 10th April 1862." In *The Political Writings of Richard Cobden*. London: Fisher Unwin.

Collini, Stefan, Donald Winch, and John Burrow. 1983. *That Noble Science of Politics: A Study in Nineteenth-century Intellectual History*. Cambridge: Cambridge University Press.

Dickens, Charles. (1846) 1977. "Charles Dickens to Thomas Hodgskin, February 2nd." In *The Letters of Charles Dickens*, Vol. 4, *1844–1846*. Edited by Kathleen Tillotson. Oxford: Clarendon Press, 487.

Drew, John, and Michael Slater. 2011. "What's in *The Daily News*? A Re-evaluation–Part 2." *The Dickensian* 483 (107): 22–39.

Dudley Edwards, Ruth. *The Pursuit of Reason: The Economist 1843–1993*. London: Hamish Hamilton.

Elliot, Ebenezer. 1840a. "Elegy." In *The Poetical Work of Ebenezer Elliot: The Corn-Law Rhymer*. Edinburgh: Tait, 103.

Elliot, Ebenezer. 1840b. "Corn-Law Hymns No. I to XX." In *The Poetical Works of Ebenezer Elliot: The Corn Law Rhymer*. Edinburgh: W. Tait.

Engels, Friedrich. (1845) 1969. *The Condition of the Working-class in England in 1844.* London: Panther Books.

Everett, Alexander Hill. 1823. *New Ideas on Population: with Remarks on the Theories of Malthus and Godwin.* London: John Miller.

Farrar, Peter Nelson. 1987. "Richard Cobden, Educationist, Economist and Statesman." PhD diss., University of Sheffield.

Fay, Charles Ryle. (1932) 2017. *The Corn Laws and Social England.* Cambridge: Cambridge University Press.

Forget, Evelyn L. 1999. *The Social Economics of Jean-Baptiste Say: Markets and Virtue.* London: Routledge.

Gordon, Barry. 1979. *Economic Doctrine and Tory Liberalism, 1824–1830.* London: Macmillan.

Gordon, Scott. 1955. "The London Economist and the High Tide of Laissez Faire." *Journal of Political Economy* 63 (6): 461–488, https:doi.org/10.1086/257722.

Grampp, William Dyer. 1960. *The Manchester School of Economics.* Stanford: Stanford University Press.

Halévy, Élie. (1903) 1956. *Thomas Hodgskin.* Translated and edited by A.J. Taylor. London: Ernst Benn.

Hilton, Boyd. (1977) 1980. *Corn, Cash, Commerce: The Economic Policies of the Tory Governments, 1815–1830.* Oxford: Oxford University Press.

Hilton, Boyd. 2006. *A Mad, Bad, & Dangerous People? England 1783–1846.* Oxford: Oxford University Press.

Hinde, Wendy. 1987. *Richard Cobden. A Victorian Outsider.* New Haven: Yale University Press.

Hirschman, Albert O. 1977. *The Passions and the Interests: Political Arguments for Capitalism Before its Triumph.* Princeton: Princeton University Press.

Hirst, Francis W. 1903. "Introduction." In *Free Trade and the Other Fundamental Doctrines of the Manchester School.* Edited by F.W. Hirst. London: Harper and Brothers.

Hodgskin, Thomas. 1820. Travels in the North of Germany. Describing the Present State of the Social and Political Institutions, the Agriculture, Manufacture, Commerce, Education, Arts and Manners in That Country, Particularly in the Kingdom of Hannover. 2 Vols. Edinburgh: Archibald Constable.

Hodgskin, Thomas. 1823. "The Spitalfields Act." *Mechanics' Magazine,* September 6.

Hodgskin, Thomas. 1824. "A History of Chemistry." *The Chemist* 1, March 13.

Hodgskin, Thomas. 1826a. "A Labourer, Effects of Repealing the Corn Laws. To the Editor of Trade's Newspaper and Mechanics' Weekly Journal." *The Trades' Newspaper, and Mechanics' Weekly Journal,* February 12.

Hodgskin, Thomas. 1826b. *Trades' Newspaper,* January 22.

Hodgskin, Thomas. 1826c. "Political Economy." *Trades' Newspaper,* January 29.

Hodgskin, Thomas. 1827a. *Popular Political Economy: Four Lectures Delivered at the Mechanics' Institution.* London: Charles Tait.

Hodgskin, Thomas. 1827b. *The Word BELIEF Defined and Explained.* London: Charles Tait.

Hodgskin, Thomas. 1843. *A Lecture on Free Trade in connexion with the Corn Laws.* London: G.J. Palmer.

Hodgskin, Thomas. 1848a. "The London Telegraph." *The London Telegraph,* February 1.

Hodgskin, Thomas. 1848b. "The London Telegraph." *The London Telegraph,* May 2.

Hodgskin, Thomas. 1850. Review of "More Verse and Prose: By the Corn-Law Rhymer." *Economist,* February 2.

Hodgskin, Thomas. 1862a. "Science–Umping Birds–Minute Philosophy." *Brighton Guardian*, January 22.

Hodgskin, Thomas. 1862b. "Science–The Passions–Progress." *Brighton Guardian*, March 12.

Hodgskin, Thomas. 1863a. "Science–Is Political Economy a Science?" *Brighton Guardian*, August 12.

Hodgskin, Thomas. 1863b. "Science–The Destiny of Society." *Brighton Guardian*, September 2.

Hollis, Patricia. 1974. "Pressure from Without: An Introduction." In *Pressure from Without in Early Victorian England*. Edited by Patricia, Hollis. London: Edward Arnold, 1–26.

Howe, Anthony. 1997. *Free Trade and Liberal England 1846–1946*. Oxford: Clarendon Press.

Hume, David. (1777) 1987. "Of the Populousness of Ancient Nations." In *Essays Moral, Political, Literary*. Edited by Eugene F.Miller. Indianapolis, IN: Liberty Fund, 377–464.

Hutt, William Harold. 1974. *A Rehabilitation of Say's Law*. Athens, OH: Ohio University Press.

Jaffe, James A. 1995. "The Origins of Thomas Hodgskin's Critique of Political Economy." *History of Political Economy* 27 (3): 493–515, https://doi.org/10.1215/00182702-27-3-493.

Jaffe, James Alan. 2000. *Striking a Bargain: Work and Industrial Relations in England 1815–1865*. Manchester: Manchester University Press.

James, Patricia. (1979) 2013. *Population Malthus: His Life and Times*. London: Routledge.

Jones, E.L. 1981. "Agriculture 1700–80." In *The Economic History of Britain since 1700. Vol. 1, 1700–1860*. Edited by Roderick Floud and Deirdre McCloskey. Cambridge: Cambridge University Press, 66–86.

Langer, Gary F. 1987. *The Coming of Age of Political Economy, 1815–1825*. Westport: Greenwood Press.

Longmate, Norman. 1984. *The Breadstealer: The Fight against the Corn Law, 1838–1846*. London: Temple Smith.

Malthus, Thomas Robert. 1798. *An Essay on the Principle of Population, as it Affects the Future Improvement of Society with Remarks on the Speculations of Mr. Godwin, M. Condorcet, and Other Writers*. London: Johnson.

Marx, Karl. 1848. *On the Question of Free Trade*. Brussels: Democratic Association of Brussels.

Marx, Karl. (1852) 1979. "The Chartists," *New York Daily Tribune*, August 25. In *Marx & Engels Collected Works, Vol. 11: Marx and Engels: 1851–1853*. Moscow: Progress Publishers.

Mayhew, Robert J. 2014. *Malthus: The Life and Legacies of an Untimely Prophet*. Cambridge: The Belknap Press of Harvard University Press.

McLaren, Angus. 1978. *Birth Control in Nineteenth-Century England*. New York: Holmes & Meier.

Mokyr, Joel. 1983. *Why Ireland Starved: A Quantitative and Analytical History of the Irish Economy, 1800–1850*. London, Allen & Unwin.

Morley, John. (1879) 1903. *The Life of Richard Cobden*. London: Fisher Unwin.

Neilson, Francis. (1951). "The Corn Law Rhymes." *American Journal of Economics and Sociology* 10 (4): 407–415. https://doi.org/10.1111/j.1536-7150.1951.tb00070.x.

O'Brien, Patrick K., and Stanley L.Engerman. 1981. "Changes in Income and its Distribution during the Industrial Revolution." In *The Economic History of Britain since 1700, Vol. I, 1700–1860*. Edited by Roderick Floud and Deirdre McCloskey. Cambridge, UK: Cambridge University Press, 164–181.

Otteson, James R. 2010. "Adam Smith and the Great Mind Fallacy." *Social Philosophy and Policy* 27 (1): 276–304, https://doi.org/10.1017/s0265052509990112.
Paley, William (1785) 2002. *The Principles of Moral and Political Philosophy*. Indianapolis, IN: Liberty Fund.
Pareto, Vilfredo. (1907) 1974. *Letter to Antonio Antonucci*, November 24. In *Scritti politici. III. Reazione, libertà, fascismo*. Edited by G. Busino. Utet: Torino, 806–812.
Petersen, William. 1971. "The Malthus–Godwin Debate, Then and Now." *Demography* 8 (1): 13–26, https://doi.org/10.2307/2060335.
Psillos, Stathis. 2011. "Regularities All the Way Down: Thomas Brown's Philosophy of Causation." In *Causation and Modern Philosophy*. Edited by Keith Allen and Tom Stoneham. London: Routledge, 227–248.
Rowe, Christopher. 2018. "William Huskisson and the Rhetoric of Free Trade." *Economic Affairs* 38 (2): 207–223. https://doi.org/10.1111/ecaf.12288.
Sally, Razeen. 1998. *Classical Liberalism and International Economic Order*. London: Routledge.
Salvadori, Neri and Rodolfo Signorino. 2013. "The Malthus versus Ricardo 1815 Corn Laws Controversy: An Appraisal." *MPRA Paper*. University Library of Munich: Germany, https://EconPapers.repec.org/RePEc:pra:mprapa:5053.
Say, Jean-Baptiste. (1803) 2002. *A Treatise on Political Economy*. Translated and edited by C.R. Prinsep. Kitchener: Batoche Books.
Say, Jean-Baptiste. 1820. *Lettres à M. Malthus, sur différents sujets d'économie politique, notamment sur les causes de la stagnation générale du commerce*. Paris: Bossange.
Smith, Adam. (1759) 1869. *The Theory of Moral Sentiments and Essays on Philosophical Subjects*. Edited by Dugald Stewart. Indianapolis, IN: Liberty Fund.
Smith, Adam. (1767) 1985. "Considerations Concerning the First Formation of Languages." In J.C. Bryce, ed. *The Works and Correspondence of Adam Smith*, Vol. 4: *Lectures on Rhetoric and Belles Lettres*. Indianapolis, IN: Liberty Fund, 201–226.
Smith, Adam. (1776) 1981. *An Inquiry into the Nature and Causes of the Wealth of Nations*. Vol. I, v. Edited by Roy H. Campbell and Andrew S. Skinner. Indianapolis, IN: Liberty Fund.
Smith, Kenneth. (1951) 2006. *The Malthusian Controversy*. London: Routledge.
Sowell, Thomas. 1972. *Say's Law: An Historical Analysis*. Princeton: Princeton University Press.
Spencer, Herbert. 1852. "A Theory of Population, Deduced from the General Law of Animal Fertility." *The Westminster Review* 57 (New Series, 2): 468–501.
Stack, David. 1998. *Nature and Artifice: The Life and Thought of Thomas Hodgskin, 1787–1869*. Martlesham: Boydell & Brewer.
Steuart, James. (1767) 1966. *An Inquiry into the Principles of Political Oeconomy*. Chicago: University of Chicago Press.
Thompson, Edward P. 1964. *The Making of the English Working Class*. New York: Vintage Books.
Thompson, Noel. 1984. *The People's Science: The Popular Political Economy of Exploitation and Crisis 1816–34*. New York: Cambridge University Press.
Vernon, James. 2014. *Distant Stranger: How Britain Became Modern*. Los Angeles: University of California Press.
Wallas, Graham. (1898) 1925. *The Life of Francis Place, 1771–1854*. London: Allen & Unwin.
Wilson, James. 1840. *Influences of the Corn Laws*. London: Longmans.

4 Free trade in banking

Some thoughts on the business cycle

As we mentioned in chapter 3, the year 1825 was difficult and dreary for many, because a bubble had burst, launching an economic crisis. Free trade was under siege, and William Huskisson's liberalizations were thought to have damaged the economy.

Such a context provided Thomas Hodgskin with plenty of food for thought, which this chapter will review. His reflections on the subject were quite parsimonious and scattered among his writings; yet they were fully consistent with his general understanding of economics and show a keen understanding of the peculiarities of banking and finance. This matters because the boom that generated the bust was, according to Nicholas Dimsdale and Anthony Hotson (2014, 32), "stimulated excessively by inept monetary and fiscal measures for which the Bank and the Treasury were responsible."

Here is the background to the bust, as outlined by Dimsdale and Hotson: Britain returned to the gold standard after the Napoleonic Wars. The economy was weak until it reached a cyclical trough in 1819 and revived thereafter, "largely in response to a rise in exports, in particular cotton textiles." Then came a boom, supported by a strong revival of financial activities and "helped by a financial stimulus brought by the authorities." By the early 1820s, the Bank of England, pushed by the government, was redeeming exchequer bonds at the same time as it was losing gold reserves. This significantly increased the liquidity in circulation (Neal 1998, 60).

In London debt securities were issued by all the independent states that had arisen in Latin America from the ashes of the Spanish Empire (Chile, Guatemala, Colombia, Argentina, Peru, Mexico). These new states, often at war with each other and destined to endure perpetual political turmoil of the kind that Joseph Conrad (1857–1924) later immortalized in his novel *Nostromo*, desperately needed to finance themselves. These deals were sometimes quite appetizing for investors: the legendary gold and silver mines of those countries attracted their attention. "The great demand in Europe for investment opportunities in Latin America, coupled with new leaders in Latin America desperate for funds to support the process of nation building (among other things), produced a surge in lending from (mostly) London to (mostly) Latin American sovereigns" (Reinhart and Rogoff 2009, 93).

To these factors, others of domestic origin were added: "The reduction of interest on government debt, and a shortage of opportunities for domestic investment in the period between the canal and the railway building eras fortuitously deflected all this extra capital into foreign loans and joint-stock ventures overseas" (Hilton [1977] 1980, 204). So "the loan bubble of 1822–25 was produced, which ended [sic] giving the British holders of foreign treasury bills their first taste of a sovereign state's default" (Neal 1998, 62).

After a surge in the stock market in the spring of 1825, on December 3rd and 12th of that same year, the London banks of Wentworth, Chaloner & Rishworth and Pole, Thornton & Co. went bankrupt, triggering a bank run and dragging along 43 corresponding country banks. Overall, there were 73 English bankruptcies (out of 770 English banks) as well as three bankruptcies in Scotland, where there were 36 banks (Kindleberger 1984, 83). At first, the Bank of England reduced its loans, to secure its reserves; but eventually it "lent money by every possible means, and in modes which we had never adopted before": on its action, Walter Bagehot (1826–1877) would shape his own ideas about the role of a central bank as lender of last resort in times of crisis (1873, 160–207).

Psychological factors always play a role in financial crises, but they are not necessarily at the center of economists' attention. It is thus particularly noteworthy that Hodgskin was concerned with the effect of expectations on markets. In early 1826, he wrote an article for the *Trades' Newspaper*, in which he warned against the psychological effects of announcing the abolition of duties. This may appear to contradict his advocacy of free trade, but it did not: his argument relates not to policies but to expectations. The boom—which had just turned to a bust—had developed thanks to the investment in commercial enterprises outside England. Explaining that the hope for fewer trade restrictions "flattered the cupidity and stimulated the enterprise, of our manufacturers and merchants," Hodgskin was probably stating the obvious. Yet he linked such growing "greed" to psychological factors. The psychology of the businessmen affected investment decisions "by talking of the increased market they were to find for their commodities. The latter eagerly hastened to supply the imaginary market. They first over-worked and over-employed their men, and then undersold each other. [As] These speculations turned out not profitable they became bankrupts, and distress among the workmen, wide-spread and alarming distress, has been the consequence" (Hodgskin 1826).

Thus Hodgskin explicitly compared the dynamics of bad investments in the ascending phase of the business cycle to a form of euphoria that grew because of deceptive signals coming from politics. The entrepreneur tends to overestimate the potential of a new market and increases production, but ends up facing the illusory nature of his prospects. This insight had consequences in Hodgskin's understanding of money. In *Popular Political Economy*, Hodgskin criticized the government-prescribed limitations to the circulation of low-denomination banknotes introduced after the panic of 1825, and maintained that the response of the legislators only managed to "augment the power of the Bank of England, which had already caused inconceivable mischief" (Hodgskin 1827, 216). In Hodgskin's view, it was hard to imagine that there was an excess supply of bank notes issued by the country banks; rather, it was the currency issued by the Bank of England that caused inflation:[1]

> It is proved, for example, by parliamentary documents, that the issues of the Bank of England have been trebled in amount since the year 1792, while the amount of the issues of Country bankers were less, immediately prior to the late revulsion in the latter end of 1825, by seven millions, than they were in 1814, and less by four millions than in 1807... . Nothing but colossal power can work colossal mischief, and if that revulsion and consequent distress were in any degree caused by paper-money, they were so vast and extensive, that nothing less than the immense power of the Bank of England, which did actually vary the amount of its issues one-sixth within a few short months, could have caused them.
> (Hodgskin 1827, 215–216)

Hodgskin could see the handiness of paper money, of which he was a strong supporter (as we will see), but he thought that if monopolized by government its mismanagement was inevitable: nothing but colossal power can work colossal mischief.

A few years later, in *The Natural and Artificial Right of Property Contrasted*, Hodgskin (1832, 155–156) would briefly revisit the subject of the cyclical trends of the economy, linking them to political cronyism:

> When we look at the commercial history of our country, and see the false hopes of our merchants and manufacturers leading to periodical commercial convulsions, we are compelled to conclude, that they have not the same source as the regular and harmonious external world. ... Starts of national prosperity, followed by bankruptcy and ruin, have the same source then as fraud and forgery. To our legal right of property we are indebted for those gleams of false wealth and real panic, which, within the last fifty years, have so frequently shook, to its centre, the whole trading world.

The reference to "our legal right of property" points to government meddling with factors of production, by supporting the legislating classes no matter what their claims. In a sense, thus, Hodgskin blames government intervention for stimulating misallocation of resources in the boom phase.

It is possible to attribute to Hodgskin a review of McCulloch's *Treatise on the Circumstances which Determines the Rate of Wages*, published in the *Economist* in 1851, when he was in charge of the book review section of the magazine. There Hodgskin pondered the issue of the economic cycle, touching in particular the theme of "waste of capital" in the years of euphoria (this time, the timespan between 1842–1846):

... in those years capital was much misapplied and wasted; and hence the revulsion of 1847–8. There was something else, therefore, besides the quantity of capital which determined the employment and the wages of labour between 1842 and 1846, and that something every person knows, was a delusive and false hope in capitalists, or those who could obtain credit, which gave a wonderful extension to employment without any corresponding increase in capital. The quantity of capital was the ultimate test, indeed, of the validity of credit; it proved the credit to have been fallacious—the hopes to have been a delusion; but in the meantime the people were employed, the wages paid and consumed.

(Hodgskin 1851, 1440)

All this does not mean that Hodgskin had a substantial theory of economic cycles. However, on these three different occasions, a number of ideas emerged:

1. the theme of the misuse of capital (the increase in production because of malinvestment);
2. the question of the "psychology" of the entrepreneur, inclined to exaggerate;
3. the "political" decision as the cause of the boom: be it an "advertising policy" that excites the greed of the capitalists or, rather, the way in which the property rights are attributed and secured by the legislating classes, which allows some people a condition of substantial irresponsibility (heads–I win, tails–you lose).

The desire for "good news" on the one hand, and the political fabrication of the same on the other, led to bad investments. Economic actors are prone to cyclical enthusiasms that can result in malinvestment. Political authorities can and do exacerbate these feelings: "cheating" businesses, so to say, with "gleams of false wealth."

Free banking

As we have seen, Hodgskin thought that knowledge could not be easily "centralized" in the hands of rulers: this was the gist of those "natural laws" that economics discovered, *contra* the pretensions of lawmakers. He thought banking no exception to the rule. The issuing of money no more "needs to be regulated by meddling statesmen, than the business of paper making," he argued (Hodgskin 1827, 218).

"Banking, or at least the issuing of bank notes, is, as it were, a new business, and while the temptations to engage in it have been very great, the correct methods for carrying it on have been imperfectly known" (Hodgskin 1827, 215). Hodgskin was fully convinced that banking requires the knowledge of the concrete circumstances of time and place, to borrow Friedrich Hayek's words; for this reason, it would be better to leave it in the hands of private bankers who are "very useful workers" (Hodgskin 1827, 206). Money, in itself, is not a product of the political order: "As money is not the offspring of legislation, so it is not by laws that its quantity or value are regulated" (Hodgskin 1827, 185).

Hodgskin may then well be considered one of the first supporters of *free banking* [2] despite not having taken part in the debate among *Banking School, Currency School* and *Free Banking School* that took place after the crisis of 1825 (see Schwartz [1987] 2008). Once again, he stood on the opposite side from Ricardo ([1824] 2004, 271–302).

The coming of an irredeemable paper currency was preceded by many historical episodes of free banking. These involved rival issuers of banknotes, where such notes were denominated in units of a common *currency standard* (the dollar, the pound, etc.) based on precious metals (typically, gold). These systems saw "the unrestricted competitive issue of specie-convertible money by unprivileged private banks" (White [1984] 1995, ix).

In her classic study on the subject, Vera Smith (1912–1976) describes free banking as

> a regime where note-issuing banks are allowed to set up in the same way as any other type of business enterprise, so long as they comply with the general company law. The requirement for their establishment is not special conditional authorisation from a Government authority, but the ability to raise sufficient capital, and public confidence, to gain acceptance for their notes and ensure the profitability of the undertaking. Under such a system all banks would not only be allowed the same rights, but would also be subjected to the same responsibilities as other business enterprises. ... Notes issued under this system would be "promises to pay," and such obligations must be met on demand in the generally accepted medium which we will assume to be gold. No bank would have the right to call on the Government or on any other institution for special help in time of need. No bank would be able to give its notes forced currency by declaring them to be legal tender for all payments, and it is unlikely that the public would accept inconvertible notes of any such bank except at a discount varying with the prospect of their again becoming convertible. A general abandonment of the gold standard is inconceivable under these conditions, and with a strict interpretation of the bankruptcy laws any bank suspending payments would at once be put into the hands of a receiver.
> (V. Smith [1936] 1990, 169–170)

Thus, the banks received deposits in metal money, offering in exchange their freely redeemable liabilities, also in the form of banknotes. The value of the monetary standard was decided by the balance of demand and supply on the gold market, but the metallic standard did not prevent the institutions where values are deposited in metallic currency from turning "from bailers to investors of deposited funds (and the corresponding change in the function of banks from bailment to intermediation)"; these changes were eventually followed by the "development of assignable and negotiable instruments of credit (inside money)" (Selgin 1988, 16–17).

Yet in such a context one could still think, as Italian economist Francesco Ferrara (1810–1900) did, that "banknotes are not money, but the simple promise of payment in money. Coins carry with them the inherent value of the metal of which they are made, while the note has no value in itself, nor does it acquire any unless it is converted, or has the certain possibility of being converted, into a certain amount of money" (Ferrara 1873, 365). In Hodgskin's words, "the term 'money price,' as applied to any commodities, only signifies the natural relation which exists at any given moment between them and a specific quantity of bullion in coin,—the use of bank notes, as long as they are payable on demand in precious metals, not altering this relation" (1827, 219).[3]

Kurt Schuler has identified about sixty historical episodes he classifies as "free banking" on the grounds that they involved "a certain amount of bank freedom, multiple note issuers, and the absence of any government-sponsored 'lender of last resort'" (Schuler 1992, 4–47). One of these was likely known to Hodgskin: Scotland had a free banking system between 1716 and 1845. There were no entry barriers for banks that wanted to issue money, there was no central bank, and the degree of supervision in the banking system was quite low. From 1765 Scottish banks were forbidden to issue banknotes worth less than one pound or bearing an "optional clause"—a device through which the banks "promised payment to the bearer, either as soon as the note should be presented, or … six months after such presentment, together with the legal interest for the said six months" (Smith [1776] 1981, II.ii, 98). Both of these regulations actually earned the approval of Adam Smith, who believed they were useful to reduce the risk of fraud and, as we would say today, to protect the less cautious money savers.[4]

Hodgskin instead rejected the arguments offered in support of any public intervention in the banking system. First, he denied the need for a single issuing institution in order to avoid fraud. The experience of those years allowed a certain optimism. According to Lawrence H. White ([1984] 1995, 36) Scottish free banking was not plagued by significant problems of counterfeiting. On the contrary: their relatively brief circulation periods made Scottish banknotes less tempting targets for counterfeitors than those issued by the Bank of England:

> The frequency of counterfeiting is related to the length of time for which each banknote remains in circulation: on the contrary, the Scottish banknotes circulated for a short time, because the other banks did not use them as cash, but returned them to the issuing institution through the clearing house, to get their countervalue in return.

Hodgskin prophesied that banknotes "issued by private individuals … will unquestionably supersede, even to a greater degree than at present, metallic money" (Hodgskin 1827, 194), yet he thought that even private coinage of metallic money, "had the matter not been interfered with" by government, would have spontaneously emerged in markets (Hodgskin 1827, 190). Alas, "it having been supposed, however, in this as in numberless similar cases, that unless the legislature made regulations, there would be only disorder and confusion, governments accordingly assumed the power of coining."

Hodgskin (1827, 194–195) thought there was no case for government claiming a monopoly of issuing; that "[e]xperience tells us, that of all false coiners, none have so sported with the confidence of mankind, under the pretence of protecting them from false coiners, as governments." Governments are inevitably seduced by monetary manipulation, because of its redistributive consequences: "By making alterations in the coin, they have altered all the relations of property." If the issue is the stability of the currency value, "the best way of keeping the metallic currency of any country steady in value, and to have a proper quantity in circulation, is to allow both bullion and coin to be freely imported and exported like all other commodities, and freely dealt with by all classes and conditions of men, like the equally useful articles of hats and shoes."

This suggests an understanding of money as something totally different from a government creation. Hodgskin's point of reference was, once again, Adam Smith. In *The Wealth of Nations* (Smith [1776] 1981, I.iv, 2), the establishing of money is seen as a by-product of the division of labor, needed because the latter would be "frequently very much clogged and embarrassed in its operations" by the use of barter.

Hodgskin was not happy with Smith's treatment of the origin of money. The language used by Smith "almost make [sic] us suppose that he regarded the invention of money as a chance occurrence; or, at least, that he had not formed any accurate idea of those specific circumstances which give rise to the employment of some one commodity as money, whenever the division of labour is introduced" (Hodgskin 1827, 181). While he borrowed from Smith an understanding of money as an intermediary in exchanges (which he does not deny being its "main utility") Hodgskin (196) stresses the functions of measuring value and serving as a "store of value."

Insofar as abandoning barter is concerned, Hodgskin offered two reasons. The first one is "inequality in the time necessary to complete different commodities." Bread is produced every day and can be immediately consumed, to meet a specific need. Other commodities, however, cannot immediately meet needs. In a barter regime. "This ... would cause the hunter or the baker to have a surplus of game or bread, before the maker of bows and arrows, or the grazier, had any commodity completed to give for the surplus game or bread" (Hodgskin 1827, 180). Money thus facilitates "the exchanges which are necessary to the continuance of division of labour" (187–188), allowing goods that have different production times to be sold and bought. Some of these goods, we would add, are used to produce other goods and are therefore less easily tradable than consumer goods. Thus "the obvious utility of division of labour suggested the means of getting over this difficulty, which consisted in the invention of money" (Hodgskin 1827, 180).

The intrinsic diversity of the types of commodities[5] is accompanied by the need to have a good estimate of relative prices.

> A bow and arrow could at no time have been precisely equal in value to each of such different things as a hut, a canoe, or a hatchet; or to an ox, a deer, a hare, or a salmon; and these things could not be exchanged for one another, without some measure to determine how much or how many of other commodities were equal in value to those which could not be divided without destroying them.
>
> (Hodgskin 1827, 180)

Money is equally as important as a unit of exchange and as a unit of measure. While the two things do not necessarily need to be the same, at least in point of theory, Hodgskin tends to equate "the employment of some one commodity as a measure of the value" and its employment as "means of exchanging all commodities" (181). This very juxtaposition suggests looking at precious metals: though "different commodities have been employed as money at different times and places" (182), there are "obvious natural circumstances" which explain "the preference universally given to the precious metals."

Such obvious natural circumstances are the peculiarities of precious metals. As Smith ([1776] 1981, I.iv, 4) noted, they "can likewise, without any loss, be divided into any number of parts, as by fusion those parts can easily be reunited again." Hodgskin emphasizes that these natural circumstances allow us to understand that the metallic nature of money is in itself the outcome of a spontaneous evolutionary process. On the matter, our author quotes Turgot (1727–1781):

> gold and silver constituted money, and universal money, and that without any arbitrary agreement among men, without the intervention of any law, but only by the nature of things. They are not, as many people imagine, signs of value; they have an intrinsic value in themselves, if they are capable of being the measure and the token of other values. This property they have in common with all other commodities which have a value in commerce. They only differ in being at the same time more divisible, more unchangeable, and of more easy conveyance than other merchandize, by which they are more commodiously employed to measure and represent the value of others.
>
> (Turgot [1766] 1785, 46–47)

For Hodgskin, the use of money "began, like division of labour, without the interference of any legislature." There is, therefore, "abundant reason to believe that the practice of coining originated with individuals, and was carried on by them before it was seized on and monopolized by governments."[6] Specifically, "Metallic money is not like an army of ruffian soldiers, the offspring of law, and the creature of governments, it is something instinctively adopted by the human race" (Hodgskin 1827, 184).[7] What happened was simply that, "having perceived the use which might be made of taking this process into their own hands," governments "forbad individuals to coin money, and declared themselves the only lawful coiners" (190).

Yet the main advantage of commodity-money lay, for Hodgskin, precisely in the fact *it is* a commodity—and, as such, part of market exchanges.[8]

> Miners will not supply these metals without an adequate payment, and other men will not pay miners unless they require the precious metals. Their want of money is *regulated by the number of exchanges to be made or the quantities of goods to be bought and sold*; and thus *the quantity of money required at any time and place, is always determined by the number of exchanges* to be made. Of course the relative value of the precious metals to other commodities determines how much of them must be *given for other things*; and the number of sales to be made within a given period, determines, as far as money is the instrument for effecting those sales—the quantity of money required.
>
> (Hodgskin 1827, 188, *italics added*)

Yet Hodgskin was aware that even the relationship between supply and demand of precious metals never sufficed to prevent the adulteration of money by states.[9] Naturally, the latter have a vested interest in using the monetary instrument for redistributive ends: this was the case in a world in which the bulk of the monetary base is still composed of coins, through seigniorage.

Hodgskin deserves credit not only for sensing the dangers of the political manipulation of money, but also for having perfectly understood that, as soon as the government had an exclusive claim on paper money, the political manipulation of money would become even easier.[10] Distinguishing between "paper money *issued, regulated, and controlled by governments*; and paper money *issued and circulated by merchants, bankers, and tradesmen, for the purposes of commerce*" (emphasis added), he warned about the risks of the first kind. Governments can, indeed, "debase the coin," whereas specie "still possesses some value, and cannot be issued in boundless excess; but paper money, which cannot be exchanged for specie, is quite valueless: and as there can be no limit to its issue, it confers on the individuals who possess the government a boundless power of working mischief" (Hodgskin 1827, 197).

More generally, on the topic of paper money, Hodgskin deemed it to be useful, provided that it did not come with a monopoly of issuance.

On the flexibility of paper money, he followed Adam Smith, according to whom the use of paper money had made it possible to economize on gold and silver. "When paper is substituted in the room of gold and silver money, the quantity of the materials, tools, and maintenance, which the whole circulating capital can supply, may be increased by the whole value of gold and silver which used to be employed in purchasing them" (Smith [1776] 1981, III.ii, 39). In short, paper emission with fractional reserves, according to Smith, served the purpose of resuscitating otherwise "dead" capital, that is of economizing on the use of resources employed in the extraction and coining of precious metals, but which could find better uses elsewhere.[11]

> The gold and silver money which circulates in any country may very properly be compared to a highway, which, while it circulates and carries to market all the grass and corn of the country, produces itself not a single pile of either. The judicious operations of banking, by providing, if I may be allowed so violent a metaphor, a sort of waggon-way through the air, enable the country to convert, as it were, a great part of its highways into good pastures and corn-fields, and thereby to increase very considerably the annual produce of its land and labour.
> (Smith [1776] 1981, II.ii, 40)

With even greater enthusiasm than Smith, Hodgskin praised the value and the effectiveness of "commercial paper money," while being well aware that, through it, a form of credit creation could take place. Banknotes are the evolution of the "promissory notes to pay certain sums of money at specific periods," that

> must have come into use almost as early as the invention of writing and the beginning of trade. The merchant who undertakes a long voyage, or the manufacturer who plans an extensive project, requires the means of subsistence and of continuing his operations till his produce can be brought to market. He accordingly borrows the goods which he needs daily, or the money to buy them, promising payment at some specific time, or when his own produce is sold. Persons are willing to supply him with this accommodation, because his future produce will be his only means of payment, and in fact the only commodities produced to exchange for what he immediately requires, and of course the only market for it.
> (Hodgskin 1827, 199–200)[12]

These practices emerged spontaneously "in every part of the civilized world, unwilled by the legislature and almost unknown to it." On the other hand,

> Governments have no commodities on the way to the market, which is the natural guarantee of all paper-money; they cannot be compelled to make payment, and they can know nothing of individuals, which knowledge is the only secure foundation for giving them credit.
> (Hodgskin 1827, 215).

Unlike Smith, Hodgskin did not even believe it was appropriate to limit the possibility of issuing low-denomination bank notes. *Popular Political Economy* was written before 1833 and the Bank Notes Act, which made Bank of England notes a legal tender everywhere but at the bank's counter where they could be redeemed, and the 1844 Bank Charter Act which expanded the exclusive issuing power of the Bank of England. However, it was written after the Country Bankers Act of 1826, which—following the scare of 1825—regulated the country banks and raised the lowest denomination banknotes from 1 to 5 pounds,[13] in addition to strengthening the prerogatives of the Bank of England. For Hodgskin,

> Whatever may have been the real object of the Acts of Parliament passed in the year 1826, to put a stop to the issuing of bank notes for one and two pounds, because Mr. Canning supposed, very ridiculously, that country bankers were usurping the king's prerogative of coining money, their effects have been to injure country and local banks, which are the best kind, and to augment the power of the Bank of England, which has already done inconceivable mischief. They are a direct violation of the principles of free trade, which the ministers profess; but as the Bank of England is under the control of government, those Acts have added to the power which it before possessed over the currency of the country. By tampering with it, the government has already inflicted vast misery on us, and no man can expect, from this added power, any other result than increased mischief.
>
> (Hodgskin 1827, 216)

These arguments stayed with Hodgskin a long time. Writing in 1864, he remarked that "the precious metals have been properly called natural money. They have been used ... universally for this purpose." But as "the government has taken on itself exclusively, in latter times, the whole business of coining," it started to play with weight and measurement as "the pound of silver has disappeared altogether, and in place of it is substituted a nominal pound,—sovereign,—which has the extraordinary weight of 123,274 grains of standard gold, the like to which there is nothing else in nature. Men worship it and commit idolatry." Such confusion was the product of "the legislature, which in this present century could adopt and maintain this ... almost absurd system of monies" (Hodgskin 1864, 2).

For Hodgskin, paper money was nothing but promissory notes and, therefore, it did not alter the monetary price. He thought that widespread use of banknotes was a development that was already taking place, therefore not to be meddled with:

> It is not a question of theory, whether paper can be substituted for gold and silver; it is not a proposed arrangement of some individuals, or of the legislature, to employ paper for metallic money; it is not a scheme of some hot-brained projector, but it is found in practice and by general agreement, that by far the greater number of exchanges can be and are actually made without using metallic money.
>
> (Hodsgkin 1827, 204)

The switch toward paper money is then, in itself, a spontaneous social evolution. If "[t]he quantity of money ... required at any time in society, depends on the quantity of business. ... [t]o keep money as much as possible steady in its value, the quantity should vary with the business to be done." This balancing process occurs naturally if the issuance of money is left to private institutions.

> As the rule, bankers only issue their notes by discounting bona fide commercial bills, which are the best possible data for judging of the quantity of business. The issue of bank notes varying with the amount of bills discounted, they being also in all cases returned to the banker, if he put too many in circulation, is, perhaps, the best method which can be imagined or devised to make the quantity of money in society vary with the quantity of business. Thus bank notes, when the issue of them is freely permitted, when no corporations are endowed by the legislature with exclusive privileges, when the issues of every banker are checked and controlled by the watchfulness of rival bankers, tend continually to prevent all those fluctuations in prices which are occasioned by alterations in the relation between the quantity of business to be transacted, and the quantity of money in circulation.
>
> (Hodgskin 1827, 210–211)

Here Hodgskin seems to endorse the so-called "real bills doctrine," namely, the theory that banks may properly create any quantity of bank notes and deposits so long as they create them only in exchange for real bills offered to them. Once again, Hodgskin followed Smith.[14] Real bills were "commercial IOUs, issued by a second firm in payment for material inputs received from a first firm higher in the structure of production, to be paid off with the proceeds of sales to a third firm lower in the structure." It was thought that, in this way, banknotes' issuance was going to be attuned with real output and demand for money. Yet, as White pointed out, proponents of such a view confused "the demand for bank notes and the demand for loanable funds." They assumed no excess of circulating banknotes was possible, because of the procedure whereby they were issued, but they disregarded that "the type of transactions by which notes are put into circulation is irrelevant to the question of whether the stock of notes is excessive" (White [1984] 1995, 121–122).

However, what Hodgskin seems most interested in emphasizing is that "the issues of every banker are checked and controlled by the watchfulness of rival bankers"; that is, competition by self-interested actors leads to a harmonious system. It is for this reason that there was no basic contradiction between a system based upon commodity-money, the value and quantity of which are regulated by "natural circumstances," and banknotes, whose quantity is likewise "determined by the number of exchanges to be made." Both things—the oscillations in price of scarce precious metals and the need to respond by issuing banknotes to the need for commercial credit—constituted the "natural" regulation of a sector that does not need external intervention. Credit operators have better information available than a central regulator will ever have. "Banking, however, let us never forget, with the issuing of bank notes, is altogether a private business, and no more needs to be regulated by meddling statesmen, than the business of paper making" (Hodgskin 1827, 218). The result of the division of work in this area appeared to Hodgskin as a thing of great charm and elegance, an authentic example of the degree of complexity that it could achieve.

Thus, in *Popular Political Economy* a contemporary reader can appreciate an admirable description of the London clearing house[15] as an example of a system based on an entirely private governance, yet perfectly able to perform such a vital function as offsetting the debtor and credit positions of the various banks.

Notes

1 In fact, we may say the first happened because of the second. If later "critics of free banking … have felt obliged to appeal to a country-banking mania to account for the events of 1825," they failed to appreciate the extent of the Bank of England's policies on country banks, which responded to an increase in the Bank of England's circulation (and hence the reserves of country banks) in the context of "a general plan for cheap money and credit expansion." See Selgin (1992, 179–180).
2 He is so considered by White ([1984] 1995, 64–65).
3 Yet, keeping in mind Hodgskin's distinction between social price and natural price,

> Money, as well as all the commodities of which it measures the value, are subject to variations in their natural price; and most commodities, including money, are unequally affected by social regulations. The money price of all commodities is consequently influenced by numerous circumstances; and it is by no means an easy task, as many people suppose, to detect the real cause of those variations in price which are of daily occurrence.
>
> (Hodgskin 1827, 234–235)

4 According to Smith, "Paper money may be so regulated as either to confine itself very much to the circulation between the different dealers, or to extend itself likewise to a great part of that between the dealers and the consumers." The first alternative is the desirable one, to reduce the risks of bankruptcy and fraud in society as a whole. If that means a limitation of economic freedom, Smith is willing to accept it because "those exertions of the natural liberty of a few individuals, which might endanger the security of the whole society, are, and ought to be, restrained by the laws of all governments" (Smith [1776] 1981, ii.ii, 94). On Smith's analysis of money and banks, see Rockoff (2013). For a riveting reconstruction of the evolution of Smith's ideas on the subject of banking regulation, in the wake of the bankruptcy of the Ayr Bank, see Goodspeed (2016) and West (1997).
5 It is perhaps excessively generous toward Hodgskin to find here a premonition of Menger's distinction between first-order goods and higher-order goods. See Menger ([1871] 2007, 51ff).
6 Whether the first coins were official private issues or not is still a matter of debate. For a useful review of such debate, see Selgin (2017).

7 In a harsh review of John Gray's (1799–1883) *Lectures on the Nature and Use of Money* in *the Economist*, Hodgskin stresses again how the adoption of gold and silver as standard preceded any legislation (Hodgskin 1848, 1058).
8 As eloquently put by Italian economist Francesco Ferrara (1873, 369):

> Does the State have any other office to be exercised on metallic money? Is the State its maker, perhaps? Do the metals of which the coin is made fall from the sky as a godsend? Is it the State that gives them value? Can the State (as it was once believed) increase, diminish, destroy, restore, this value at will? Does the State hand it out as if it was spring water? None of the above. The coin, which the State has manufactured, is a pure and simple commodity, which passes through his hands as every commodity passes through any hands.

9 "They have either mixed the precious metals with baser materials, or they have divided them into smaller pieces, certifying at the same time by their public seals, or by the busts of their chiefs, that the coin remained of the same value" (Hodgskin 1827, 192).
10 It is worth pointing out that

> While currencies were largely metallic, the potential gain from currency debasement was limited; debated coins would eventually circulate at a discount in comparison with full-bodied coins. Moreover, since taxes and other payments due to the sovereign were often fixed in nominal amount, the sovereign was likely to be a net monetary credit over a not-too-distant time horizon and would therefore have little incentive to create a prolonged inflation.
> (Glasner 1998, 37)

11 When, therefore, by the substitution of paper, the gold and silver necessary for circulation is reduced to, perhaps, a fifth part of the former quantity, if the value of only the greater part of the other four-fifths be added to the funds which are destined for the maintenance of industry, it must make a very considerable addition to the quantity of that industry, and, consequently, to the value of the annual produce of land and labour (Smith [1776] 1981, II.ii, 86).
12 The crucial and primal difference between promissory notes and banknotes is that, if banknotes are used, "he who will make the payment is the same person who promises it" (Ferrara 1873, 360).
13 As Kurt Schuler (2011) points out, one pound appears to be a very small amount today but, at the time, it could mean the equivalent of a two weeks' salary for a worker.
14 Smith has been seen as the "first thoroughgoing exponent of the Real Bills doctrine" (Mints 1945, 23).
15 In London there is a place called the Clearing House, at which the clerks of the different banking-houses meet at one specific time every day, to balance all accounts between these houses; and as almost all merchants and dealers of every description make all their payments by means of bills payable at some banker's, or by checks drawn on a banker; as they all have their money paid into a banker's, and as a considerable quantity of business originating in the country is transacted or settled for in town, not only by far the larger quantity of all the payments of every description arising from the trade of the metropolis, but also from the trade of a large part of the country, are made by the London bankers; the consequence is, that they have daily

immense sums to pay to each other. In 1810, according to evidence given before the Bullion Committee, the amount settled on ordinary days at the London Clearing House, between the different bankers, was at least five millions sterling; and on settling days, at the Stock Exchange, this amount was frequently fourteen millions. By means, however, of the clerks of the different banking-houses meeting at the Clearing House, and only paying the balance of their respective accounts, 220,000l. was the whole amount of money or bank notes required to pay the enormous sum of five millions sterling daily. The bankers of the metropolis are the agents for paying the greater part of the bills in circulation; so that, in fact, the chief money transactions of all England are settled by the insignificant sum just mentioned. Even this, it is supposed on good grounds, may and will be dispensed with. Such is a specimen of the natural and vast system of co-operating production; which, unknown and unmarked by us, is continually extended, and continually simplified. So much nonsense is spoken in Parliament, and written in the world at large, about bankers and bank notes, that it is right to add, that this beneficial simplification is the result of banking, and of employing commercial paper-money.

(Hodgskin 1827, 208–209)

References

Bagehot, Walter. 1873. *Lombard Street: A Description of the Money Market*. London: King.

Dimsdale, Nicholas H., and Anthony Hotson. 2014. "Financial Crisis and Economic Activity in the UK since 1825." In *British Financial Crises since 1825*. Edited by Nicholas H. Dimsdale and Anthony Hotson. Oxford: Oxford University Press, 9–23.

Ferrara, Francesco. 1873. "La questione de' banchi in Italia." *Nuova Antologia* 24 (October): 351–384.

Goodspeed, Tyler Beck. 2016. *Legislating Instability: Adam Smith, Free Banking, and the Financial Crisis of 1772*. Cambridge: Harvard University Press.

Glasner, David. 1998. "An Evolutionary Theory of the State Monopoly over Money." In *Money and the Nation State: The Financial Revolution, Government and the World Monetary System*. Edited by Kevin Dowd and Richard H. Timberlake. New Brunswick: Transaction, 21–45.

Hilton, Boyd. (1977) 1980. *Corn, Cash, Commerce: The Economic Policies of the Tory Governments 1815–1830*. Oxford: Oxford University Press.

Hodgskin, Thomas. 1826. "Effects of Repealing the Corn Laws. To the Editor of Trades' Newspaper and Mechanics' Weekly Journal." *The Trades' Newspaper, and Mechanics' Weekly Journal*, February 12.

Hodgskin, Thomas. 1827. *Popular Political Economy: Four Lectures Delivered at the Mechanics' Institution*. London: Tait.

Hodgskin, Thomas. 1832. *The Natural and Artificial Right of Property Contrasted: A Series of Letters, addressed without permission to H. Brougham, Esq. M.P. F.R.S.* London: B. Steil.

Hodgskin, Thomas. 1848. "Review of John Gray, Lectures on the Nature and Use of Money (Edinburgh: Adam and Charles Black)." *Economist*, September 16.

Hodgskin, Thomas. 1851. Review of *A Treatise on the Circumstance which Determine the Rate of Wages and the Condition of the Labouring Classes*. By J.R. McCulloch. *Economist*, December 27.

Hodgskin, Thomas. 1864. "Science-Counting, Measuring and Weighing." *Brighton Guardian*, April 20.

Kindleberger, Charles P. 1984. *A Financial History of Western Europe*. London: George Allen & Unwin.

Menger, Carl. (1871) 2007. *Principles of Economics*. Auburn: Ludwig Von Mises Institute.

Mints, Lloyd. 1945. *A History of Banking Theory in Great Britain and the United States*. Chicago: University of Chicago Press.

Neal, Larry. 1998. "The Financial Crisis of 1825 and the Restructuring of the British Financial System." *Federal Reserve Bank of St. Louis Review* 80 (3): 53–76, https://doi.org/10.20955/r.80.53-76.

Reinhart, Carmen M. and Kenneth S. Rogoff. 2009. *This Time Is Different: Eight Centuries of Financial Folly*. Princeton: Princeton University Press.

Ricardo, David (1824) 2004. "Plan for the Establishment of a National Bank." In *The Works and Correspondence of David Ricardo*. Edited by Piero Sraffa. Indianapolis, IN: Liberty Fund, 271–302.

Rockoff, Hugh. 2013. "Adam Smith on Money, Banking, and the Price Level." In *The Oxford Handbook of Adam Smith*. Edited by Christopher J. Berry, Maria Pia Paganelli, and Craig Smith. Oxford: Oxford University Press, 307–332.

Schuler, Kurt. 1992. "The World History of Free Banking: An Overview." In *The Experience of Free Banking*. Edited by Kevin Dowd. London: Routledge, 7–47.

Schuler, Kurt. 2011. "Sir Walter Scott, Advocate of Free Banking." *Alt-M*, http://www.alt-m.org/2011/06/10/sir-walter-scott-advocate-of-free-banking/.

Schwartz, Anna J. (1987) 2008. "Banking School, Currency School, Free Banking School." In *The New Palgrave Dictionary of Economic*. Edited by Steven N. Durlauf and Lawrence E. Blume. London: Palgrave Macmillan.

Selgin, George A. 1988. *The Theory of Free Banking: Money Supply under Competitive Note Issue*. London: Rowman & Littlefield.

Selgin, George A. 1992. "Bank Lending 'Manias' in Theory and History." *Journal of Financial Services Research* 6: 169–186, https://doi.org/10.1007/BF01046629.

Selgin, George A. 2017. "Lord Keynes' Contra White on the Beginnings of Coinage." *Alt-M*, https://www.alt-m.org/2017/08/30/lord-keynes-contra-white-on-the-beginnings-of-coinage/.

Smith, Adam. (1776) 1981. *An Inquiry into the Nature and Causes of the Wealth of Nations*, Vol. II. Edited by Roy H. Campbell and Andrew S. Skinner. Indianapolis, IN: Liberty Fund.

Smith, Vera C. (1936) 1990. *The Rationale of Central Banking and the Free Banking Alternative*. Indianapolis, IN: Liberty Fund.

Turgot, Anne Robert Jacques. (1766) 1785. *Reflections on the Formation and Distribution of Wealth*. London: Spragg.

West, Edwin G. 1997. "Adam Smith's Money and Banking Regulation: A Case of Inconsistency." *Journal of Money, Credit, and Banking* 29 (1):127–134, https://doi.org/10.2307/2953690.

White, Lawrence Henry. (1984) 1995. *Free Banking in Britain: Theory, Experience, and Debate, 1800–1845*. Cambridge: Cambridge University Press.

5 Between liberalism and anarchism

Private property, good and bad: Hodgskin as a Lockean

Thomas Hodgskin's political theory is based upon the assumption that political power is per se an instrument of domination—and that it is sought and defended precisely as such. Those who make laws, he writes, "appropriate wealth in order to secure power." The legislative classes are those "whose possessions depend not on nature, but on the law, perceiving that law alone guarantees and secures their possessions, and perceiving that government as the instrument for enforcing obedience to the law and thus for preserving their power and possessions" (Hodgskin 1832, 49).

These views, stated in *The Natural and Artificial Right of Property Contrasted* (1832), were also present, as we have seen, in Hodgskin's *Labour Defended* (1825). They stayed with him over the years, as he served as a parliamentary reporter for a number of papers and as a collaborator with the Hansard Parliamentary Debates. Exposure to parliamentary life did little to sweeten Hodgskin's tooth for politics.

The Natural and Artificial Right of Property Contrasted, published in 1832, was the third of his pamphlets and his true political manifesto. The book collects eight letters that he wrote in 1829 to Lord Brougham—the "parliamentary arm" of the philosophical radicals—and published "without his permission."[1] Only two years before, in 1830, Brougham had assumed the office of Lord Chancellor. This chapter will look more closely at that pamphlet as well as other articles that reflect his political philosophy.

As the title suggests, this work is a reflection on the right to property. Hodgskin distinguishes between a "natural" property right and an "artificial" one. This was not something unique to Hodgskin. "Work, industriousness, economy, skill, inspiration and all other similar qualities, exercised in an honourable and honest way, are the foundations of a description of property" wrote Percy Bysshe Shelley (1792–1822), who saw property as always linked to individual worth and endeavor (Shelley [1820] 1920, 60). In contrast, an "artificial" right to Shelley consisted of "concessions by the feudal lord, whose right on the property thus assigned was based on conquest or oppression." This entails a distinction between private property rights as they ought to be—emerging under "just" conditions—and property rights as they were legislated, so to say, by history.

Whereas Shelley was giving voice to his anarchist streak, Hodgskin was more interested in politics. The scope of his political aim is clearly revealed when one considers the public figure he chose as an opponent. Henry Brougham was not a conservative politician; on the contrary, he was a liberal reformer, one of the first "Edinburgh reviewers,"[2] an ambitious champion of the middle rank, a patron of universal education, "the tribune of the people, the scourge of the judges on the northern circuit and the most formidable debater in the House of Commons" (Stewart 1985, 1). While Brougham was not part of Jeremy Bentham's inner circle,[3] he was nonetheless sure that "The Age of Law Reform and the Age of Jeremy Bentham are one and the same" (Brougham 1838, 287).[4] As Albert V. Dicey ([1917] 2008, 120) wrote in a classic study, "when, for people of common sense and civic spirit it became obvious that law needed a radical reform, the reformers of the time felt the need for an ideal and a program. Both were provided by Bentham and his school." Brougham was a champion of these legal reforms.

Brougham's path had crossed Hodgskin's a few times. Brougham had participated in the birth of the Mechanics' Institute in London, backing the venture and including a liberal donation (Stewart 1985, 185). In 1826, he founded the Society for the Diffusion of Useful Knowledge, which sought to disseminate "useful knowledge" in the newly emerging classes through printing and distribution of low-cost publications. Recruited by James Mill, Hodgskin worked for the Society as a proofreader, but his employment quickly came to an end, in that period in which, as we saw, Hodgskin put some distance between himself and Francis Place and the Benthamites. If there was bad blood between Hodgskin and Brougham, however, it was mainly due to *The Rights of Industry, Capital and Labour*, the pamphlet written against *Labour Defended* and published by the "Society for the Diffusion of Useful Knowledge." Hodgskin thought Brougham himself was the author, even though it was actually written by its publisher, Charles Knight (Hodgskin 1832, 165–166).

It would be wrong, however, to consider *The Natural and Artificial Right of Property Contrasted* as the work of a man frustrated in his ambitions and therefore eager to get back at an estranged friend.[5] These letters affirm a philosophy. Hodgskin was targeting Benthamism, intending to reaffirm in its stead a liberalism of a Lockean inspiration, founded on natural law. Its interpretation of such natural law liberalism made him radically skeptical of any attempt to use political power to improve the condition of people's lives. In a sense, Hodgskin wanted to wage battle with reformist liberalism in the name of a radical *laissez-faire* approach.

The first battlefield where he sought his enemy was one that inspired the book's title: the nature of property. In this text, whatever people may have expected of the author of *Labour Defended*, Hodgskin takes care to emphasize that he favours the right of property, as long as it is the proper and right one. He distances himself from "individuals, such as Beccaria and Rousseau—and sects, some existing at present, such as Mr. Owen's cooperative societies, the Saint Simonians in France, and the Moravians, who have asserted that all the evils of society arise from a right of property, the utility of which they have accordingly and utterly denied" (Hodgskin 1832, 24). He wants to defend the right to property and, specifically, a theory of property rights akin to John Locke's, rooting them in natural laws.

> If ... I did not suppose, with Mr. Locke, that nature establishes such a right—if I were not prepared to shew that she not merely establishes, but also protects and preserves it, so far as never to suffer it to be violated with impunity—I should at once take refuge in Mr. Bentham's impious theory, and admit that the legislator who established and preserved a right of property, deserved little less adoration than the Divinity himself.
> (Hodgskin 1832, 24)

A government cannot establish "rights"; were it able to do so, it would be worthy of "adoration." But then those "rights" established by governments would not be worthy of the name. The fact that rights have their source in natural law is the cause of Hodgskin's skepticism toward government-made law. He wishes to make clear, "stronger than I think he [John Locke] has done, the fact, that, antecedently to all legislation, and to any possible interference by the legislator, nature establishes a law of appropriation by bestowing, as she creates individuality, the produce of labour on the labourer" (Hodgskin 1832, 28). Natural property therefore predates civil state and political decisions.

Calling on natural law to justify the right of property, however, requires an explanation of how an individual's property can come to be in a state of nature. As is well known, for John Locke (1632–1704) the model upon which every type of appropriation is designed is the ownership of land. If land has been given to all men communally, anything a single man "removes from the state in which nature has provided it and left it, anything to which he mixes his work, and to which he adds something of his own, by virtue of this becomes his property" (Locke [1688] 2014, 207).

For Hodgskin, too, "the occupation of land is the basis on which all other property rights are founded" (Hodgskin 1857, 5). His views are modelled on Locke's: in 1851, Hodgskin reviewed, in the *Economist*, Herbert Spencer's *Social Statics*. Spencer takes an anti-Lockean position. He considers the appropriation of the land a violation of the "law of equal freedom" and believes that "the right to use the land" can be guaranteed through a system of "rent" of the soil by individuals, while the whole nation would maintain the ownership (Hodgskin 1851, 115).[6] Hodgskin deeply admired the work of his younger colleague but on this subject he believed that Spencer's solution was "not at all satisfactory," falling into a "misunderstanding" that shows "a rather extraordinary inconsistency in a very logical author" (Hodgskin 1851, 120).[7] To attribute the land "to the collegial property of the communities, and to make it a monopoly of the nations" (Hodgskin 1832, 121) is a conceptual error to Hodgskin. "The author's mistake could stem from having confused the free use of the faculties of every individual with the free use of the land" (1832, 122). The source of property, for Hodgskin, remains self-ownership.

Like Locke, Hodgskin considered ownership legitimate because it develops out of self-ownership. There is a "natural right to property, founded on the fact that labor is necessary to produce whatever bears the name of wealth, which right of property exists, with all its consequences, like the principles from which it flows, at all times and places" (Hodgskin 1832, 40–41). That such natural property rights ought to be cogent is clear whenever "new wealth" is being created. The difference between the two kinds of property right is not chronological: the right of natural property does not concern resources appropriated at the dawn of history; the artificial property right has nothing to do with the more complex realities of modern society. In fact, the development of modern industry suggests that there must exist a natural relationship between the effort and initiative of individuals and their reward; this is because the alternative, a distribution of punishments and rewards by means of political power, could not guarantee the continuous creation of novelties by human beings.

> ... as new wealth is formed, and as labour multiplies the conveniences of life, mingling with all the things of creation, and modifying them so as to adapt them to the supply of our wants, a new relation between man and all surrounding objects is called into existence. As the legislator cannot beforehand provide means to secure the enjoyment of this new relation ... if nature did not at all times provide motives for respecting the new relation of man to the work of his hands, as it is continually called into existence by the creation of new wealth, society could not hold together.
> (Hodgskin 1832, 40)

Legislation cannot but appropriate things which are already in existence: it may fit, paradoxically, a "static" world, one without innovation. In contrast, novelties require a creative effort that can only come from individuals. The "true" right of property, the natural one, sets incentives that are vital in the case of new instruments and inventions being supplied. "The natural wants of man, particularly of food and clothing, are the natural stimulus to exert this power; and the means of gratifying them, which it provides, is the natural reward of the exertion" (Hodgskin 1832, 27). Hodgskin does not deny that, in a natural state, "a savage, stronger than the labourer or more cunning, may undoubtedly take the fruit of his industry from him by force or fraud." But he thinks that, more often than not, things are going to end quite differently:

> Nature creates the majority of individuals nearly equal in bodily strength, skill, and capacity, and gives to all nearly the same facilities for acquiring knowledge; and thus, making it generally more difficult and dangerous to take from another, than for each, by his labour, to provide for himself, she creates in all men motives to respect that right of property which she, by bestowing on labour all its produce, everywhere establishes, and everywhere makes known.
> (Hodgskin 1832, 30)

In his book *The Word BELIEF*, Hodgskin explains that "all our states of consciousness ... proceed ... in as certain a succession, and follow as regular laws, though, on account of their multiplicity and complexity, that succession and these laws have not in all cases yet been traced, as any of the physiological phenomena of our bodies" (Hodgskin 1827a, 46). Hodgskin was, like Locke, a sensualist: sensorial data, appropriately mediated by the process of association, constitute the contents of individual knowledge.

In *The Natural and the Artificial Right of Property Contrasted*, Hodgskin cites Locke's Second Treatise of Government on the limits to the process of appropriation in the state of nature: "As much land as a man tills, sows, improves, cultivates and can use the products of, so much is his property" (Locke, [1688] 2014, 208). Also, Locke writes:

> The measure of property Nature has well set, by the extent of men's labour and the conveniency of life. No man's labour could subdue or appropriate all, nor could his enjoyment consume more than a small part; so that it was impossible for any man, this way, to entrench upon the right of another or acquire to himself a property to the prejudice of his neighbour, who would still have room for as good and as large a possession (after the other had taken out his) as before it was appropriated.
>
> ([1688] 2014, 210)

In actual history, however, appropriation took place in other ways than those outlined by Locke. Not by chance, one of the most relevant political myths in the history of English radicalism is the "Norman Yoke."[8] It can be summarized as follows: before 1066, the Anglo-Saxons lived as free citizens and governed themselves through representative institutions. The Norman conquest deprived them of their freedom, reducing them to mere subjects. Along with the conquest came a redistribution of land that delivered England into the hands of a few big landowners. All concessions, starting with the Magna Carta, painfully obtained from the heirs of the ancient oppressors, have only partially restored that original state of freedom. As Luigi Marco Bassani (2002, 55) explained, "this metahistorical theory ... also had a clear purpose inspired by the principles of natural law: the free Saxons were men endowed with all their rights, lived in equality and freedom; while since the era of the Norman conquest there had been a continuous decline in the Saxon state of natural freedom."

Big landowners are considered the last beneficiaries of the ancient Norman conquest. But whatever the amount of historical truth in the notion of a "Norman yoke," it is apparent that the existing distribution of property rights in land is often intertwined with political decisions. Hence the necessity of a historical account to amend the more theoretical, Lockean view of how property comes to be. We may say that, if Hodgskin's theory of ownership is the same as Locke's, the history of property he refers to comes from the Scottish Enlightenment thinkers—and, more precisely, from their stadial theory of history.[9] From this theory, Hodgskin borrows the idea not only that the unintended consequences of intentional actions can be socially beneficial but that the evolution of commercial relations and modes of production can produce "progress" even in political institutions.[10]

A most relevant treatment of how landownership and the evolution of political institutions interact is offered by Smith in the third book of the *Wealth of Nations*. The concentration of land ownership, for Smith, could be traced back to "when the German and Scythian nations overran the western provinces of the Roman empire" (Smith (1776) 1981, III.ii 509). Then "the chiefs and principal leaders of those nations acquired or usurped to themselves the greater part of the lands of those countries. A great part of them was uncultivated; but no part of them, whether cultivated or uncultivated, was left without a proprietor. All of them were engrossed, and the greater part by a few great proprietors."

So far as land is considered not just a mere factor of production but also a strategic element to preserve power and ensure protection from possible enemies, a peculiar practice for inheritance prevails: "The law of primogeniture ... came to take place ... for the same reason that it has generally taken place in that of monarchies, though not always at their first institution. That the power, and consequently the security of the monarchy, may not be weakened by division, it must descend entire to one of the children" (Smith (1776) 1981, III.ii, 509).

From the law of primogeniture logically descends the practice of the entail: both help the ruling classes keep their hold on land rent. For Smith, "When great landed estates were a sort of principalities, entails might not be unreasonable."[11] Not so much in the modern era:

> They are founded upon the most absurd of all suppositions, the supposition that every successive generation of men have not an equal right to the earth, and to all that it possesses; but that the property of the present generation should be restrained and regulated according to the fancy of those who died perhaps five hundred years ago.
> (Smith [1776] 1981, III.ii, 511–512)

The issue of inheritance law is of crucial importance. It is indeed central in the argument against artificial law established by the ruling classes for their own benefit. In the *Letters of Sydney*, generally attributed to John Millar (1735–1801), we read that

> Not satisfied with directing the disposal of land after their decease, some have aimed at perpetuating their power, by preventing their successors from alienating the estate, or from changing a long line of succession which they chose to appoint. Nothing can be more absurd; a dead man cannot for ever retain the right of property, which, from its own nature, must be as fully vested in the present possessor, as it was in those who preceded him.
> (Millar 1796, 224)

It is thus easy for Hodgskin to deduce that "primogeniture and entails, cherished by all the legislating classes of Europe, were intended to preserve landed estates entire" (Hodgskin 1832, 81). This attempt to protect the rulers' properties, he acknowledges, has been "thwarted" (ibid.) since, over time, both small and large estates have been eroded in size. This happened, in Hodgskin's view, because that "artificial" appropriation of land (i.e., obtained not through work but through violence, albeit "legal") proved to be anachronistic.[12]

If the concentration of properties occurred, à la Smith, because of the need to defend them, yet it did not positively affect the land's economic performance. Indeed, big estates "are, almost in every case, worse cultivated than the surrounding country" (Millar 1796, 174). Smith noted that "To improve land with profit, like all other commercial projects, requires an exact attention to small savings and small gains, of which a man born to a great fortune, even though naturally frugal, is very seldom capable. The situation of such a person naturally disposes him to attend rather to ornament which pleases his fancy than to profit for which he has so little occasion" (Smith [1776] 1981, III.ii 512–513). Similarly, for Hodgskin the parcelling of lands would have a specific rationale linked to the increasing productivity that the middle classes, being able to acquire legitimate titles of land ownership too, would accomplish. A more productive agriculture "consumes" less land and, conversely: having smaller plots available compels them to innovate.[13]

Against "scientific" government

Hodgskin's anti-utilitarianism is by and large an assault on the idea that attempts to achieve a better government are useful. Indeed, as Alexander Gray (1882–1968) pointed out, Hodgskin "has the liberal distrust of the State, which in the anarchist becomes an obsession" (Gray 1946, 278). This radical skepticism stops a step shy of openly advocating the extinction of the state. Hodgskin does not advocate it because everything in his thinking leads him to be wary of those who come up with detailed recipes and, on the contrary, to trust in the autonomous, spontaneous development of society.[14] At the inn of the future, Hodgskin does not even order a beer.

Written before *The Natural and Artificial Right of Property Contrasted*, Hodgskin's *Travels in the North of Germany* are a treasure trove of comments on German political institutions. While Hodgskin writes widely on German society, he frequently makes points that have political implications. These points will later reverberate in his political philosophy. Consider how Hodgskin describes Prussian provincial governments:

> They are what may be called *scientific* governments [emphasis added], in which a unity of design and of purpose pervades the whole.... The powers of these provincial governments extend to every thing that can well be subjected to regulation; and they issue, in consequence, an abundance of orders. I have seen directions from them for the people to kill sparrows, how many pigeons

a man may keep, not to steal trees, to preserve deer, forbidding straw to be exported out of the province; they order midwives to be placed, and sworn in faithfully to discharge their duties; they fix the sum to be given them for their service; they tell the farmers they ought to extirpate weeds; they direct agricultural operations; they ascertain the yearly produce of the land, that measures may be taken, in time, to prevent famine.

(Hodgskin 1820b, I, 388)

The ambition of "scientific knowledge" for Hodgskin reveals the ruling classes' presumption of knowing too much. Eventually, it will lead them to act on the basis of contingent and imperfect knowledge, jeopardizing the future development of society. This problem lies at the core of Hodgskin's criticism of governments as institutions: they are faulty, imperfect, and ultimately irreformable, whatever "science" you may apply to them.

Again in the *Travels*, he comments that

Creating a legislative assembly presupposes the need to make laws, and encourages that desire to legislate that has already proved to be a source of many evils. ... The doctrines of political economy have taught us that there are laws of nature that eminently produce prosperity.

(Hodgskin 1820b, I, 464)

For Hodgskin (1820b II, 98), "the evils of society cannot be remedied by acts of parliament." His polemic against utilitarianism boils down to this: he sees as fundamentally unrealistic, if not altogether utopian, to imagine that whatever mischief is made by legislation can be amended using the very same means. In a sense, Hodgskin is bringing the concept of self-interest into political analysis, assuming that political actors are uniformly led by their immediate interest rather than allegiance to grander principles. For this reason, he sees "the first and chief object proposed [by these political actors] is to preserve the unconstrained dominion of the law over the minds and bodies of mankind .... No misery indeed is deemed too high a price to pay for his supremacy, and for the quiet submission of the people" (Hodgskin 1832, 44).

Some thirty-five years after the publication of the *Travels*, the 71-year-old Hodgskin gave two lectures on crime, in which—thanks to a meticulous knowledge of crime and conviction statistics that he carefully gleaned from the *Economist*—he argued that a spirit of emulation for the well-to-do classes pushes the poor to commit crimes against property. The fact that those at the top of the social pyramid can acquire resources by taxing all others pushes those at the bottom to resort to the "taxation of the poor," i.e., theft. At the end of the second lecture Hodgskin announced that he was preparing to publish a *Demonstration of the Absurdity of the Legislation* (Hodgskin 1857, 26). This work never saw the light of day, even though Hodgskin kept actively writing for another eleven years. And yet we can say that such logical demonstration is actually the intellectual workshop of a lifetime.

His total distrust of the mere possibility of any positive legislative development explains why Hodgskin was so inimical to the utilitarians. In a rush of intellectual emancipation from the dogmas of the past, the utilitarians denied the doctrine of natural rights (rights are only positive, i.e., the product of legislative action) and aimed to use the tools of legislation to achieve the political goals of radicalism. For them, the pursuit of happiness by every individual in the absence of government can only result in mutual attempts at subjugation. The fact that we have rights, that is, freedoms for some that are configured as duties for others, is only possible in the presence of an overarching political entity, i.e., a figure capable of governing the relationship between individuals according to criteria of certainty.

This distrust of a central authority does not imply an appreciation for customary law, rather than "rational" legislation. Both are totally alien to Hodgskin. If the utilitarians insist on codifying norms and producing good legislative initiatives—not least because "the conjunction of the theory of natural rights with the tradition of common law represents for them the constitution of a conservative" block, "both cultural and political" (Hodgskin 1832, 137)— Hodgskin interprets the authentic theory of natural rights as an eminently acceptable alternative to the status quo. In this scheme, common law is sometimes put on the same level as legislation, as a simple instrument of domination. He informs us that "Numberless are the statutes and the decisions at common law, having the force of statutes, intended solely to secure [the] rights and privileges" of the ruling classes (51). The judges are considered integral parts of that "great evil" that is the government (156).

Indeed, precisely from the fact that "our judges having worked out a system, by deciding cases as they were brought before them, partly following previous decisions, and partly straining them to meet, according to their ideas, the equity of each particular case," he infers "that our laws have not created the right of property such as it is, which now exists among us; they have followed, and followed with a very lingering pace, and at a great distance, the various slow and successive improvements which intervened between the first appropriation of the land, and our present right of property" (Hodgskin 1832, 127–128). Hodgskin willingly admits that there exist "discrepancies between the law relating to property, ... and the actual right of property," but he rejects the idea that anything good could come from the parliamentary committees gathered to mend the laws:

> it would be more rational for your commissioners, first of all to enquire into the rights which now exist, not in law books, but among the people, and to ascertain, from the alterations which have taken place in past times, what the future alterations are likely to be; and finally, to try and adapt the law, so as to make it oppose as few impediments as possible, to the bringing about the results ordained by nature, in gradually restoring the natural right of property.
>
> (Hodgskin 1832, 129)

In other words, the only space for legitimate and useful legal intervention is that which consists in repealing existing interventions, making room for spontaneous, societal developments.

This is of particular relevance when dealing with the government of the economic realm. Hodgskin's criticism of utilitarians was by and large a critique of all those who "brought economic policy into Parliament." Hodgskin, who certainly knew them in his years doing parliamentary reporting, is willing to recognize their effort "to replace their imperfect knowledge, as a basis for legislation, with the even more imperfect knowledge … of previous legislators" (Hodgskin 1827b, 40). Yet, as we saw in chapter 3, for him political economy must seek to discover laws of a very general nature; it cannot respond to particular questions, specific to the particular circumstances of time and place in which production takes place. Government intervention can only worsen the allocation of resources in society, both because it is inevitably a self-interested intervention, which therefore benefits the ruling classes,[15] and because it can only be based on partial and incomplete information.

For the Utilitarians, "the rationalization of society as a function of the progressive improvement of the conditions of its members cannot be a spontaneous, evolutionary process, but appears in the form of a re-establishment and makes institutional planning necessary" (Di Sciullo 2004, 57). Hodgskin stands on the other side of the barricade: he thinks that the progressive improvement of the conditions of the members of society can only be the result of a spontaneous process.

Public opinion and the middle classes

The best that formal law can do, therefore, is not to intrude or prevent the spontaneous evolution of social behavior and institutions. In a sense, anarchism here encounters conservatism in the sense that, since legislation is considered a means that cannot be used to improve society, one finds itself close to the option of doing nothing. Indeed, Hodgskin quotes Edmund Burke (1729–1797) approvingly:

> When the legislature fulfils its functions in the best possible manner, it only embodies the customs of the community in a legal and precise form of words, lending the sanction of its clear and delightful phraseology to the opinions and rights already existing among its subjects. "In reality the real purpose of legislative power is to follow the public inclination without forcing it," is the accurate definition of legislation, given by Mr. Burke, "give orientation, form, technical capacity and specific sanction to the general feeling of the community. When it goes beyond it, its authority becomes precarious, regardless of its rights."
>
> (Hodgskin 1832, 113)[16]

The reference to the "public inclination" makes it clear that Hodgskin is thinking of a different agent for reform in society than government: namely, public opinion.

Public opinion, a concept of paramount importance in nineteenth-century liberalism, reflects shared ideas and points of view that freely evolve within society. This evolution makes it difficult to clearly define public opinion. While "underlying the shared reverence for 'public opinion' was a struggle between its competing appropriations by the contending political camps" (Wahrman 1995, 195) classical liberals tended to assume that it overlapped with the judgment of the middle classes. So did James Mill, who maintained that "the middle rank ... is that portion of the community of which, if the basis of Representation were ever so far extended, the opinion would ultimately decide" (Mill [1823] 1992, 41). As noted by Alan S. Kahan (2003, 85), "The 1830s and 1840s ... was a period when class-oriented, especially middle-class-oriented language flourished throughout Europe." The middle class was not necessarily defined by income or capital, but by "practicing a certain lifestyle, acquiring and displaying certain moral values" (166). Given such values, which sharply distinguish them from the landed classes but elevate them above the working classes, the middle ranks can be understood as speaking for the common interests of society against the exclusive class interest of the ruling aristocracy.

Deirdre McCloskey[17] associated the emergence of global economic growth with a "Bourgeois Revaluation," that, is a growing appreciation of mercantile and artisanal professions, which little by little begin to be seen as honorable endeavors. Such a phenomenon sees the bourgeoisie come on the stage with a strong cultural identity, associated with values such as progress, desert, self-reliance. Historian Henry Thomas Buckle (1821–1862), a paragon of Victorian liberalism, spoke in similar terms of the emergence of "a middle or intellectual class" that did not fancy itself busy with "war or theology." The activity of such persons

> was turned against the abuses of government, and caused a series of rebellions, from which hardly any part of Europe escaped; and finally, that in the eighteenth and nineteenth centuries, it has extended its aim to every department of public and private life, diffusing education, teaching legislators, controlling kings, and, above all, settling on a sure foundation that supremacy of Public Opinion, to which not only constitutional princes, but even the most despotic sovereigns, are now rendered strictly amenable.
> (Buckle [1857] 2011, 189–109)

That public opinion was stronger in a society with a growing and more robust middle class was a concept dear also to William A. Mackinnon (1784–1870), author of the first work featuring the words "Public Opinion" in its title. Mackinnon argued that public opinion and civilization "depended on each other" and that the former was strong and rooted where there was not an excessive imbalance between classes. Unlike the uproar of crowds, public opinion needs adequate means to be spread, and genuine knowledge, pondered by experts. Mackinnon ([1846] 1849, I, 8) defines public opinion as "the idea that, on a certain subject, belongs to the best informed, most intelligent and moral people: such idea is gradually understood and spread among people, who adopt it as their own feeling."[18] It is strengthened in the most technologically advanced societies, which allow both the formation of a robust middle class and a more fluid circulation of information. Indeed, the presence "of a large, well-educated and prosperous middle class, together with a free press and popular education" were seen as "sufficient guarantees" of the political influence of the middle ranks (Fontana 1985, 43).

This does not mean that public opinion was without its enemies. Public battles—"parliamentary reform, free trade, and dissent" (Hollis 1974, 12)—were controversial and challenged the position of the ruling class. Furthermore, the very idea of members of society petitioning Parliament seemed to challenge the latter's role: at the beginning of the century, public opinion was deemed as "illegitimate, unnecessary or both" but later became "a necessary tool of social reform, a necessary aid to government, evidence of healthy public concern" (26). With the benefit of hindsight, in 1867 William Gladstone could indeed recognize that "'agencies out of doors' ... formed and matured public opinion, and were therefore 'the legitimate expressions of the people, by which bad legislation is to be corrected'" (Hansard 1867, as quoted in Hollis 1974, 5). One generation earlier, a parliamentarian's view of, say, the Anti-Corn Law League would have been less positive and the parliamentarian more irritated.

Perhaps not unsurprisingly for a man whose professional life was journalism during the heyday of political gazettes, Hodgskin (1832, 110[fn]) makes public opinion the only legislator he is willing to accept. He considers it an effective means of exercising control over governments' action—and, in the longer term, of doing away with governments at all. The idea that public opinion was to keep abuse in check was broadly shared. As Patricia Hollis observed, reformers "were not reluctant to use large language," invoking "the language of sin, of the identity of public and private morality"—"whatever was morally wrong could not of course be politically right" (Hollis 1974, 7). This point—the rejection of a double standard applying different principles to those in government and to the governed—is a central theme for Hodgskin. Public opinion, he writes, "not the judges, conferred on the press its rights and privileges; and public opinion, against the inclination of the judges, continually maintains and extends them" (Hodgskin 1832, 111). It therefore appears as the whole of the convictions of those who live in a certain political community, and therefore it makes the "rights" of their neighbors cogent, recognizing them spontaneously. The principles of natural law are bonded with those of mutual consent by virtue of the very nature of social order, which for our author means "the vast scheme of social production, mutual dependence, and mutual service, which grows out of the division of labour," which "precedes all the plans of the legislator, to regulate or preserve it" (77). This view of an intricate and never-ending fabric of *mores* and mutually agreed upon views and norms reminds us of a story by Jorge Luis Borges (1899–1986) in which the utopian project of a world parliament goes awry. Yet its supporters realize that "The Parliament of the World began with the first moment of the world and it will go on when we are dust. There's no place on Earth where it does not exist" (Borges [1975] 1977, 47).

That public opinion is the instrument best suited for a context marked by a growing middle class is particularly clear in some articles that Hodgskin wrote for the *Brighton Guardian*. These articles were written in the 1860s, twenty years after the repeal of the corn laws. The new classes had gradually gained ground: in 1867 Disraeli promoted the second Reform Act, which further expanded suffrage by extending it to artisans and skilled workers. Some of the battles to break the grip of the aristocracy had been won, but they coincided with that "spirit of reform" so dear to radical philosophers, determined as they were to use law as a lever for social advancement. That, in Hodgskin's vision, was an illusion destined to be shattered.

He noticed that "Of late years the middle classes have been gaining influence over legislation" but he points out that [if] "we put out of view the abolition of some old and notoriously mischievous laws—such as the Corn and Navigation laws—modern legislation is by no means creditable to the middle classes" (Hodgskin 1865b). In principle, Hodgskin struggled to accept the idea that a particular class may be more circumspect and able to legislate for the whole social body. If indeed "in our time it is very much the custom, because the Government has been occasionally forced into a right path by the popular action, to ascribe most of its acts, particularly war, to the influence of the people, [nonetheless] the people, whether middle or lower classes, are not made wise by sharing in the power of the Government" (Hodgskin 1865a).[19]

Nonetheless, the arrival of the middle classes on the scene is in itself positive for an economic reason. The rise of the middle classes, in fact, provides a hint to answer the question "how can the multitude be raised to comparative opulence?" (Hodgskin 1863, 2). Historically, "the burgher class ... practising new and improved arts, taught them to the serfs whom they invited or rescued from the dominion of the feudal lords" (2). The bourgeoisie create new knowledge and develop new ideas and modes of production which they then hand on to their subordinates, but above all they determine, with the increasingly important role played by exchanges, a growing division of labor. Such "progress" puts the old aristocracies into crisis. The middle classes rose with the emergence of the mercantile spirit, which "pervades in some degree all orders and ranks and by the influence of habit and example it is communicated, more or less, to every member of the community" (Millar 1818, II, 777).[20]

It is precisely in this diffusion of the mercantile spirit that the germs of freedom reside. The progress of the division of labor means that people are driven "to acquire expertise in particular trades and professions and, instead of becoming employees of someone, find it more profitable to work on their own and sell the product of their work" (Millar 1771, 237). In doing so, John Millar explains, a widespread sense of independence develops and, with it, a sort of "jealousy of freedom."[21]

> The more a nation progresses in wealth and refinement of customs, the more it has the opportunity to employ a greater number of merchants, traders and artisans and, as people belonging to the humblest classes come to find themselves in a position of greater independence on the financial level, they begin to experience those feelings of freedom that are natural to the human soul and that only need can suppress. Having less need of the favour and protection of the powerful, these classes no longer need to care to obtain them, therefore their dedication is directed, mainly, to acquire the professional qualities useful in the practice of their trade. The ideas that they had formed during their primitive servile status are consequently gradually forgotten, giving way to habits of different kinds.
>
> (Millar 1771, 237)

Hodgskin likewise enthusiastically saluted the achievements of the middle classes and, in particular, all those political upheavals that seemed to question the old European order. The attitude initially taken by the paper he edited in 1848, the *London Telegraph*, toward the events in France is particularly significant. Hodgskin, by then a fully mature journalist and no longer a political activist with literary aspirations as he had been during his stint at *The Chemist*, was the paper's editor-in-chief and on page two commented on current events.

The *London Telegraph* lasted but a few months; it was, however, 1848, and there was nothing better than the revolutionary trends all over Europe to rekindle Hodgskin's hopes, convinced as he was that the era in which people are governed "by the cat-o'-nine-tails and the gallows" (Hodgskin 1848e, 2) was coming to an end. Since the revolt in Palermo, in January, the year was shaping up to be a particularly turbulent one. And if the young Marx and Engels traveled across Europe to stoke the revolutionary flames as best as they could, in London the sixty-something Hodgskin was perfectly up to date with what was happening on the continent. Reading these articles today reveals the reaction of an author whose liberalism was tinged with anarchic strokes, but who nonetheless was part of the liberal philosophical tradition and looked suspiciously on any attempt at steering the economy in a more public direction.

In particular, the *London Telegraph* immediately considered the revolution in France the first step toward a future of freedom throughout Europe, and toward the total collapse of political regimes based on the power of the aristocracy and on the extensive use of coercion. For Hodgskin, François Guizot (1787–1874), the historian turned prime minister of Orléanist France, "is an honest believer, like the great majority of Europe, in the virtue and necessity of a coercive and what is called a paternal government." He was "at once a great historian, a great philosopher, and a great minister. But the system he undertook to guide, we must say, in spite of the majority of Europe, is founded in error" (Hodgskin 1848b, 2). Louis Philippe's France was the domino piece that, with its own collapse, would bring down all the other European states:

"The greatest revolution of our time, the overthrow of the whole system of government, founded on coercion, has been more completely and suddenly accomplished than we ventured yesterday to hope" (Hodgskin 1848a, 2).

The tone of the *London Telegraph* changed with the passing of time, alternating a general support for the French attempt and much admiration for leaders such as Lamartine with a certain skepticism about specific initiatives as the newly proclaimed republic began to legislate. On the urging of Louis Blanc (1811–1882), on February 25th the provisional government committed itself to "guaranteeing the existence of labourers through labour" and allowed the establishment of the *ateliers nationaux*, public workshops. The aim was to reabsorb the idle and restive labor force through large public works and infrastructure.[22] In the words of a scholar who was not without sympathy for the attempt:

> The scheme had been conceived as "true socialism" in action with male residents of Paris offered either decently paid, public works-style jobs or generous unemployment benefit. But the result was that tens of thousands of workers, idlers and chancers and opportunists moved to Paris hoping to profit from this gigantic system of out relief, while furious private employers had to hike wages to compete.
>
> (Hunt 2010, 63)

Blanc became Hodgskin's *bête noire*. Hodgskin's criticism of Blanc concerned matters of political economy: he urged the French revolutionaries to reread the works of Say and Bastiat, the great French masters who should have inspired their actions.[23] He was well aware that, in 1848, "the hungry belly is the most furious and invincible of democrats" (Hodgskin 1848f, 2), but not all the answers to the rightful resentment of the workers were equally acceptable.

In particular, Hodgskin wrote on March 16, Louis Blanc's decrees "concerning labour are complete violations of individual liberty." If "laws have been formerly made in order to give advantage, to masters and employers," that does not mean that "they should now be made to confer an advantage on workmen. That is class legislation." Blanc's experiment is juxtaposed to the corn laws, of all things, established to "enrich the landed aristocracy" and whose effect was to expose landowners to general hatred, since it put them "in the invidious position of limiting the food of the people." It is understandable, Hodgskin noted, that a revolution

> which was made in great part by, and for the workmen, should confer advantages on them [but] that it may work to their advantage, it must not begin by confiscating the property of employers, and by laying restrictions on their honest and honourable industry. The mischievous industry which requires to be checked and frowned down is unnecessary legislative interference with the rights of individuals.
>
> (1848c, 2)

In the ateliers so dear to Blanc, Hodgskin insightfully noticed not a "syndicalist" system of popular participation in company management, but an attempt to "lay down the rule that it is the duty of the bureaucracy to find employment and wages for all the children that are born; but every person who has examined the subject ridicules such as pretentious, and knows that the bureaucracy cannot be more than such as a task" (1848g, 2).

The opening of public workshops presupposed a scheme in which the state would be the one "to take care of everything." Blanc "deals with human beings as if Nature had made no difference betwixt them, and they were all to be modelled by the ideas of one Louis Blanc" (Hodgskin 1848i, 2). For Hodgskin, it was a matter of fact that "Monsieur Louis Blanc will soon have to give it up, acknowledge that social order is not provided for by it; and if provided for at all, must be by a far higher power than bureaucracy" (1848g, 2). "LouisBlancism" became synonymous with interventionism. The *London Telegraph* came to accuse the conservative *Times of London* of the same sin, when it also did "demand that the state will provide for the destitute people."

Upon learning that Lamartine (1790–1869), on the occasion of a meeting with the Société d'Economie Politique, had declared that democratic institutions would have to change the face of political economy, making it the "science of fraternity," Hodgskin's reaction was utter outrage:

> This assumption of power in the democratic republic, to make a science different from what it is, that is, to alter and change the laws of nature which the scientific men attempt to explain and expound—appears to us the most extraordinary instance of ignorance and assumption in a public man we have ever met with.
>
> (Hodgskin 1848h)[24]

To those who argued that political economy was not a political science, it is understandable that the very idea of a "Ministry of Labour" (another of Blanc's proposals) would sound shocking.

The controversy against the ateliers and Blanc did not exhaust the extent of Hodgskin's criticism of the revolution in France, which, for example, also involved issues of a monetary nature.[25] In June, he took some rather surprising stances (1848k, 2). He justified the new insurrection ("The horrible scenes therefore now taking place in Paris are less the consequence of the overthrow of the monarchy than of the perverted education the people received under that and the empire") but, most of all, he chastised Lamartine's attempt to leave Louis Napoleon out of the Parliament. "Were Louis Napoleon allowed to take his seat in the Assembly, that a fortnight would suffice to extinguish him: now he will be made of importance … and the proscription of the man … will be a fatal blow to the peace of France" (Hodgskin 1848j, 2).

Hodgskin's radicalism had been tempered by his long experience as a parliamentary reporter: he knew how to be suddenly reflective, and above all he never lost sight of the long-term objectives. This is why he prophesied—correctly—that any attempt to keep the future Napoleon III at bay could only strengthen him. That is why he saluted the victory of moderates in the elections: once again, two cheers for the middle classes. A socialist breakthrough would reveal a form of "class government" of one class in spite of the other and, at the same time, would frighten the rest of society, strengthening the enemies of the middle classes; in other words, consolidating the old powers.

The middle classes were valuable, in Hodgskin's eyes, for what they represented about social progress, and their political position was in some ways a consequence of that.

> In natural society—society depending on mutual help and the division of labour in which all share and by which all profit—no classes have adverse interests; but in political society, founded on the rule of one or a few over the many, the middle classes have interests adverse to those both above and below them.
>
> (Hodgskin 1848m)

Hodgskin crushed the very idea of a political "mediation" between the different social demands. It is very clear where he traced the line: everything that is by voluntary agreement, "natural society," which depends on mutual agreement and the division of labor, is legitimate and potentially produces harmonious outcomes. To damage society by an intervention "external" to the society itself, by decisions that are independent of the mutual agreement between individuals and are artificially imposed from above, is inevitably a harbinger of imbalances and injustices. Such is the lesson that he drew from his familiarity with political economy, and on the basis of which he endeavored to analyze political facts. An article from September 1848, published in the *Economist* and which we should certainly attribute to Hodgskin, reminded the French interim government that

> Liberty is the sum and substance of all the deductions of political economy. ... The science is slowly assented to by statesmen of the old school, precisely because it is the science of liberty, demonstrating, in opposition to the host of theories and a multitude of assumptions, not only that individuals may be entrusted with freedom, and the state be safe, but that by which there can be no safety. Thus the science of wealth, which the ignorant men in Paris are to put down in the name of liberty, is empathically the science of liberty.
>
> (Hodgskin 1848m)

On the basis of these principles, in 1825 Hodgskin had defended the workers' freedom of association. Later, on the same premises, he championed the freedom of contract of the bourgeoisie.

Notes

1 This Hodgskin makes clear in the subtitle: *A Series of Letters, addressed without permission, to H. Brougham, Esq. M.R.F.R.S. &c. (now the Lord Chancellor) by the Author of "Labour Defended Against the Claims of Capital."*
2 But Walter Bagehot ([1855] 1879, 40) remarked, "He [Brougham] was connected with the Whigs, but he never was one. His impulsive ardour is the opposite of their coolness; his irregular, discursive intellect contrasts with their quiet and perfecting mind."
3 According to Robert Stewart (1985, 89), "Brougham's amour propre would not suffer him to accept the fawning attendance which Bentham asked of his acolytes."
4 The relationship between Brougham and Bentham was actually complex. See Stephen (1900, 225–227).
5 Stack (1998, 138–155) examines the hypothesis in detail, situating it in the context of Hodgskin's passage from radical pamphlets to Whig journalism, but he believes it is difficult to imagine any implied malice on Hodgskin's behalf.
6 On the issue of Spencer's approach to the property in land, see Mingardi (2007).
7 It is a bit paradoxical that a thinker of Hillel Steiner's insight has suggested that young Spencer would support the nationalization of land, "strongly influenced by Thomas Hodgskin" (Steiner 1981, 561).
8 A priceless analysis of the various forms assumed by the political myth of the "Norman yoke" can be found in Hill (1954).
9 Hodgskin himself wrote to Francis Place (1820): "I therefore looked at Hume's History of England, Robertson's Charles V, Millar's Historical View, Kames' Sketches, Adam Smith, and so on, and all of them admit that almost all of Europe was formerly cultivated by servants."
10 "The four-stage theory, at least at the beginning of his career, usually took the form of a development theory that incorporated the idea of some kind of 'natural' or 'normal' movement through different modes of subsistence" (Meek 2011, 173).
11 In contrast, in Millar's *Letters of Sydney*, we read that "No possible reason can be assigned why the firstborn should succeed to a greater portion than his brothers, far less why he should altogether exclude them from the inheritance" (Millar 1796, 59).
12 This does not mean at all that Hodgskin's fight against primogeniture was fruitless, especially if we bear in mind that in those years "primogeniture found renewed favour with a few political economists who were more concerned with the dangers of redistribution than with inefficient landowners. Malthus, for example, defended primogeniture and entail" (Horne 1990, 173).
13 As Pacheco (1990, 141) notes, Hodgskin imagines a distribution of land made of smaller plots, which leave plenty of space for other crops. He does not specify "how this subdivision will occur, but it seems plausible to assume that it will be the fair trade of the land to ensure that it happens."
14 Obviously such an approach can be disappointing. For example, Peter Riley (2013, 11) wrote that this "laissez-faire approach of simply waiting for technological progress to produce moral reform, based on an inherent understanding of natural law, offers up a vision of permanent complaint accompanied by inaction."
15 Hodgskin (1868) strongly believes that the "current distribution of wealth," unbalanced in favour of the idle classes, is pernicious, but is equally convinced that establishing state enterprises and public monopolies could only worsen it further.
16 Burke's quotation is from Burke ([1777] 1904, 38).
17 See in particular McCloskey's *Bourgeois Trilogy* (2007, 2010, and 2016).
18 Reviewing the third edition of the book in the *Economist*, Hodgskin (1848n, 1481) expressed admiration for this work, which emphasized that "research on the progress of civilization is a research into the causes that influence the formation of public opinion."

19 It should be stressed that this remark came much later than 1848. Instead, from the experience of the newly formed French Republic, Hodgskin hoped to draw signals of responsibility and intelligence from the popular government. For this reason, for example, the *London Telegraph* writes about having learned "with inexpressible satisfaction, though it is only what we expected from the growing good sense and political knowledge of the French, that the elections are likely to turn out generally very much in favour of the moderate party" (Hodgskin 1848h).
20 While Hodgskin tends to see only benefits in a growing division of labor, both Smith and Millar acknowledge certain problems: it cannot really be argued that the Scottish illuminists depicted a rose-tinted "commercial society."
21 As a perceptive scholar of Millar pointed out, freedom for Millar "meant freedom from subserviency to arbitrary dominance however imposed—whether by an irresponsible monarch, by a landlord, a titled nobleman, a robed justice on the bench, a priest in the confessional, or a guardian of the orthodoxy of men's religious beliefs. It meant freedom from the very essence of servility in every relationship of life." This conception of freedom "called for the promotion and perfecting and guarding of free institutions" (Lehmann 1960, 64–65).
22 Blanc's original idea was different: the *atelier* had to be a factory managed by associated workers. The foundation of the first *atelier* had to rely on the State, to make the necessary capital available, but the public funding would expire within a year, time considered sufficient for the individual factories to be able to sustain themselves. For its advocate, the new model would in time show such superior efficiency that it would soon include private industries.
23 "Their own teacher, M. Say, will inform them that the produce of one man's labour is the market for the produce of another; their other excellent and living teacher, M. Bastiat, will convince them that all services can only be paid for by other services" (Hodgskin 1848c).
24 In a commentary on the same episode, in an *Economist* article attributable to Hodgskin, it is observed that "Lamartine and Carnot can be left without delay to the justice and satire of Monsieur Bastiat and his colleagues" so absurd is the idea that "the republic can alter a science!" (Hodgskin 1848l, 479). In his pamphlet *La Loi*, Frédéric Bastiat ([1850] 2007, 17) reports of an exchange with Lamartine. "He wrote to me one day that 'Your doctrine is only half of my program; you have remained at liberty, I have moved on to fraternity.' I replied: 'The second half of your program will destroy the first.'"
25 On March 15, the Bank of France suspended the convertibility of the banknotes, a measure also considered by Hodgskin (1848d) as "inevitable" but also "the establishment of a system of authorised paper money, representing nothing but the interests of the government or of the issuers, of which no man can at present foretell the consequences." Marx ([1895] 1969, 22) wrote: "The interim government ... established the forced circulation of banknotes. It did more: it converted all the provincial banks into branches of the Banque de France .... Thus the February revolution consolidated and directly extended the bankruptcy that it was supposed to break down."

References

Bagehot, Walter. (1855) 1879. "The First Edinburgh Reviewers." In *Walter Bagehot, Literary Studies*. London: Longmans, 1–40.
Bastiat, Frédéric. (1850) 2007. *The Law*. Auburn: Ludwig Von Mises Institute.
Bassani, Luigi Marco. 2002. *Il pensiero politico di Thomas Jefferson. Libertà, proprietà e autogoverno* [*The Political Thought of Thomas Jefferson: Liberty, Property, and Self-Government*]. Milan: Giuffré.

Borges, Jorge Luis. (1975) 1977. *The Book of Sand*. New York: Dutton.

Brougham, Henry. 1838. "Law Reform." In *Speeches of Henry Lord Brougham, upon questions relating to public rights, duties, and interests; with historical introductions, and a critical dissertation upon the eloquence of the ancients*. Vol. II. Edinburgh: Black, 287–532.

Buckle, H.T. (1857) 2011. *History of Civilization in England*. Cambridge: Cambridge University Press.

Burke, Edmund. (1777) 1904. *A Letter to the Sheriffs of Bristol*, edited by James H. Moffatt. Philadelphia-New York: Hinds, Noble & Eldredge.

Dicey, Albert V. (1917) 2008. *Lectures on the Relation between Law and Public Opinion in England during the Nineteenth Century*. Indianapolis, IN: Liberty Fund.

Di Sciullo, Franco. 2004. *La critica e il progetto. Aspetti e problemi politici dell'utilitarismo classico* [*The Criticism and the Project: Aspects and Problems of Classical Utilitarianism*]. Milan: Giuffré.

Fontana, Biancamaria. 1985. *Rethinking the Politics of Commercial Society: The Edinburgh Review 1801–1832*. Cambridge: Cambridge University Press.

Gray, Alexander. 1946. *The Socialist Tradition: Moses to Lenin*. London: Greens.

Hill, Christopher. 1954. "The Norman Yoke." In *Democracy and the Labour Movement. Essays in Honour of Dona Torr*. Edited by John Saville. London: Lawrence & Wishart, 11–66.

Hodgskin, Thomas. 1820. Letter to Francis Place, May 18.

Hodgskin, Thomas. 1820b. *Travels in the North of Germany. Describing the Present State of the Social and Political Institutions, the Agriculture, Manufacture, Commerce, Education, Arts and Manners in That Country, Particularly in the Kingdom of Hannover*. 2 Vols. Edinburgh: Archibald Constable.

Hodgskin, Thomas. (1825) 1964. *Labour Defended Against the Claims of Capital*. London: Hammersmith Bookshop.

Hodgskin, Thomas. 1827a. *The Word BELIEF Defined and Explained*. London: Charles Tait.

Hodgskin, Thomas. 1827b. *Popular Political Economy: Four Lectures Delivered at the Mechanics' Institution*. London: Tait.

Hodgskin, Thomas. 1832. *The Natural and Artificial Right of Property Contrasted. A Series of Letters, addressed without permission to H. Brougham, Esq. M.P. F.R.S.* London: B. Steil.

Hodgskin, Thomas. 1848a. "The London Telegraph." *London Telegraph*, February 26.

Hodgskin, Thomas. 1848b. "The London Telegraph." *London Telegraph*, March 4.

Hodgskin, Thomas. 1848c. "The London Telegraph." *London Telegraph*, March 16.

Hodgskin, Thomas. 1848d. "The London Telegraph." *London Telegraph*, March 17.

Hodgskin, Thomas. 1848e. "The London Telegraph." *London Telegraph*, March 18.

Hodgskin, Thomas. 1848f. "The London Telegraph." *London Telegraph*, April 12.

Hodgskin, Thomas. 1848g. "The London Telegraph." *London Telegraph*, April 13.

Hodgskin, Thomas. 1848h. "The London Telegraph." *London Telegraph*, April 27.

Hodgskin, Thomas. 1848i. "The London Telegraph." *London Telegraph*, May 5.

Hodgskin, Thomas. 1848j. "The London Telegraph." *London Telegraph*, June 13.

Hodgskin, Thomas. 1848k. "The London Telegraph." *London Telegraph*, June 26.

Hodgskin, Thomas. 1848l. "The Political Economy of the French Government." *Economist*, April 29.

Hodgskin, Thomas. 1848m. "The Science of Liberty, Equality, and Fraternity." *Economist*, May 6.

Hodgskin, Thomas. 1848n. "Review of William Mackinnon, History of Civilization and Public Opinion. By Wm. Alex. MacKinnon, M.P., F.R.S., Third edition. Charles Ollier, Southampton Street, Strand." *Economist*, December 30.

Hodgskin, Thomas. 1851. "Review of Herbert Spencer, Social Statics; or, the Conditions Essential to Human Happiness Specified, and the First of them Developed." *Economist*, February 8.

Hodgskin, Thomas. 1857. *Our Chief Crime: Cause and Cure, Second Lecture on What Shall We Do with Our Criminals*. London: Groombridge and Sons.

Hodgskin, Thomas. 1863. "Science—Growth of a Middle Class." *Brighton Guardian*, August 19.

Hodgskin, Thomas. 1865a. "Modern Political Action." *Brighton Guardian*, February 22.

Hodgskin, Thomas. 1865b. "The Middle Classes as Legislators." *Brighton Guardian*, June 7.

Hodgskin, Thomas. 1868. "State Monopolies." *Brighton Guardian*, August 26.

Hollis, Patricia. 1974. "Pressure from Without: An Introduction." In *Pressure from Without in Early Victorian England*. London: Edward Arnold.

Horne, Thomas A. 1990. *Property Rights and Poverty: Political Argument in Britain 1605–1834*. Chapel Hill: University of North Carolina Press.

Hunt, Tristram. 2010. *The Frock-Coated Communist: The Revolutionary Life of Friedrich Engels*. London: Allen Lane.

Kahan, Alan S. 2003. *Liberalism in Nineteenth-Century Europe: The Political Culture of Limited Suffrage*. London: Palgrave-Macmillan.

Lehmann, William C. 1960. *John Millar of Glasgow 1735–1801: His Life and Thought and His Contributions to Sociological Analysis*. Cambridge: Cambridge University Press.

Locke, John. (1688) 2014. *Two Treatises of Government*. Indianapolis, IN: Liberty Fund.

Mackinnon, William. (1846) 1849. *History of Civilisation and Public Opinion*. London: Henry Colburn.

McCloskey, Deirdre N. 2007. *The Bourgeois Virtues: Ethics for an Age of Commerce*. Chicago: University of Chicago Press.

McCloskey, Deirdre N. 2010. *Bourgeois Dignity: Why Economics Can't Explain the Modern World*. Chicago: University of Chicago Press.

McCloskey, Deirdre N. 2016. *Bourgeois Equality: How Ideas, Not Capital or Institutions, Enriched the World*. Chicago: University of Chicago Press.

Marx, Karl. (1895) 1969. "The Class Struggles in France 1848–1850." In *Karl Marx and Friedrich Engels. Selected Works*, Vol. 1, Moscow: Progress Publishers.

Meek, Ronald L. 2011. *Social Science and the Ignoble Savage*. Cambridge, UK: Cambridge University Press.

Mill, James. (1823) 1992. "On Government." In *James Mill, Political Writings*. Edited by Terence Ball. Cambridge: Cambridge University Press.

Millar, John. 1771. *Observations concerning the Distinction of Ranks in Society*. Dublin: T. Ewing.

Millar, John. 1796. *Letters of Sydney, on Inequality of Property. To which is added, a Treatise of the Effects of War on Commercial Prosperity*. Edinburgh: Office of the Scots Chronicle.

Millar, John. 1818. *An Historical View of the English Government: From the Settlement of the Saxons in Britain, to the Revolution in 1688: to which are Subjoined, Some Dissertations Connected with the History of the Government, from the Revolution to the Present Time*. Vol. 2. London: J. Mawman.

Mingardi, Alberto. 2007. "Il tema della proprietà nel pensiero di 'Herbert Spencer.'" *Il Politico* 72 (2): 63–96.

Pacheco, Emilio. 1990. "Utility and Rights: The Science of Morals in Britain in the First Half of the Nineteenth Century." Ph.D. diss. University of Oxford.

Riley, Peter. 2013. *Making Another World Possible: Anarchism, Anti-capitalism and Ecology in Late 19th and Early 20th Century Britain*. New York: Bloomsbury.

Shelley, Percy Bysshe. (1820) 1920. *A Philosophical View of Reform*. Oxford: Oxford University Press.

Smith, Adam. (1776) 1981. *An Inquiry into the Nature and Causes of the Wealth of Nations*. Edited by Roy H. Campbell, and Andrew S. Skinner. Indianapolis, IN: Liberty Fund.

Stack, David. 1998. *Nature and Artifice: The Life and Thought of Thomas Hodgskin, 1787–1869*. Martlesham: Boydell & Brewer.

Steiner, Hillel. 1981. "Liberty and Equality." *Political Studies* 29 (4): 555–569, https://doi.org/doi:10.1111/j.1467-9248.1981.tb01324.x.

Stephen, Leslie. 1900. *The English Utilitarians*. Vol. 1. *Jeremy Bentham*. London: Duckworth.

Stewart, Robert. 1985. *Henry Brougham 1778–1868: His Public Career*. London: Bodley Head.

Wahrman, Dror. 1995. *Imagining the Middle Class. The Political Representation of Class in Britain, c. 1780–1840*. Cambridge: Cambridge University Press.

Conclusion

If we do remember Thomas Hodgskin today, shall we think of him as a forerunner of modern socialism? I hope readers will agree by now that when Beatrice and Sidney Webb described Karl Marx as Thomas Hodgskin's "distinguished student," they were making a mistake. But it was a lucky one, in a sense, since it helped keep alive some interest in our author, whose name otherwise would barely have emerged from the fog of nineteenth-century anonymous journalism.

David Stack (1998, 205) contends that the path that leads from Hodgskin to Hayek is "just as tortuous as [from Hodgskin] to Marx." In this book I have tried to argue that the path from Hodgskin to Hayek is far smoother. Hodgskin did not metamorphose from anti-capitalist to anti-protectionist. His economics define him as a full-fledged classical liberal thinker.

But one may well wonder what influence, if any, he exercised on this tradition of thought. The answer is, not much, directly. His early association with the workers' movement paradoxically put him into a no-man's land. While his contributions to working-class magazines made him an interesting figure for students of socialism, Max Beer (1864–1943), the historian of British socialism, soon realized that "Hodgskin was no socialist. He preferred competition in the midst of institutions and opinions as free as man can form them" ([1919] 1984, 206). Indeed, while the word "socialism" was used in a much different way when Hodgskin was writing, without being associated with what later came to be the tenets of Marxism, he could not be seen sympathetically by later upholders of that flag, who share an ambitious view of government and a lack of faith in markets' self-correcting virtues. Indeed, scholars who should have been friendlier to Hodgskin's understanding of government as dangerous and the market as beneficial kept away from his work. In his *The Counter-revolution of Science*, the great champion of twentieth-century classical liberalism, F.A. Hayek (1899–1992), briefly mentions him without having apparently read him, just to single him out as a British follower of Saint-Simon (Hayek 1955, 239).

Whatever influence Hodgskin thus exerted on classical liberals, then, was a *mediated one*. His first biographer, Élie Halévy, identified another possible disciple of Hodgskin's: Herbert Spencer. There were personal bonds between the two and they both suggest to us the outline of a particular tradition of classical liberalism.

Herbert Spencer and Thomas Hodgskin

In this book, I have suggested that Hodgskin's *laissez-faire* was in tune with his support and care for the working class. He foresaw that modern economic growth could eventually raise the living standards of the poor, and he was a partisan of innovation and machinery. At the same time, his politics were rooted in a profound distrust of any government intervention, including "scientific" government, promoted by liberals who shared a utilitarian foundation for their liberalism.

Seeing Hodgskin in connection to Spencer may help us place him within a specific political "family," that of the non-utilitarian liberals. They were a minority in the nineteenth century and in the country (England) that saw the triumph of the utilitarian liberals, who succeeded in twisting law in a more libertarian direction. For Halévy ([1903] 1956, 169), Hodgskin was "the first—before Herbert Spencer—to found a philosophy of free trade basing it on the critique of Bentham's philosophy of law." Both Hodgskin and Spencer were exposed to the latter: indeed without the support of Benthamite Francis Place, Hodgskin could not have established himself as a journalist and found a place, however precarious, in the republic of liberal arts.

Spencer began to write in the 1840s, when utilitarianism and liberalism were almost synonymous. He called himself a "rational," not "empirical," utilitarian.[1] "Rational" utilitarianism is meant to be an "indirect" utilitarianism: it evaluates different social situations with respect to the utility that they produce, but refuses to pursue political strategies aimed at "the greatest happiness for the greatest number" because such attempts at social engineering are inevitably spoiled by a partial understanding of reality.

Yet Spencer's relations with the utilitarian intellectual stars of his era were more nuanced and less vitriolic than Hodgskin's. When Spencer's *Synthetic Philosophy*, published as a series of pamphlets, appeared to be a failure, the intervention of John Stuart Mill and other friends, who offered to buy a number of copies as a whole, enabled him to continue in his endeavors (Spencer 1904, II, 132–137).

Nonetheless, Spencer has been labeled "the most formidable of Bentham's liberal critics."[2] In *Social Statics* he tackles utilitarianism head-on, emphasizing what he sees as its inevitably collectivist nature. Having conceived their system around the pursuit of "the greatest possible happiness for the greatest possible number of individuals," the theorists of utilitarianism pursue "the benefit of the mass, not of the individual." Spencer declines to use their toolbox. The original sin of what Spencer called the *expediency philosophy* lies in the fact that it "chooses as its object the laws of Parliament and uses the statesman as an architect" (Spencer 1851, 15). Bentham's utilitarianism "takes government into partnership—assigns to it entire control of its affairs—enjoins all to defer to its judgment—makes it in short the vital principle, the very soul of its system." The utilitarian theorists sin by an excess of presumption; they assume they can rely on data which in fact they do not have at all:

> Considering that men as yet so imperfectly understand man—the instrument by which, and the material on which, laws are to act—and that a complete knowledge of the unit—man, is but a first step to the comprehension of the mass—society, it seems obvious enough that to educe from the infinitely-ramified complications of universal humanity, a true philosophy of national life, and to found thereon a code of rules for the obtainment of "greatest happiness" is a task far beyond the ability of any finite mind.
>
> (Spencer 1851, 13)

Social Statics was written during the few months that Spencer spent at the *Economist*, as a journalist. He was not yet thirty; Hodgskin was more than twice his age. They came from very different worlds: Hodgskin had known military discipline because his father had forced him, as a child, into the Royal Navy, he was self-educated, he had travelled across Europe, he had struggled in every way to make a living out of what he wrote, he had listened, in person, to the lessons of the Scottish philosophers as well as those of Jean-Baptiste Say, he was an avid reader. In contrast, Spencer adored his father, had developed his political ideas thanks to his father and uncle, who were teachers and educated him, he was on the trail of religious dissent, he was a lazy reader, his main life experience amounted to having worked as an "engineer" for the British railways. If they shared some beliefs, there was a lot that divided them.

Spencer quotes Hodgskin only three times in his autobiography. He informs us that, when he was at the *Economist*, he spent a few nights "with my coadjutor Mr. Hodgskin, who wrote the reviews and a good part of the leading articles" (Spencer 1904, I, 347), and that he had browsed some of the books that came in to be reviewed, before they ended up in the hands of his senior colleague (Spencer 1904, I, 351).

The third occurrence is more interesting and comes from a letter from Spencer to his father, in which he informs us that neither his publisher John Chapman "nor Mr. Hodgskin" approve of *Demostatics* as a title for Spencer's first political treatise and that, on the contrary, "Mr. Hodgskin quite approves of Social Statics, which he thinks would be a very good title. I am going to consult with Chapman about it. What is your objection to it?" (Spencer 1904, I, 359). And *Social Statics* it was.

Apparently, Spencer valued Hodgskin's opinion: he consulted with him even before the publisher and his beloved father, on a topic that was crucial and very dear to him, such as the title of his first real book.[3] From a letter discovered by Mark Francis, we know that Spencer thanked Hodgskin, upon sending him a copy fresh from the press, for helping him avoiding "various mistakes."[4] On the same occasion, he politely urged Hodgskin, of whom Spencer himself recalls in the *Autobiography* that he personally wrote almost all the reviews of the *Economist*, to talk about it in that newspaper, even though he acknowledged how it might be difficult for him to review the work of a friend.

Hodgskin swiftly contributed a very positive review of *Social Statics*. It was rather petty of Spencer not only to fail to acknowledge it explicitly in his *Autobiography*, even though it appeared in a newspaper to which he was also contributing, but also to make a broad comment that "when reviews at length came, I was disappointed by their superficial character" (Spencer 1904, I, 360). Indeed, he wrote a review of his own and added it to the *Autobiography* to show how reviewers should have behaved.[5] Hodgskin (1851, 112–111) celebrated Spencer as the author of what was "at once novel and elaborate, precise and logical, a very comprehensive and complete exposition of the rights of men in society," also written in "language that sparkles with beauties." The main merit that he credits him with is precisely having refuted the utilitarian theory. On the other hand, in the review he expressed reservations regarding the stance taken by Spencer on the subject of land ownership and, against his younger colleague, reaffirmed a Lockean position. Nonetheless, it is an extremely positive article, the kind of review that an author at his debut could only welcome with enthusiasm—and gratitude.

Many years later, however, in replying to one of Hodgskin's daughters, Mary,[6] Spencer categorically denied that there was any particular intellectual chemistry between them. Urged by Mary, Spencer admitted that the two had actually spent some time together, including "a Christmas Eve (or New Year's Eve)." But, he told her, his intellectual elaboration was completely autonomous: Spencer had already written the letters, later collected in *The Proper Sphere of Government*, in which he explained to his dissenting readers why, from the separation between Church and State, strict liberal principles had to descend in terms of war, colonies, international trade. His conversations with Hodgskin added little:

> The intercourse we had daily at the *Economist* office consisted of remarks about passing incidents, especially such as bore upon misgovernment and overgovernment, in which remarks we habitually found ourselves in agreement. That he exercised any influence over my opinions I deny.
> (Herbert Spencer to Mary Hodgskin, March 22, 1903)

Our memory can trick us. In a letter to Hodgskin from 1849, when he was working at *The Economist* and writing *Social Statics*, Spencer implies a much closer familiarity than he acknowledged in the later correspondence with Mary Hodgskin. Spencer not only refers to "our debates on Friday evening," but acknowledged that he "opened your treatise on *Natural and Artificial Right of Property* [*sic*] with some trepidation" because giving a philosophical foundation to rights was also the objective of the manuscript on which he was working on, which would later become *Social Statics*.[7] Already on that occasion, however, Spencer noted that although the conclusions of the two books were similar, "we do not get there by the same process."

Was then Spencer ungenerous toward his old friend? It seems so. There is a 1855 letter in which Spencer addresses his correspondent as "My dear

Hodgskin" and, mentioning he was reading a book by Samuel Bailey (1791–1870),[8] asks him for some clarification about the theory of the mind as a process of association and classification (Herbert Spencer to Thomas Hodgskin, April 16, 1855). Both subjects (of particular importance, since Spencer's *Principles of Psychology* was published in 1855) and the tone give the impression of a non-episodic acquaintance.

It is true that Spencer was very jealous of the originality of his ideas, on which he constantly insists not only in the *Autobiography* but also in a short text, "The Filiation of Ideas," conceived as a "proper criticism" of his own work (Spencer [1899] 1908). On the other hand, he was also extremely precise in accounting for things he had read and digested. Spencer's interests as a reader tended toward natural sciences, anthropology, and travel books. The attention he devoted to political philosophy is scarce.[9] It is very likely that, before meeting Hodgskin, he had no knowledge of the latter's radical essays.

The relationship cooled on both sides, possibly with some resentment on Hodgskin's, as his wife is credited with the comment that Spencer was "one of those men" who took advantage of her husband's "brains and knowledge as well as of his books" (Taylor 1955, 102). In one of his last articles, almost twenty years after they worked together, Hodgskin quoted his old *protégé*, providing a synthesis of the Spencerian principle of evolution, or the idea of moving from simple and homogeneous structures to complex and heterogeneous structures, and emphasizing how this constituted further proof of the need to limit "ignorant and rude interference" on the natural order. Nonetheless, Hodgskin (1867, 2) regarded this as an "unphilosophical" approach. In another article, he reiterated his old criticisms of Spencer's theory of appropriation (1862, 2).

The anti-utilitarianism of Spencer and Hodgskin

What did Spencer take from Hodgskin, or at least develop from his exchanges with him? Can we see those ideas as the kernel of a non-utilitarian classical liberal tradition?

In part, Spencer's association with Hodgskin may have led him to consider the idea that public opinion is the ultimate tribunal of society. Skeptical toward "reforms" of all kinds, Hodgskin thought that the spontaneous evolution of society could lead to the obsolescence of positive law, which he considered as a chain that should be left to rust. Spencer devotes his entire political and sociological research to the way society changes and, in particular, to the way in which it evolves between the two different polarities of "military society" and "industrial society." In his view, institutions "depend on character and, although they may change in their superficial aspects, cannot be changed in their essential nature more quickly than it is possible to change that character" (Spencer 1904, II, 365). For Spencer, society's evolution is based on a harmonious development of institutions and "public opinion." The utilitarian pretense of scientific government can do little to improve people's conditions if it precedes genuine social change. According to Spencer, "the properties of the aggregate are determined by the properties of its units." Thus "so long as the characters of citizens remain substantially unchanged, there can be no substantial changes in the political organization which has slowly been evolved by them." Although human nature is not fixed, for Spencer ([1873]1896, 111, 109) it "can be modified but very slowly," so attempts to bring about radical political changes in a short time "will inevitably fail."

This seems to echo some of Hodgskin's own views, those that form his rationale for non-interventionism. Spencer's is a general outlook that has consequences for judging democracy. In the synthesis of an influential Spencerian scholar, "political institutions could have been democratised only to the extent that individuals had embraced a more appropriate sense of justice and were therefore ready to respect the freedom (and property) of others" (Taylor 1992, 65). Spencer's vision is perhaps more nuanced than Hodgskin's, but the widespread ideas, the appreciation of this or that social function, everything that contributes to inform the public opinion at some point in time—all Hodgskin's ideas—play a crucial role in it.

The point where Hodgskin and Spencer really converge, however, is another: they both were able to establish a social theory on the most fundamental of the discoveries of political economy. Hodgskin considered the weight assigned by Adam Smith to the division of labor exaggerated and he had the ambition to enrich that perspective, emphasizing the importance of the social division of knowledge. But both things, at least in Hodgskin's view, actually go together. His is a defense of the *complexity* of the social sphere against presumptuous and therefore inopportune public interference. What does such complexity translate into, if not a more and more branched division of labor? What does new and greater knowledge produce, if not an ever-growing specialization?

One could say that this is also the core of Spencer's social theory. The latter is less pamphlet-like and assertive, embellished by abundant sociological trappings and strengthened by comparison with the best available knowledge on the evolution of primitive societies. But a harsh critic such as Giovanni Papini (1881–1956) was not wrong when he wrote that Spencer learned from political economy "that what characterizes progress is the division of labour" (Papini 1906, 204). Specialization and division of labor are eminently adaptive. For Spencer, just as for Hodgskin, the growing division of labor forced an ever-increasing interdependence: more complicated production requires that people constantly rely on each other, only in this way can each person increase the number of needs they actually manage to satisfy.

It could be said that in Spencer this assumption becomes a complete social theory. It informs indeed his understanding of evolution as "a shift from an indefinite incoherent homogeneity to a defined coherent heterogeneity, which accompanies the dissipation of motion and the integration of matter" (Spencer [1862] 1867, 360). In Hodgskin there are tidbits of journalism, various annotations (which may read as prescient to us) on the division of labor in the industrial world, ideas never brought to full maturation but that echo the sentiments of his classical liberalism. However, it is not far-fetched to assume that those conversations about "too much government" during his time at the *Economist* did germinate in Spencer more than he was willing to admit.

It may be evocative to consider Spencer and Hodgskin as the core of a tradition in classical liberalism, in which the Smithian emphasis on a growing division of labor and the understanding of its benefits become the main argument for individual liberty. The main, albeit not the only argument; Hodgskin—as we have seen—shared the language of natural law liberalism. Yet Spencer and Hodgskin both wrote in what was, to borrow A.V. Dicey's words, "the era of utilitarian reform" when "legislation was governed by the body of opinion, popularly, and on the whole rightly, connected with the name of Bentham" ([1917] 2008, 45). While Hodgskin had no disciple, if we do not consider Spencer as such, Spencer had a few—British "Individualists" who adopted his language and carried his flag. But that was a minority tradition in the history of liberalism, one not blessed with the same fecundity as the liberalism of the Benthams and the Mills. There are, nonetheless, elements of this philosophy that later came to surface again, for example in F.A. Hayek's liberalism.

A distinct tradition of classical liberalism?

David Stack strongly emphasized Hodgskin's deism as the key to understanding his thought. Supporting Stack's claim there is, above all, the lexicon found in Hodgskin's latest articles, written for the *Brighton Guardian* when he was over seventy years old, in which the reference to the natural order as determined by the "Creator" is constant.[10] But what kind of natural order was, insofar as politics are concerned, Hodgskin defending?

For one thing he does not conceive an idea of "nature" as coinciding with any particular political order. Michael Oakeshott (1901–1990) observed that the modern European state was "so empirical a construction" and "so manifestly a contingent collection of human beings" that "seeking a 'natural' unity in it would seem to deny its most notable feature" (Oakeshott 2006, 412). Those who tried to appeal to "nature" to justify the modern political order are, in fact, trying to conceal its artificiality. Hodgskin, on the contrary, thinks of "nature" as a self-regulating social order beyond politics. This "eco-system" should not be disturbed precisely because the knowledge of the legislator will always be limited and partial. The "nature" of a changing society and—if the concept of "evolution" is still lacking—the idea of progress, on the other hand, can both be found in Hodgskin's thought: a "natural" progress in the sense of "spontaneous," not oriented from any "visible hand."[11]

This approach is not without its problems. In a world where the state continually interferes, how shall we move to political arrangements that respect and allow for spontaneous order? In discussing guild laws in Germany, Hodgskin (1820, II, 185) considered that they ought to be abolished and yet "it ought not ... to be the government which should abolish them.

Its interference is above all things to be deprecated, and its only duty on this subject is to refuse its support to them [guild regulations], and leave them to be abolished by the rest of society refusing to submit to them." In Hodgskin a radical distrust for the state becomes also a diffidence toward "reform" when politically pursued.

In contemporary times, authors like Hayek have been more pragmatic and supported efforts to restore what they deemed as proper conditions of a market economy. But government is indeed a much bigger and complex enterprise now than it was at the time Hodgskin vigorously denounced it. By which, I mean that advocates of limiting it are understandably keen on any effort to do so, given that there is only a a faint hope that government may ever really get smaller.

Hodgskin and Spencer could be considered part of a tradition of thought whose leading light, one century later, is Hayek. If Spencer and Hayek share "the aspiration of embedding the defence of liberty in a broad evolutionary framework" (Gray [1981] 1998, 103)—what brings together Hodgskin and Hayek is their understanding of the importance of knowledge in a market economy—and its dispersion thorough society. Hodgskin wrote *Popular Political Economy* one century before Hayek, who, with his teacher Ludwig von Mises (1881–1973), engaged in the so-called socialist calculation debate, arguing the superiority of a market economy in allowing for the best possible use of available resources. They challenged the possibility that a benevolent planner could plan production more satisfactorily than individual, self-interested businessmen. They maintained that the relevant knowledge (the knowledge that should inform *concrete* production in the *concrete* world) is scattered through society and best available to those closer to production itself. In due course, Hayek extended his polemics to the "fatal conceit" of managing society from the top.

This is, as we saw, the gist of Hodgskin's anti-statist argument: rulers do have at best very imperfect knowledge, certainly way too imperfect to attempt to steer society in this or that direction hoping to accomplish the common good. In writing that "No man can say how industry may be rendered most productive; for this is the continually varying result of the practical knowledge of all mankind" (Hodgskin 1827, 40), Hodgskin was using a language later libertarian writers in economics would much appreciate.

I am in no way suggesting that any para-genealogy of Hayek's thought that includes Hodgskin and Spencer is a truthful sketch of the Austrian economist's ideas. I am pointing to some affinities, as John Gray ([1981] 1998, 103) did many years ago in the case of Hayek and Spencer. Possibly Hayek never read Spencer,[12] almost certainly he never read Hodgskin,[13] yet similarities between them exist.

Needless to say, the Hayekian understanding of knowledge is far more nuanced than Hodgskin's ever was. But a twentieth-century Nobel laureate in economics should not, perhaps, be compared with a nineteenth-century self-taught journalist.

Such convergence may simply suggest that these are themes of significance, which are likely to be tackled in similar ways by authors who share an interest in individual liberty and economic progress. If knowledge is, as Hodgskin thought, a collective effort, such resemblance is not surprising: in a sense, it only shows that the theme is greater than those mastering it, no matter how great they are.

That the above-mentioned points are enough to sketch the contours of a particular tradition in classical liberalism is a matter of contention. Perhaps such a distrust of those on top, the idea that they can achieve no success in planning a great society, is a pre-political instinct: it is a sort of sentiment that comes before a certain set of ideas, and without which it is impossible even to consider those ideas. Spencer thought that you could not have any idea of liberty without a sentiment of liberty, since "when adequately strong the appropriate emotion prompts resistance to interference with individual action, whether by an individual tyrant or by a tyrant majority,"[14] but that was not always the case. This liberal sensibility is perhaps stronger in Hodgskin than in any other author. This book has argued that classical liberalism is the tradition in political thought to which Thomas Hodgskin belongs, and of which he should be considered a genuine champion.

Notes

1 See Weinstein (1998).
2 Likewise George H. Smith (2013, 158) on Spencer and Thomas Hodgskin.
3 Spencer had already published, in 1843, *The Proper Sphere of Government*, a pamphlet in which he put together a series of letters he sent to *The Nonconformist*.
4 Herbert Spencer to Thomas Hodgskin, January 13, 1851, quoted in Francis (1978, 321). Francis dates the letter January 13, 1850, and it is thus filed at the Seymour Library of Knox College. Nonetheless, this would be impossible, since *Social Statics* (the frontispiece of which reads 1851) according to Spencer was printed in December 1850. In reality, that "0" could well be a "1," and as such it must be interpreted according to the contents of the letter.
5 It is worth mentioning that Spencer's autobiography was published posthumously.
6 Hodgskin's family moved to the U.S. after his death, but Mary still visited England from time to time (Taylor 1955, 101[fn]).
7 Herbert Spencer to Thomas Hodgskin, October 22, 1849, quoted in Francis (1978, 321).
8 It was probably Bailey (1855).
9 For example Spencer does not quote Locke much. The one major political works in which the author of the *Two Treaties of Government* is mentioned by Spencer is *Social Statics*. This could indeed be evidence of Hodgskin's influence.
10 Earlier references are less conspicuous. In *Labour Defended* the word "Creator" appears once and so does the word "God"; in *Popular Political Economy* the word "Creator" occurs twice ("God" occurs five times, including expressions such as "thank God" and "God knows"). In *The Natural and the Artificial Right of Property Contrasted*, in light of the declared intention to contrast natural and artificial property rights, the occurrences are more numerous (about twenty) but "God" is openly considered synonymous with "Nature."
11 Economist Renzo Fubini (1904–1944) suggested a similar interpretation. He found affinities between Hodgskin and Italian economist Francesco Ferrara because of the

"repeated opposition—assumed as the foundation of all the arguments, without distinction, of the English thinker—of the 'natural order' to the 'artificial order'" (Fubini 1937, 2).
12 "Hayek assured me that he had never read Spencer, and I'm sure this was the case" (Gray 2015).
13 The reference, in *The Counter-revolution of Science*, is to Halévy's book.
14 Herbert Spencer to Moncure D. Conway, December 12, 1893, now in Conway (1904, II, 395).

References

Bailey, Samuel. 1855. *Letters on the Philosophy of the Human Mind*. London: Longman.
Beer, Max. (1919) 1984. *A History of British Socialism*. Nottingham: Spokesman.
Conway, Moncure Daniel. 1904. *Autobiography. Memories and Experiences*. London: Cassel & Company.
Dicey, Albert V. (1917) 2008. *Lectures on the Relation between Law and Public Opinion in England during the Nineteenth Century*. Indianapolis, IN: Liberty Fund.
Duncan, David. 1908. *The Life and Letters of Herbert Spencer*. New York: D. Appleton and Company.
Francis, Mark. 1978. "Herbert Spencer and the Myth of Laissez-Faire." *Journal of the History of Ideas* 39 (2): 317–328, https://doi.org/10.2307/2708783.
Fubini, Renzo. 1937. "Rileggendo Ferrara: Ferrara e Proudhon." *Giornale degli Economisti e Rivista di Statistica* 77 (1): 1–17.
Gray, John. (1981) 1998. *Hayek on Liberty*. London: Routledge.
Gray, John. 2015. "John Gray: The Friedrich Hayek I Knew, and What He Got Right—and Wrong." *New Statesman*. July 30, https://www.newstatesman.com/politics/2015/07/john-gray-friedrich-hayek-i-knew-and-what-he-got-right-and-wrong.
Halévy, Élie. (1903) 1956. *Thomas Hodgskin*. Translated and edited by A.J. Taylor. London: Ernst Benn.
Hayek, Friedrich A. von. 1955. *The Counter Revolution of Science: Studies on the Abuse of Reason*. Glencoe, IL: Free Press.
Hodgskin, Thomas. 1820. *Travels in the North of Germany. Describing the Present State of the Social and Political Institutions, the Agriculture, Manufacture, Commerce, Education, Arts and Manners in That Country, Particularly in the Kingdom of Hannover*. 2 Vols. Edinburgh: Archibald Constable.
Hodgskin, Thomas. 1827. *Popular Political Economy: Four Lectures Delivered at the Mechanics' Institution*. London: Tait.
Hodgskin, Thomas. 1851. "Review of Herbert Spencer, Social Statics; or, the Conditions Essential to Human Happiness Specified, and the First of them Developed." *Economist*, February 8.
Hodgskin, Thomas. 1862. "Science—the Right of Property in Land–Mr Spencer's Theory." *Brighton Guardian*, October 8.
Hodgskin, Thomas. 1867. "Former Ignorance—Present Knowledge." *Brighton Guardian*, April 24.
Oakeshott, Michael. 2006. *Lectures in the History of Political Thought*. Exeter: Imprint Academy.
Papini, Giovanni. 1906. *Il crepuscolo dei filosofi*. Milano: Società editrice lombarda.
Smith, George H. 2013. *The System of Liberty*. Cambridge: Cambridge University Press.

Spencer, Herbert. 1851. "Review of Herbert Spencer, *Social Statics; or, the Conditions Essential to Human Happiness Specified, and the First of them Developed*." *Economist*, February 8.

Spencer, Herbert. (1862) 1867. *First Principles*. London: Williams and Norgate.

Spencer, Herbert. (1873) 1896. *The Study of Sociology*. New York: D. Appleton and Company.

Spencer, Herbert. (1899) 1908. "The Filiation of Ideas." In *The Life and Letters of Herbert Spencer*. Edited by David Duncan. New York: D. Appleton and Company, 304–365.

Spencer, Herbert. 1904. *An Autobiography*. London: Williams and Norgate.

Stack, David. 1998. *Nature and Artifice: The Life and Thought of Thomas Hodgskin, 1787–1869*. Martlesham: Boydell & Brewer.

Taylor, Arthur J. 1955. "The Originality of Herbert Spencer." *University of Texas Studies in English* 34, 101–106.

Taylor, Michael W. 1992. *Men Versus the State: Herbert Spencer and Late Victorian Individualism*. Oxford: Clarendon Press.

Weinstein, David. 1998. *Equal Freedom and Utility: Herbert Spencer's Liberal Utilitarianism*. Cambridge: Cambridge University Press.

Index

Anti-Corn Law League 81–84, 85–89
Ashton, Thomas 32, 49
association, freedom of 35, 130
Autobiography (Spencer) 138–139, 140

Bailey, Samuel 140
banking system 101–110
barter 104–105
Bassani, Luigi Marco 118
Bastiat, Frédéric 69, 128, 132
Becker, Gary S. 56–57
Beer, Max 136
Bentham, Jeremy 5, 6, 25–26, 115, 137
Berg, Maxine 46
Birkbeck, George 7, 66
Blanc, Louis 128–129
Böhm-Bawerk, Eugen von 37, 41, 43
Borges, Jorge Luis 125–126
Bourgeois Revaluation 124
Briggs, Asa 68
British Royal Navy 11–26
Brougham, Henry 6, 8, 114, 115, 118
Brown, Thomas 71
Buckle, Henry Thomas 124
Burke, Edmund 123
Byrn Jr., John 25

Cannan, Edwin 39
capital: accumulation of 50–51; business cycles 100–101; definitions 37; as exploitation 53; Hodgskin's socialism 33–36; human capital 50–58; and labour 34–35, 40–42; and machinery 43–50; and privilege 36–43; types of 56
capitalists, Industrial Revolution 52–55
captains of the navy 22–23
Chapman, John 138
Chartist movement 82

chemistry, history of 71
Clapham, J. H. 76
class *see* social class
Cobden, Richard 81–84, 86–88
Conrad, Joseph 98
corn laws: Anti-Corn Law League 81–84; opposition by Hodgskin 76–84; public opinion 126, 128
cottage industry 44
currency, free banking 101–110

Dancy, J. Ross 17
Danson, John Towne 83–84
Darwin, Charles 74
deism 142
demand and supply 72–74
Demonstration of the Absurdity of the Legislation (Hodgskin) 121
Dicey, Albert V. 26, 115, 142
Dickens, Charles 83
Dimsdale, Nicholas 98
division of labor: forced labor 20; freedom 126–127; Hodgskin's view 18, 46–47, 141–142; knowledge-guided labor 70, 72, 74–75, 77; machinery 43, 45–47; privilege and capital 39, 42; Smith, Adam 18, 46–47, 142; supply and demand 72–74

economic growth 48–49, 51–52, 69, 124, 137
The Economist 8–9, 84, 138–139
education: *An Essay on Naval Discipline* 24; self-education of the masses 6–7
Edwards, Ruth Dudley 9
Engels, Friedrich 33, 41, 58
An Essay on Naval Discipline (Hodgskin) 10–26

Index

Farrar, Peter Nelson 84
Feinstein, Charles 49
Ferguson, Adam 18
Ferrara, Francesco 92, 103, 111, 144
financial crises 99; *see also* business cycles
forced enlistment (impressment) 11, 13–25
forced labor 13–14, 20–22
Fourier, Charles 33
Foxwell, H. S. 33
Francis, Mark 138
Frederick, John 3–4
free banking 101–110
free trade: banking 101–110; business cycles 98, 99; corn laws 77–81; manifesto of Hodgskin 84–89
freedom: of association 35, 130; division of labor 126–127; impressment 11, 13–25
French Revolution 127–128

Gray, Alexander 120
Gray, James 4
Gray, John 33, 143
Griffin, Emma 49
Guizot, François 127

Halévy, Élie 5, 33, 136
Hall, Charles 46
Hayek, Friedrich 101–102, 136, 142, 143
Hicks, John 49
Hinde, Wendy 83
Hodgskin, Mary 139
Hollis, Patricia 125
Hotson, Anthony 98
human capital 50–58
Hume, David 14, 77–78
Huskisson, William 68, 79–80, 98
Hutt, William H. 72

idealism, Anti-Corn Law League 81–82
impressment 11, 13–25
indirect utilitarianism 137
Industrial Enlightenment 51–52
Industrial Revolution: accumulation of capital 50–51; capitalists and entrepreneurs 52–53; cultural context 52; living standards 32, 76; machinery 43–45
inheritance law 119–120
innovation: accumulation of capital 50–51; knowledge-guided labor 69–76; scientific advancement 51–55
intellectual work 55–56
interventionism 129

investment, debt securities 98–99
'invisible hand' 36, 71

Knight, Charles 35–36
knowledge: intellectual work 55–56; 'scientific' government 120–123; Society for the Diffusion of Useful Knowledge 115
knowledge-guided labor 69–76, 77

labor: and capital 34–35, 40–42; capital and privilege 36–54; knowledge-guided 69–76, 77; and machinery 38; manual and intellectual work 55; slavery 13–14, 20–22
Labour Defended against the Claims of Capital (Hodgskin) 32, 57, 114, 115
laissez-faire 66, 137
land ownership 119–120
Landes, David 44–45
Latin America, investment opportunities 98–99
Lecture on Free Trade (Hodgskin) 86
legislation: corn laws 76–84, 81–84, 126, 128; natural law 41, 67, 101, 115–116, 142; public opinion 126; purpose of 114, 115, 117, 119, 122–123
liberalism 137, 142–144
living standards 32, 48–49, 76, 137
Locke, John 115, 116, 118–119
London Telegraph 127–128
'LouisBlancism' 129
Lovett, William 82

machinery: Hodgskin's perspective 43–50; and labor 38
Mackay, Charles 9–10
Mackinnon, William A. 124–125
MacLeod, Christine 7, 54
Malthus, Thomas 67, 73, 75, 87
Marx, Karl 33, 44, 45, 136
McCloskey, Deirdre 50–51, 54, 124
McCulloch, J. R. 100
Menger, Anton 33
Menger, Carl 110
middle class: living standards 50; public opinion 123–130
'military society' 140
militia, voluntary 17–18
Mill, James 5, 6, 34, 115, 124
Mill, John Stuart 33, 137
Millar, John 126–127
Mokyr, Joel 51–52
money as unit of exchange 101–110

The Natural and Artificial Right of Property Contrasted (Hodgskin) 114, 115–116, 118, 139
natural law 41, 67, 101, 115–116, 142
natural price 37–38, 75–76
naval discipline, *An Essay on Naval Discipline* 10–26
Newcomen, Thomas 53–54
newspapers, history of 6–7, 8–10
'Norman Yoke' 118–119

Oakeshott, Michael 142
Owen, Robert 33, 46

Paley, William 23
paper currency 101–110
Papini, Giovanni 141
Parker, Peter 3
Place, Francis: friendship with Hodgskin 4–6, 8; labor and capital 40; political economy 66
'Plug Plot' 83
political economy 66–69, 114–115, 129
Popular Political Economy (Hodgskin) 48, 57, 66–67, 70, 79–80, 88, 107–108, 143
population theories: growth rate 74–76; knowledge-guided labor 72–76; Malthus, Thomas 67, 73, 75; political economy 67
power: capital and privilege 39–40; legislation 114
private property 114–120
privilege, and capital 36–43
property rights 114–120
protectionism 78–79, 83
public opinion 123–130, 140

rational utilitarianism 137
real bills doctrine 109
Ricardian socialism 33, 40
Ricardo, David 33, 43, 75
Robertson, Joseph Clinton 7, 8
Rogers, Nicholas 12–13
Royal Navy, *An Essay on Naval Discipline* 11–26
Russell, Bertrand 34

Sally, Razeen 77–78
Say, Jean-Baptiste 5–6, 19, 69, 73
Schuler, Kurt 103
'scientific' government 120–123, 140–141
Scottish Enlightenment 17
self-education, working class 6–7

self-ownership 116–117
Shelley, Percy Bysshe 114–115
Shipley, Conway 2
skilled labor 48; *see also* knowledge-guided labor
slave labor 13–14, 20–22
Smith, Adam: capital and privilege 36–43; corn laws 77–78; currency 105, 106–107; division of labor 18, 46–47, 142; Hodgskin's admiration for 36; knowledge-guided labor 70, 72, 74–75; labor and capital 34–35, 37–38; land ownership 119–120; naval discipline 14; naval recruitment 20–21; standing army 18
Smith, Vera 102
social class: Anti-Corn Law League 81–82; capital and privilege 39–40; corn laws 78–79, 81; free trade 84–85; Industrial Revolution 52; living standards 49–50; *see also* working class
social price 38, 75–76
Social Statics (Spencer) 138–139
socialism: Hodgskin's theory of 32–36, 40, 66; living standards 48–49
Society for the Diffusion of Useful Knowledge 115
Spencer, Herbert 9, 116, 136–140
Stack, David 2–3, 9, 36, 73, 136, 142
standards of living 48–49, 76, 137
stock market 99
supply and demand 72–74

Thompson, E. P. 35, 43, 45
Thompson, Noel W. 33
Thompson, William 33
Towers, Joseph 15
trade *see* free trade
Trades' Newspaper 68–69
Travels in the North of Germany (Hodgskin) 78, 120–121
Turgot, Anne Robert Jacques 105

utilitarianism: Hodgskin's stance 5–6, 120–123, 140–142; types of 137
utopian socialism 33

voluntary militia 17–18

wages 49; *see also* living standards
Watt, James 53–56, 70
Weaver, Richard 18

Webb, Beatrice 136
Webb, Sidney 136
White, Lawrence H. 103
Wilson, James 9

The Word BELIEF Defined and Explained (Hodgskin) 71, 118
working class: free trade 85; labour 36; self-education 6–7